The New iPad®

PORTABLE GENIUS

by Paul McFedries

WILEY

John Wiley & Sons, Inc.

The New iPad® Portable Genuis

Published by
John Wiley & Sons, Inc.
10475 Crosspoint Blvd.
Indianapolis, IN 46256
www.wiley.com

Published simultaneously in Canada

ISBN: 978-1-118-17303-9

Manufactured in the United States of America

10 9 8 7 6 5 4 3 2 1

For general information on our other products and services or to obtain technical support, please contact our Customer Care Department within the U.S. at (877) 762-2974, outside the U.S. at (317) 572-3993 or fax (317) 572-4002.

Wiley publishes in a variety of print and electronic formats and by print-on-demand. Some material included with standard print versions of this book may not be included in e-books or in print-on-demand. If this book refers to media such as a CD or DVD that is not included in the version you purchased, you may download this material at http://booksupport.wiley.com. For more information about Wiley products, visit www.wiley.com.

Library of Congress Control Number: 2011938581

WILEY

Credits

Senior Acquisitions Editor
Stephanie McComb

Project Editor
Amanda Gambill

Technical Editor
John Smith

Senior Copy Editor
Kim Heusel

Editorial Director
Robyn Siesky

Business Manager
Amy Knies

Senior Marketing Manager
Sandy Smith

Vice President and Executive Group Publisher
Richard Swadley

Vice President and Executive Publisher
Barry Pruett

Project Coordinator
Patrick Redmond

Graphics and Production Specialists
Joyce Haughey
Andrea Hornberger
Sennett Vaughan Johnson
Mark Pinto

Quality Control Technicians
Lindsay Amones
Rebecca Denoncour

Proofreading and Indexing
Melissa D. Buddendeck
BIM Indexing & Proofreading Services

About the Author

Paul McFedries is a full-time technical writer. Paul has been authoring computer books since 1991 and has more than 75 books to his credit. Paul's books have sold more than four million copies worldwide. These books include the Wiley titles *iPhone 4S Portable Genius; Macs Portable Genius Second Edition; MacBook Air Portable Genius Third Edition; Switching to a Mac Portable Genius Second Edition; Teach Yourself VISUALLY Macs Second Edition; Twitter Tips, Tricks, and Tweets Second Edition;* and *The Facebook Guide for People Over 50*. Paul is also the proprietor of Word Spy (www.wordspy.com), a website that tracks new words and phrases as they enter the English language. Paul encourages everyone to drop by his personal website at www.mcfedries.com, or to follow him on Twitter at www.twitter.com/paulmcf and www.twitter.com/wordspy.

Acknowledgments

Being a freelance technical writer is an awesome vocation: You get to work at home; you get to set your own schedule; and you get to help other people understand and use technology, which is a warm-fuzzy-feeling generator. But perhaps the best part of technical writing is getting to be among the first not just to use, but to really *dive into,* the latest and greatest software and hardware. The hardware side is often the most fun, because it means you get to play with gadgets, and that's a gadget geek's definition of a dream job. So to say I had a blast researching and writing about the iPad redefines the word *understatement.* What self-respecting gadget guy wouldn't have a perma-grin while poking and prodding the iPad to see what it can do?

And what self-respecting technical writer wouldn't be constantly shaking his head in admiration while working with the amazing editorial team at Wiley? Skip back a couple of pages to see the complete list of the team who worked so hard to bring you this book. The people I worked with directly included Senior Acquisitions Editor Stephanie McComb, who found a way for me to realize my dream of writing an iPad book; Project Editor Amanda Gambill, whose mind seems to be constantly generating eyebrow-raisingly good suggestions; and Senior Copy Editor Kim Heusel, whose judicious and just-so editing makes me look like a much more competent writer than I am. Thanks to all of you for your hard work and unmatched competence.

Contents

chapter 4

How Do I Configure My iPad?   52

chapter 3

How Can I Protect My iPad?   36

chapter 5

How Can I Get More Out of
iPad Web Surfing?   78

chapter 6

How Do I Make the Most
of E-mail on My iPad?   106

chapter 7

How Can I Have Fun
with iPad Photos? 134

Introduction

It's not often that a device comes along and changes pretty much everything: The wheel, the clock, the printing press, the telegraph, the telephone, the TV, the PC. A couple of hands are all you need to count the technological inventions that have set the world on its ear in the past. Is it hyperbole to add the iPad to that list? Perhaps, but lots of smart people are betting the bank that the iPad is not only the most prominent landmark in a new computing landscape, but that it is, at the same time, forming that landscape. No, we're not quite into what some are calling the post-PC era, but thanks to the iPad and the legions of imitators it has spawned, that era isn't as far into the future as you might think.

Are you ready to embrace that future? Certainly your purchase of an iPad signals that you, for one, are ready to welcome your new tablet overlords. But when times change, the people who thrive in the new world are those who master the technologies that are driving that change. As you'll soon find out (if you haven't already), your iPad is almost comically simple to use right out of the box. It's slick, elegant, and just so easy: a tap here, a tap there, and away you go.

Yes, the *basics* of the iPad are a snap to pick up, but one of the secrets of the iPad's tremendous success is that the basics are a mere starting point. Your iPad is almost impossibly thin, but it has its depths: hidden settings, obscure features, out-of-the-way preferences, and little-known techniques. The usefulness of some of these features is debatable at best, but many of them can help you work faster, easier, and more efficiently. Rather than groping blindly through these dark iPad alleys, you might consider making an appointment at your local Apple Store's Genius Bar. More often than not, the on-duty genius will give you good advice on how to get more out of your iPad investment. The Genius Bar is a great thing, but it isn't always a convenient thing. You usually have to make an appointment, drag yourself down to the store, perhaps wait for your genius, get the advice you need (or the problem looked at, or whatever), and then make your way back home.

In some cases, you may need to leave your iPad for a while (the horror!) to get a problem checked out and hopefully resolved.

What you really need is a version of the Genius Bar that's easier to access, more convenient, and doesn't require tons of time or leaving your iPad in the hands of a stranger. What you really need is a *portable* genius that enables you to be more productive and solve problems wherever you and your iPad happen to be hanging out.

Welcome to *The New iPad Portable Genius*. This book is like a mini Genius Bar all wrapped up in an easy-to-use, easy-to-access, and eminently portable format. In this book, you learn how to get more out of your iPad by accessing all the really powerful and timesaving features that aren't obvious at a casual glance. You also learn how to avoid your iPad's occasional annoying character traits and, in those cases where such behavior can't be avoided, you learn how to work around it. Finally, you learn how to prevent iPad problems from occurring and, just in case your preventative measures are for naught, you learn how to fix many common problems yourself. This edition also includes updates on most of the new features in the third-generation iPad and iOS 5.1.

This book is for iPad users who know the basics but want to take their iPad education to a higher level. It's a book for people who want to be more productive, more efficient, more creative, and more self-sufficient (at least as far as the iPad goes). It's a book for people who use their iPad every day, but who would like to incorporate it into more of their day-to-day activities. It's a book I had a blast writing, so I think it's a book you'll enjoy reading.

How Do I Connect My iPad to a Network?

You can do plenty of things locally on your iPad without having to reach out and touch some remote site or service. You can jot some notes, add appointments, edit contacts, or just play around with the iPad settings. However, I'm willing to bet you didn't fork over the bucks for an iPad just so you could use the Notes app. Whether it's the web to go on a surfin' safari, the App Store or iBookstore to grab some content, or Google Maps to find your way, the iPad comes alive when it's connected to a network.

Connecting to a Wi-Fi Network

As you see a bit later in this chapter, the cellular-enabled iPad automatically connects to cellular networks. At first, things aren't automatic when it comes to Wi-Fi connections. As soon as you try to access something on the Internet — a website, your e-mail, a Google map, or whatever — your iPad scours the surrounding airwaves for Wi-Fi network signals. If you've never connected to a Wi-Fi network, or if you're in an area that doesn't have any Wi-Fi networks you've used in the past, you see the Select a Wi-Fi Network dialog, as shown in Figure 1.1. (If you don't see the Select a Wi-Fi Network dialog, you can still connect to a wireless network; I cover this later in this chapter.)

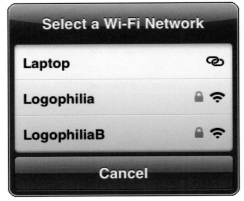

1.1 If you're just starting out on the Wi-Fi trail, your iPad displays a list of nearby networks.

This dialog displays a list of the Wi-Fi networks that are within range. For each network, you get three tidbits of data:

- **Network name.** This is the name that the administrator has assigned to the network. If you're in a coffee shop or similar public hot spot and you want to use that network, look for the name (or a variation thereof) of the shop.

- **Password-protected.** If a Wi-Fi network displays a lock icon, it means the network is protected by a password and you need to know that password to make the connection.

- **Signal strength.** This icon gives you a rough idea of how strong the wireless signals are. The stronger the signal (the more bars you see, the better the signal), the more likely you are to get a fast and reliable connection.

Making your first connection

Follow these steps to connect to a Wi-Fi network:

1. **Tap the network you want to use.** If the network is protected by a password, your iPad prompts you to type it, as shown in Figure 1.2.

2. **Use the keyboard to type the password.**

3. **Tap Join.** The iPad connects to the network and adds the Wi-Fi network signal strength icon to the status bar.

To connect to a commercial Wi-Fi operation — such as those you find in airports, hotels, and convention centers — you almost always have to take one more step. In most cases, the network prompts you for your name and credit card data so you can be charged for accessing the network. If you're not prompted right away, you will be as soon as you try to access a website or check your e-mail. Type your information and then enjoy the Internet in all its Wi-Fi glory.

1.2 If the Wi-Fi network is secured with a password, use this screen to type it.

Caution Because the password box shows dots instead of the actual text for added security, this is no place to demonstrate your iPad speed-typing prowess. Slow and steady wins the password typing race (or something).

Connecting to known networks

If the Wi-Fi network is one that you use all the time — for example, your home or office network — the good news is your iPad remembers any network to which you connect. As soon as a known network comes within range, your iPad makes the connection without so much as a peep. Thanks!

Stopping incessant Wi-Fi network prompts

The Select a Wi-Fi Network dialog is a handy convenience if you're not sure whether a Wi-Fi network is available. However, as you move around town, you may find that dialog popping up all over the place as new Wi-Fi networks come within range. One solution is to wear your finger down to the bone with all the constant tapping of the Cancel button, but there's a better way: just tell your iPad to shut up already with the Wi-Fi prompting. Here's how:

1. **On the Home screen, tap Settings.** The Settings screen appears.
2. **Tap Wi-Fi.** iPad opens the Wi-Fi Networks screen.

3. **Tap the Ask to Join Networks switch to the Off position, as shown in Figure 1.3.**
   Your iPad no longer prompts you with nearby networks. Whew!

1.3 Toggle the Ask to Join Networks switch to Off to put a gag on network prompts.

Okay, I hear you ask, if I'm no longer seeing the prompts, how do I connect to a Wi-Fi network if I don't even know it's there? That's a good question, and here's a good answer:

1. **On the Home screen, tap Settings.** Your iPad displays the Settings screen.

2. **Tap Wi-Fi.** The Wi-Fi Networks screen appears and the Choose a Network list shows you the available Wi-Fi networks.

3. **Tap the network you want to use.** If the network is protected by a password, your iPad prompts you to type it.

4. **Use the keyboard to type the password.**

5. **Tap Join.** The iPad connects to the network and adds the Wi-Fi network signal strength icon to the status bar.

Connecting to a hidden Wi-Fi network

Each Wi-Fi network has a name — often called the Service Set Identifier, or SSID — that identifies the network to Wi-Fi-friendly devices such as your iPad. By default, most Wi-Fi networks broadcast the network name so you can see and connect to it. However, some Wi-Fi networks disable network name broadcasting as a security precaution. The idea here is that if an unauthorized user can't see the network, he or she can't attempt to connect to it. However, some devices can pick up the network name when authorized computers connect to it, so this is not a foolproof security measure.

You can still connect to a hidden Wi-Fi network by manually entering the connection settings. You need to know the network name, its security and encryption types, and the password. Here are the steps to follow:

1. **On the Home screen, tap Settings to open the Settings screen.**

2. **Tap Wi-Fi.** You see the Wi-Fi Networks screen.

3. **Tap Other.** Your iPad displays the Other Network screen, as shown in Figure 1.4.

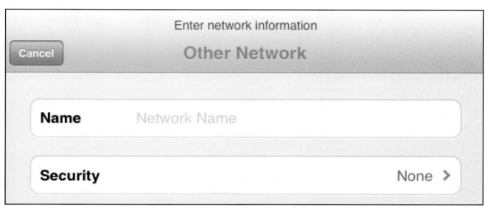

1.4 Use the Other Network screen to connect to a hidden Wi-Fi network.

4. **Type the network name in the Name text box.**

5. **Tap Security to open the Security screen.**

6. **Tap the type of security used by the Wi-Fi network: WEP, WPA, WPA2, WPA Enterprise, WPA2 Enterprise, or None.** If you're not sure, try WPA2, which is the most common type for home networks.

7. **Tap Other Network to return to the Other Network screen.** If you chose WEP, WPA, WPA2, WPA Enterprise, or WPA2 Enterprise, your iPad prompts you to type the password.

8. **Use the keyboard to type the password.**

9. **Tap Join.** The iPad connects to the network and adds the Wi-Fi network signal strength icon to the status bar.

Turning off the Wi-Fi antenna

The iPad Wi-Fi antenna is constantly on the lookout for nearby Wi-Fi networks. That's useful because it means you always have an up-to-date list of networks to check out, but it takes its toll on the iPad battery. If you know you won't be using Wi-Fi for a while, you can save some battery juice for more important pursuits by turning off the iPad Wi-Fi antenna. Here's how:

1. **On the Home screen, tap Settings.** The Settings screen appears.
2. **Tap Wi-Fi.** The Wi-Fi Networks screen appears.
3. **Tap the Wi-Fi switch to the Off position, as shown in Figure 1.5.** Your iPad disconnects from your current Wi-Fi network and hides the Choose a Network list.

1.5 If you don't need Wi-Fi, turn off the antenna to save battery power.

When you're ready to resume your Wi-Fi duties, return to the Wi-Fi Networks screen and tap the Wi-Fi switch to the On position.

Tethering to an iPhone Internet connection

If you have a Wi-Fi-only iPad, you might think you're stuck if you're out and about, need to use the Internet, and there's no Wi-Fi in sight. If you have an iPhone that's running iOS 4.3 or later, then you can work around this problem by using a nifty feature called Personal Hotspot, which enables you to configure your iPhone as a kind of Internet hub or gateway device — something like the hotspots that are available in coffee shops and other public areas. You can connect your iPad to your iPhone via Wi-Fi and your iPad can then use the iPhone cellular Internet connection to get online. This is often called *Internet tethering*.

This sounds too good to be true, but it's real — I swear. The downside (you just knew there had to be a downside) is that additional usage charges apply. In the United States, for example, AT&T offers a SmartPhone Tethering plan that costs $45 per month, which is $20 more than the next lowest priced plan (although you also get an extra 2GB of data). Similarly, Verizon offers a tethering option that costs an extra $30 per month but includes unlimited tethering data.

Your first step down the Personal Hotspot road is to activate the feature on your iPhone. Here's how it's done:

1. **On the iPhone Home screen, tap Settings.** The Settings screen appears.

2. **Tap Personal Hotspot.** iPhone opens the Personal Hotspot screen.

3. **Tap the Personal Hotspot switch to the On position.** If you don't have the Bluetooth antenna turned on, your iPhone asks if you want to turn it on.

4. **Tap Wi-Fi and USB Only.**

5. **Personal Hotspot generates a Wi-Fi password automatically (see Figure 1.6).** You can set your own by tapping Wi-Fi Password, typing the new password, and then tapping Done.

1.6 When you activate Personal Hotspot, the iPhone generates a password for you.

With Personal Hotspot enabled on your iPhone, follow these steps to connect your iPad to it via Wi-Fi:

1. **On your iPad, display the list of nearby wireless networks.**

Note If you have a third-generation iPad with 4G, you can use it as a Personal Hotspot if your data plan allows for Internet tethering. To set it up, tap Settings, tap Personal Hotspot, and then tap the Personal Hotspot switch to On.

2. **In the network list, click the one that has the same name as your iPhone, as shown in Figure 1.7.** Your device prompts you for the Wi-Fi password.

1.7 To make a Wi-Fi connection to the iPhone hotspot, display the list of wireless networks and then select your iPhone.

3. **Type the Personal Hotspot Wi-Fi password and then tap OK.** In the status bar, your iPad shows the Personal Hotspot icon, which is two interconnected rings (see Figure 1.8), and your iPhone shows Personal Hotspot: 1 Connection, as shown in Figure 1.9.

1.8 When your iPad is tethered, it shows the Personal Hotspot icon in the status bar.

1.9 Your iPhone tells you when someone is tethered to its Internet connection.

Working with Cellular Network Connections

Connections to a cellular network are automatic and occur behind the scenes. As soon as you switch on your 4G-enabled iPad, it checks for a 4G signal. If it finds one, it connects to it and displays the 4G icon, as well as the connection strength in the status bar (the more bars, the better). If your current location doesn't do the 4G thing, your iPad tries to connect to a 3G network. If that works, you see the 3G icon in the status bar, as well as the signal strength. If there's no 3G network within range, your iPad looks for an EDGE network instead. If that works, you see the E icon in the status bar (plus the usual signal strength bars). If none of that works, you see No Signal, so you might as well go home.

Tracking cellular data usage

Having a data plan with a cellular provider means never having to worry about getting access to the network. However, unless you're paying for unlimited access (lucky you!), you should be worrying about going over whatever maximum amount of data usage your plan provides per month. That's because going over your data max means you start paying through the nose for each megabyte, and you can run up a hefty bill in no time.

To avoid that, keep track of your cellular data usage by following these steps:

1. **On the Home screen, tap Settings.** The Settings screen appears.

2. **Tap General.** Your iPad displays the General options screen.

3. **Tap Usage.** Your iPad displays the Usage screen.

4. **Tap Cellular Usage.** Your iPad displays the Cellular Usage screen.

5. **Examine the Sent and Received values in the Cellular Network Data section.**

Genius

The iPad cellular usage values are meaningful only if they correspond to your monthly data cycle with your provider. Check with your cellular provider to see which day of the month your data resets. On that day, follow the previous steps to open the Cellular Usage screen, and then tap Reset Statistics. When the iPad asks you to confirm, tap Reset.

Disabling data roaming

Data roaming is an often convenient cellular plan feature that enables you to surf the web, check and send e-mail, and exchange text messages when you're outside your provider's normal coverage area. The downside is that roaming charges are almost always eye-poppingly expensive. They're often several dollars per minute, depending on where you are and what type of service you're using. Not good!

Unfortunately, if you have the iPad Data Roaming feature turned on, you may incur massive roaming charges even if you never use the device! That's because your iPad still performs background checks for things like incoming e-mail messages and text messages, so a week in some far-off land could cost you hundreds of dollars without even using the device. Again, not good!

To avoid this insanity, turn off Data Roaming when you don't need it. Follow these steps:

1. **On the Home screen, tap Settings.** The Settings screen appears.
2. **Tap Cellular Data.** The Cellular Data screen appears.
3. **Tap the Data Roaming On/Off button to change this setting to Off.**

Turning off the cellular antenna

The iPad cellular antenna is constantly on the lookout for a connection. That's handy because it means you always have access whenever you're in a cellular network coverage area. However, this constant searching uses up your iPad battery like crazy. If you're on a Wi-Fi network or you don't need a cellular network connection for a while, you can preserve precious battery life by turning off the cellular antenna. To do so, follow these steps:

1. **On the Home screen, tap Settings.** The Settings screen appears.
2. **Tap Cellular Data.** The Cellular Data screen appears.
3. **Tap the Cellular Data switch to the Off position.** Your iPad disconnects from your cellular connection.

When you're ready to get back on the cellular highway, return to the Cellular Data screen and tap the Cellular Data switch to the On position.

Switching Your iPad to Airplane Mode

When you board a flight, aviation regulations in most countries are super-strict about disallowing not only cell phone calls, but also wireless signals of *any* kind. This means your iPad is a real hazard to sensitive airline equipment because it also transmits Wi-Fi and Bluetooth signals, even if there are no Wi-Fi receivers or Bluetooth devices within 30,000 feet of your current position.

Your pilot or friendly flight attendant will suggest that you simply turn off your device. Sure, that does the job, but darn it, you have an iPad, which means there are plenty of things you can do outside of its wireless capabilities, such as listen to music or an audiobook, watch a show, view photos, and much more.

So how do you reconcile the no-wireless-and-that-means-you regulations with the multitude of wireless-free iPad apps? You put your iPad into a special state called Airplane mode. This mode turns off the transceivers — the internal components that transmit and receive wireless signals — for the iPad cellular antenna, Wi-Fi, and Bluetooth features. With your iPad now safely in compliance with federal aviation regulations, you're free to use any app that doesn't rely on wireless transmissions.

To activate airplane mode, tap settings on the Home screen and the Settings screen appears. Tap the Airplane Mode On/Off switch to turn this setting On, as shown in Figure 1.10. Your iPad disconnects your cellular network and your wireless network (if you have a current connection). Notice, as well, that while Airplane mode is on, an airplane icon appears in the status bar in place of the signal strength and network icons.

1.10 When your iPad is in Airplane mode, an airplane icon appears in the status bar.

How Do I Keep My iPad in Sync?

Your iPad weighs a bit less than a pound and a half (a tiny bit more with a cellular chip shoehorned inside), so it's as portable as a computer can get. This means you often have it with you when you venture out, but hello? Aren't you forgetting something? You were just about to waltz outside without any of your *data*. Your contacts, calendars, bookmarks, music, videos, and other media are on your main computer. Why not take them with you? You can if you sync that data with your iPad. How to do so is covered in this chapter.

Connecting Your iPad to Your Computer

When the iPad was first released, it looked as though we might have finally arrived at that glorious day when computers and devices could just sort of *sense* each other's presence and begin a digital conversation without requiring something as inelegant as a *physical* connection. Ugh. However, despite the fact that the fancy-schmancy iPad supported *two* wireless technologies — Wi-Fi (see Chapter 1) and Bluetooth (see Chapter 4) — exchanging data between it and a Mac or PC still required a wired connection.

Well, I'm happy to report that those days are behind us. Sort of. Yes, you can still use a cable to connect your iPad and your computer, but iOS 5 now also supports *wireless* connections via Wi-Fi. The next couple of sections provide the details.

Connecting via USB

Although iOS 5 supports Wi-Fi syncing, USB connections are still important for those times when you want to use iTunes to change your sync settings. To make an old-fashioned USB-style connection, you can proceed in a couple of ways:

- **USB cable.** Use the cable that came with your iPad to attach the USB connector to a free USB port on your Mac or Windows PC. Then, attach the dock connector to the 30-pin connector port on the bottom of the iPad.

- **Dock.** If you shelled out the bucks for an optional iPad dock (a regular dock or a keyboard dock), plug it in to a power outlet. Using the iPad cable, attach the USB connector to a free USB port on your Mac or Windows PC and then attach the dock connector to the 30-pin connector port on the back of the dock. Now, insert your iPad into the dock cradle.

Connecting via Wi-Fi

As long as your iPad and your computer are connected to the same Wi-Fi network, the Wi-Fi connection happens automatically, but only if you prepare your iPad. Specifically, you need to follow these steps:

1. **Connect your iPad to your computer.**
2. **When your iPad appears in the iTunes Devices list, click it.**

3. **In the Summary tab, select the Sync with this iPad over Wi-Fi check box.**

4. **Click Apply.** iTunes configures your iPad to sync over Wi-Fi.

5. **Eject and then disconnect your iPad.**

6. **Shut down and restart iTunes.**

7. **Turn off your iPad and then turn it back on.** Your iPad appears in the iTunes Devices list without being physically connected to your computer.

After you do all of the above, you're ready to sync over Wi-Fi, which I describe a bit later in this chapter.

Syncing Your iPad Automatically

Depending on the storage capacity of your iPad — 16GB, 32GB, or 64GB — you may be able to cram all of your computer's iPad-friendly digital content onto the iPad hard drive. If that sounds like the way you want to go, then you can take advantage of the easiest of the iPad syncing scenarios, in which you don't have to pay any attention in the least: automatic syncing. (If that does *not* sound like the way you want to go, no worries: see the section on syncing your iPad manually a bit later in this chapter.) Because you know all the iPad-able content on your Mac or Windows PC is going to fit, all you have to do is turn on your iPad and connect it to your computer.

Caution I've found that syncing can sometimes fail if your iPad is open to an app settings screen when you launch the sync. Press the Home button to ensure that no settings or apps are open before trying to sync.

Yup, that's all there is to it! iTunes opens automatically, connects to your iPad, and begins syncing. As an added bonus, the USB port also begins charging the iPad battery. Note these two things while this is happening, as shown in Figure 2.1:

-   **You see your iPad in the iTunes Devices list.**

-   **You see Syncing "*iPad*" in the iTunes status area (where *iPad* is the name of your iPad).**

17

Eject

2.1 When you connect your iPad, iTunes springs into action and starts syncing.

Note, too, that iOS 5 offers a welcome little perk: you can now use your iPad while the sync is running. When the sync is done, you need to do two things:

- **In iTunes, click the Eject icon beside your iPad in the Devices list (see Figure 2.1).**
- **Remove the dock connector from the iPad 30-pin connector port.**

Bypassing the automatic sync

Sometimes, you may want to connect your iPad to your computer, but you don't want it to sync automatically. I'm not talking about switching to manual syncing full time; I get to that in a second. Instead, I'm talking about bypassing the sync one time only. For example, you may want to connect your iPad to your computer just to charge it (assuming you either don't have the optional dock or you don't have it with you). Or perhaps you just want to use iTunes to eyeball how much free space is left on your iPad or to check for updates to the iPad software.

Whatever the reason, you can tell iTunes to hold off on the syncing by using one of the following techniques:

- **Mac.** Connect the iPad to the Mac, and then quickly press and hold the Option and ⌘ keys.

- **Windows.** Connect the iPad to the Windows PC, and then quickly press and hold the Ctrl and Shift keys.

When you see that iTunes has added your iPad to the Devices list, you can release the keys. Note, however, that you don't need to use iTunes to see how much free space is left on your iPad. On the Home screen, tap Settings, tap General, and then tap About. In the About screen that slides in, the Available value tells you how many gigabytes (or megabytes) of free space you have left.

Troubleshooting automatic syncing

Okay, so you connect your iPad to your computer and then nothing. If iTunes isn't already running, it refuses to wake up from its digital slumbers. What's up with that?

A couple of things could be the problem. First, connect your iPad, switch to iTunes on your computer, and then click your iPad in the Devices list. On the Summary tab, as shown in Figure 2.2, make sure the Open iTunes when this iPad is connected check box is selected.

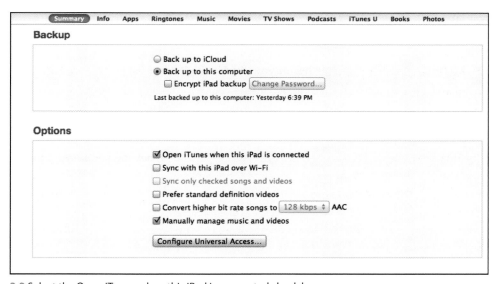

2.2 Select the Open iTunes when this iPad is connected check box.

19

If that check box was already selected, you need to delve a bit deeper to solve the mystery. Follow these steps:

1. **Open the iTunes preferences:**
   - **Mac.** Choose iTunes ⟹ Preferences, or press ⌘+. (period).
   - **Windows.** Choose Edit ⟹ Preferences, or press Ctrl+. (period).

2. **Click the Devices tab.**

3. **Deselect the Prevent iPods, iPhones, and iPads from syncing automatically check box.**

4. **Click OK to put the new setting into effect and enable automatic syncing again.**

Syncing Your iPad Manually

When you first connected your iPad to iTunes, the brief setup routine included a screen that asked if you wanted to automatically sync certain content, such as music and photos. If you activated a check box for a particular type of content, iTunes configured the iPad to sync *all* of that content. That's fine, but depending on how much content you have, you might end up throwing a lot of stuff at your iPad.

One fine day, you'll be minding your own business, performing what you believe to be a routine sync operation, when a dialog like the one shown in Figure 2.3 rears its nasty head.

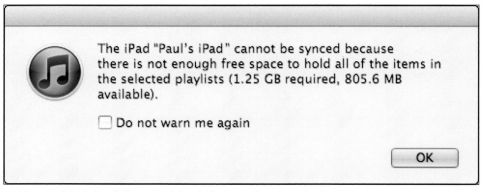

The iPad "Paul's iPad" cannot be synced because there is not enough free space to hold all of the items in the selected playlists (1.25 GB required, 805.6 MB available).

☐ Do not warn me again

OK

2.3 You see this dialog if iTunes can't fit all of your stuff on your iPad.

Groan! This most unwelcome dialog means just what it says: you don't have enough free space on your iPad to sync all the content from your computer. You can handle this in a couple of ways:

- **Remove some of the content from your computer.** This is a good way to go if your iPad is really close to having enough space. For example, the dialog says your computer wants to send 100MB of data, but your iPad has only 98MB of free space. Get rid of a few megabytes of stuff on your computer, and you're back in the sync business.

- **Synchronize your iPad manually.** This means that you no longer sync everything on your computer. Instead, you handpick which playlists, podcasts, audiobooks, and so on are sent to your iPad. It's a bit more work, but it's the way to go if there's a big difference between the amount of content on your computer and the amount of space left on your iPad.

Syncing manually means that you handle the syncing yourself for the various content types: contacts, calendars, e-mail, bookmarks, music, podcasts, audiobooks, eBooks, photos, videos, and apps. You do this using the other tabs in the iPad window: Info, Music, Photos, and so on. To learn the specifics for each type of data, see the following chapters:

- **Safari bookmarks.** See Chapter 5.
- **E-mail account info.** See Chapter 6.
- **Mail application notes.** See Chapter 6.
- **Photos.** See Chapter 7.
- **eBooks.** See Chapter 8.
- **Music, podcasts, and audiobooks.** See Chapter 9.
- **Movies and TV shows.** See Chapter 10.
- **Contacts.** See Chapter 11.
- **Calendars.** See Chapter 12.

Once you have your sync settings straight, click Sync to actually perform the synchronization.

Syncing Your iPad Via Wi-Fi

The ability to sync your iPad with your computer without a wire in sight is one of the nicest new iOS 5 features. If you're sitting in your easy chair or relaxing on the front porch, who wants to get up, go to the computer, connect your iPad, and then run a sync just to get, say, the latest podcasts? With iOS 5, as long as your iPad is on AC and is connected to the same Wi-Fi network as your computer, you can run the sync by barely moving a muscle.

Follow these steps to sync with iTunes right where you are by using Wi-Fi:

1. **Make sure your computer is running and connected to the same Wi-Fi network as your iPad.**

2. **On the iPad Home screen, tap Settings.** The Settings app appears.

3. **Tap General.**

4. **Tap iTunes Wi-Fi Sync.**

5. **Tap Sync Now.** Your iPad syncs with iTunes on your computer.

Taking Syncing to a Higher Level

Syncing data between your iPad and your Mac or PC isn't complicated Most of the time it's a straight connect-and-sync task (or, in the Wi-Fi case, it's a straight sync task). I'm loath to add complexity to such an admirably simple procedure, but you need to know how to handle the main sync challenges that might come your way. The next few sections show you how to handle sync conflicts, deal with large sync changes, replace and refresh iPad data, and merge and sync data from two or more computers.

Handling sync conflicts

When you sync information between your iPad and a computer, you might think it's exclusively new data that's being transferred: new songs, new contacts, new calendar appointments, and so on. However, the sync also includes edited or changed data. For example, if you change someone's e-mail address on your iPad, the next time you sync, iTunes updates the e-mail address on the computer, which is exactly what you want.

However, what if you already changed that person's address on the computer? If you made the same edit, it's no big deal because there's nothing to sync. But what if you made a different edit? Ah, that's a problem, because now iTunes doesn't know which version has the correct information. In that case, it shrugs its digital shoulders and passes off the problem to a program called Conflict Resolver, which displays the dialog shown in Figure 2.4.

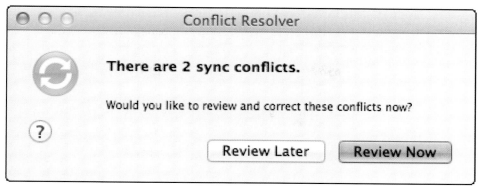

2.4 If you make different edits to the same bit of information on your iPad and your computer, the Conflict Resolver springs into action.

If you want to deal with the problem now, click Review Now. Conflict Resolver offers you the details of the conflict. For example, in Figure 2.5 you can see that a contact's work e-mail address is different in Address Book and on the iPad. To settle the issue once and for all (you hope), click the correct version of the information, and then click Done. When Conflict Resolver tells you it will fix the problem during the next sync, click Sync Now to make it happen right away.

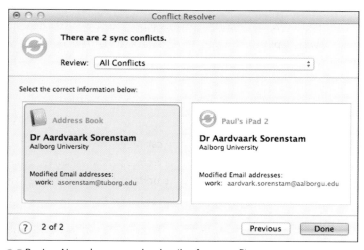

2.5 Review Now shows you the details of any conflicts.

Handling large iPad-to-computer sync changes

Syncing works both ways: Not only does your iPad receive content from your computer, but your computer also receives content from your iPad. For example, if you create any bookmarks, contacts, or appointments on your iPad, those items are sent to your computer during the sync.

However, it's implied that the bulk of the content flows from your computer to your iPad, which makes sense because for most things it's a bit easier to add, edit, and delete stuff on the computer. That's why if you make lots of changes to your iPad content, iTunes displays a warning that the sync is going to make lots of changes to your computer content. The threshold is five percent, which means that if the sync changes more than five percent of a particular type of content on your computer — such as bookmarks or calendars — the warning appears. For example, Figure 2.6 shows the Sync Alert dialog you see if the sync will change more than five percent of your contacts or groups. In this example, the sync will change more than 25 percent of the contacts.

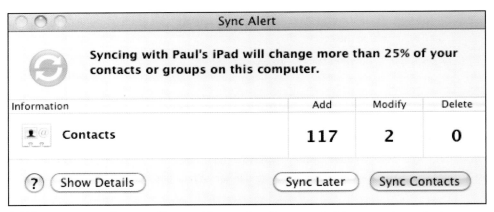

2.6 iTunes warns you if a sync will mess with more than five percent of the computer content.

If you're expecting this (because you did change lots of stuff on your iPad), click the Sync *Whatever* button, where *Whatever* is the type of data: Bookmarks, Contacts, and so on. If you're not sure, click Show Details to see what the changes are. If you're still scratching your head, click Sync Later to skip that part of the sync.

If you're running iTunes for Windows, you can either turn off this warning or adjust the threshold. (For some unfathomable reason, iTunes for the Mac doesn't offer this handy option.)

Follow these steps:

1. **Choose Edit ⇨ Preferences, or press Ctrl+, (comma).** The iTunes dialog appears.

2. **Click the Devices tab.**

3. **If you want to disable the sync alerts altogether, deselect the Warn When check box.** Otherwise, leave that check box selected and move to Step 4.

4. **Use the Warn When *Percent* of the Data on the Computer will be Changed list to set the alert threshold, where *Percent* is one of the following:**

   - **any.** Select this option to see the sync alert whenever syncing with the iPad will change data on your computer. iPad synchronizations routinely modify data on the computer, so be prepared to see the alerts every time you sync. (Of course, that may be exactly what you want.)

   - **more than *X*%.** Select one of these options — your choices are 5% (the default), 25%, and 50% — to see the alert only when the sync will change more than *X* percent of some data type on the computer.

5. **Click OK to put the new settings into effect.**

Removing and replacing iPad data

After you know what you're doing, syncing contacts, calendars, e-mail accounts, and bookmarks to your iPad is a relatively bulletproof procedure that should happen without a hitch each time. Of course, this is technology you're dealing with, so hitches do happen every now and then. As a result, you might end up with corrupt or repeated information on your iPad.

Or perhaps you've been syncing your iPad with a couple of different computers (see the section on syncing media with two or more computers later in this chapter) and you decide to cut one of them out of the loop, and use a single machine for all of your syncs.

In both of these scenarios, you need to replace the existing information on your iPad with a freshly baked batch of data. Fortunately, iTunes has a feature that lets you do exactly that. Here's how it works:

1. **Connect your iPad to your computer.**

2. **In the iTunes Devices list, click the iPad.**

3. **Click the Info tab.**

4. **Select the Sync check boxes for each type of information with which you want to work (contacts, calendars, e-mail accounts, bookmarks, or notes).** If you don't select a check box, iTunes won't replace that information on your iPad. For example, if you like your iPad bookmarks just the way they are, don't select the Sync Bookmarks check box.

5. **In the Advanced section, select the check box beside each type of information you want to replace.** Figure 2.7 shows five check boxes: Contacts, Calendars, Mail Accounts, Bookmarks, and Notes.

Advanced

Replace information on this iPad
- ☐ Contacts
- ☐ Calendars
- ☐ Mail Accounts
- ☐ Bookmarks
- ☐ Notes

During the next sync only, iTunes will replace the selected information on this iPad with information from this computer.

2.7 Use the check boxes in the Advanced section to decide which information to replace on your iPad.

6. **Click Apply.** iTunes replaces the selected information on your iPad.

Note If a check box in the Advanced section is disabled, it's because you didn't select the corresponding Sync check box. For example, if the Sync Notes check box is deselected, the Notes check box is disabled in the Advanced section.

Merging data from two or more computers

Long gone are the days when our information resided on a single computer. Now it's common to have a desktop computer (or two) at home, a work computer, a smartphone (such as an iPhone), and, of course, your iPad. It's nice to have all that digital firepower, but it creates a big problem: You end up with contacts, calendars, and other information scattered over several devices. How are you supposed to keep track of it all?

The latest solution from Apple is iCloud (I talk about it later in this chapter), which provides seamless information integration across multiple computers, including Macs and Windows PCs.

If you don't have an iCloud account, you can still achieve a bit of data harmony. That's because iTunes offers the welcome ability to *merge* information from two or more computers on the iPad.

For example, if you have contacts on your home computer, you can sync them with your iPad. If you have a separate collection of contacts on your notebook, you can also sync them with your iPad, but iTunes gives you two choices:

- **Merge Info.** With this option, your iPad keeps the information synced from the first computer and merges it with the information synced from the second computer.
- **Replace Info.** With this option, your iPad deletes the information synced from the first computer and replaces it with the information synced from the second computer.

Follow these general steps to set up your merged information:

1. **Sync your iPad with information from one computer.** This technique works with contacts, calendars, e-mail accounts, and bookmarks.
2. **Connect your iPad to the second computer.**
3. **In iTunes, click your iPad in the Devices list.**
4. **Click the Info tab.**
5. **Select the Sync check boxes that correspond with information already synced on the first computer.** For example, if you synced contacts on the first computer, select the Sync Contacts check box.
6. **Click Apply.** iTunes displays a dialog like the one shown in Figure 2.8.

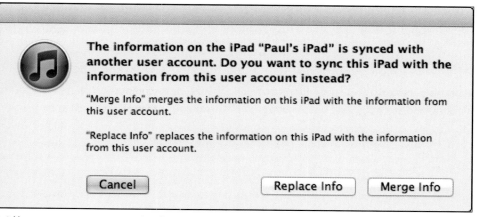

The information on the iPad "Paul's iPad" is synced with another user account. Do you want to sync this iPad with the information from this user account instead?

"Merge Info" merges the information on this iPad with the information from this user account.

"Replace Info" replaces the information on this iPad with the information from this user account.

Cancel   Replace Info   Merge Info

2.8 You can merge contacts, calendars, e-mail accounts, and bookmarks from two or more computers.

7. **Click Merge Info.** iTunes syncs your iPad and merges the computer's information with the existing information from the first computer.

Syncing media with two or more computers

It's a major drag, but you can't sync the same type of content to your iPad from more than one computer. For example, suppose you're syncing photos from your desktop computer. If you then connect your iPad to another computer (your notebook, for example), crank up iTunes, and select the Sync Photos from check box, iTunes coughs up the dialog in Figure 2.9. As you can see, iTunes tells you that if you go ahead with the photo sync on this computer, it will blow away all your existing iPad data!

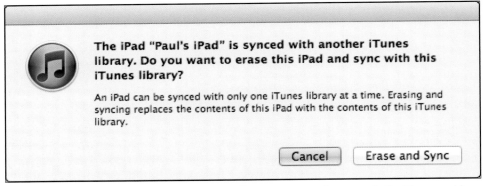

The iPad "Paul's iPad" is synced with another iTunes library. Do you want to erase this iPad and sync with this iTunes library?

An iPad can be synced with only one iTunes library at a time. Erasing and syncing replaces the contents of this iPad with the contents of this iTunes library.

Cancel   Erase and Sync

2.9 Syncing the same type of content from two different computers is a no-no in the iTunes world.

So there's no chance of syncing the same iPad with two different computers, right? Not so fast, my friend. Let's try another thought experiment. Suppose you're syncing your iPad with your desktop computer, but you're not syncing Movies. Again, you connect your iPad to your notebook (or whatever), crank up iTunes, and select the Sync Movies check box. Hey, no ominous warning dialog! What gives?

The deal here is that if iTunes sees that you don't have any examples of a particular type of content (such as movies) on your iPad, it lets you sync that type of content, no questions asked.

In other words, you *can* sync your iPad with multiple computers, although in a roundabout kind of way. The secret is to have no overlapping content types on the various computers you use for the syncing. For example, let's say you have a home desktop computer, a notebook computer, and a work desktop computer.

Here's a sample scenario for syncing your iPad with all three machines:

- **Home desktop (music and video only).** Select the Sync music check box in the Music tab, and select all the Sync check boxes in the Movies tab. Deselect the Sync check boxes on the Photos and Podcasts tabs.

- **Notebook (photos only).** Select the Sync photos from check box on the Photos tab. Deselect all the Sync check boxes in the Music, Podcasts, and Movies tabs.

- **Work desktop (podcasts only).** Select the Sync box in the Podcasts tab. Deselect the Sync check boxes in the Music, Photos, and Movies tabs.

Syncing Your iPad with iCloud

When you go online, you take your life along with you, of course, so your online world becomes a natural extension of your real world. However, just because it's online doesn't mean the digital version of your life is any less busy, chaotic, or complex than the rest of your life. The Apple iCloud service is designed to ease some of that chaos and complexity by automatically syncing your most important data — your e-mail, contacts, calendars, and bookmarks. Although the syncing itself may be automatic, setting it up is not, unfortunately. The rest of this chapter shows you what to do.

iCloud works particularly well with the iPad, because when you're on the town or on the road, you need data pushed to you. To ensure your iPad works seamlessly with your iCloud data, you need to add your iCloud account and configure the iPad iCloud sync settings.

Setting up your iCloud account on your iPad

Start by setting up your iCloud account on your iPad:

1. **On the Home screen, tap Settings.** Your iPad opens the Settings screen.
2. **Tap Mail, Contacts, Calendars.** The Mail, Contacts, Calendars screen appears.
3. **Tap Add Account.** The Add Account screen appears.
4. **Tap the iCloud logo.** Your iPad displays the iCloud screen, as shown in Figure 2.10.
5. **Tap the Apple ID text box and type your iCloud e-mail address.**
6. **Tap the Password text box and type your iCloud password.**
7. **Tap Next.** Your iPad verifies the account info and then asks if you want to allow iCloud to use your location.

2.10 Use the iCloud screen to configure your iCloud account on your iPad.

8. **Tap OK.** Allowing iCloud to use your location enables you to use the Find My iPad feature, which I discuss in Chapter 3. Your iPad displays the iCloud screen, as shown in Figure 2.11.

9. **For each type of data you want pushed to your iPad, tap the corresponding switch set to On.**

10. **If, after tapping a switch to On, your iPad asks if you want to merge previous synced data with your iCloud data, tap Merge.**

11. **Tap Save.** Your iPad returns you to the Mail settings screen with your iCloud account added to the Accounts list.

2.11 Use this iCloud screen to activate many features, including contacts, calendars, and bookmarks.

Setting up iCloud synchronization on your iPad

The *cloud* part of iCloud means that no matter where you are, your e-mail messages, contacts, and calendars get pushed to your iPad and remain fully synced with all your other devices. Your iPad comes with this push feature turned on, but if you want to double-check this, or if you want to turn off push in order to concentrate on something else, you can configure the setting by following these steps:

1. **In the Home screen, tap Settings.** The Settings screen appears.

2. **Tap Mail, Contacts, Calendars.** The Mail, Contacts, Calendars screen appears.

3. **Tap Fetch New Data.** Your iPad displays the Fetch New Data screen, as shown in Figure 2.12.

2.12 You use the Fetch New Data screen to configure iCloud synchronization on your iPad.

4. **If you want iCloud data sent to you automatically, tap the Push switch to the On position.** Otherwise, tap Push to the Off position.

5. **If you turned push off (or if your iPad includes applications that don't support push), tap the frequency with which your iPad should fetch new data: Every 15 Minutes, Every 30 Minutes, Hourly, or Manually.**

Setting up iCloud synchronization on your Mac

If you want to keep your Mac in sync with the iCloud push services, you need to add your iCloud account to the Mail application and configure your Mac's iCloud synchronization feature.

Follow these steps to get your iCloud account into the Mail application:

1. **In the Dock, click the Mail icon.** The Mail application appears.

2. **Choose Mail ⇨ Preferences to open the Mail preferences.**

3. **Click the Accounts tab.**

4. **Click +.** Mail displays the Add Account dialog.

5. **Type your name in the Full Name text box.**

6. **Type your iCloud e-mail address in the Email Address text box.**

7. **Type your iCloud password in the Password text box.**

8. **Click Create.** Mail verifies the account info and displays the Account Summary screen.

9. **Select the check box beside each type of data you want to set up.**

10. **Click Create.** Mail returns you to the Accounts tab with the iCloud account added to the Accounts list.

Macs were made to sync with iCloud, so doing so should be a no-brainer. To ensure that's the case, you need to configure your Mac to make sure iCloud sync is activated, and that your e-mail accounts, contacts, and calendars are part of the sync process. Follow these steps to set your preferences:

1. **Click the System Preferences icon in the Dock.** Your Mac opens the System Preferences window.

2. **In the Internet & Wireless section, click the iCloud icon.** The iCloud preferences appear, as shown in Figure 2.13.

2.13 Click your iCloud account, and then select the items you want to sync.

3. **Select the check box beside each data item you want to sync with your iCloud account, particularly the following push-related items:**

   ● **Mail & Notes**

   ● **Contacts**

   ● **Calendars**

   ● **Bookmarks**

   ● **Photo Stream**

   ● **Documents & Data**

Configuring your iCloud account on your Windows PC

iCloud is happy to push data to your Windows PC. However, unlike with a Mac, your Windows machine wouldn't know iCloud if it tripped over it. To get Windows hip to the iCloud thing, you need to do two things:

● **Download and install the latest version of iTunes.**

● **Download and install the iCloud Control Panel for Windows, which you can find here: http://support.apple.com/kb/DL1455.**

With that done, you now configure iCloud to work with your Windows PC by following these steps:

1. **On the Windows PC that you want to configure to work with iCloud, choose Start ⇨ Control Panel to open the Control Panel window.**

2. **Double-click the iCloud icon.** If you don't see this icon, first open the Network and Internet category. The iCloud Preferences window appears.

3. **Use the Apple ID text box to type your iCloud address.**

4. **Use the Password text box to type your iCloud password.**

5. **Click Sign In.** Windows signs in to your account and then displays the iCloud control panel, as shown in Figure 2.14.

2.14 Use the iCloud control panel to set up your Windows PC to work with iCloud.

6. **Select the check box beside each type of data you want to sync.**

7. **Click Apply.**

Note

After you sign into iCloud for the first time, you might see a Windows Security Alert dialog box telling you that Windows Firewall is blocking a program. Make sure that the Private networks check box is selected, the Public networks check box is deselected, and then click Allow access.

How Can I Protect
My iPad?

Your iPad is a tablet, but that humble word doesn't even begin to capture the true nature of the device. After all, you use your iPad to surf the web, send and receive e-mail and text messages, manage your contacts and schedules, take pictures and shoot videos, and much more. This remarkable versatility also means that your iPad is jammed with tons of information about you. Although you might not store the nuclear launch codes on your iPad, chances are what *is* on there is pretty important to you. Considering this, you should definitely take steps to protect your iPad.

Protecting Your iPad with a Passcode

When your iPad is asleep, the device is locked in the sense that tapping the touchscreen or pressing the volume controls does nothing. This sensible arrangement prevents accidental taps when the device is in your pocket or rattling around in your backpack or handbag. To unlock the device, you either press the Home button or the Sleep/Wake button, drag the Slide to Unlock slider, and you're back in business.

Note If you have a third-generation iPad or an iPad 2 and an Apple Smart Cover, you can also lock/unlock your iPad by opening the Smart Cover. If you frequently remove the Smart Cover and don't want to unlock your iPad, you can turn off the automatic lock. To do so, tap Settings, tap General, and then tap the iPad Cover Lock/Unlock switch to Off.

Unfortunately, this simple technique means that anyone else who gets his mitts on your iPad can also be quickly back in business — *your* business! If you have sensitive or confidential information on your device, or want to avoid digital joyrides that run up massive roaming or data charges, you need to truly lock your iPad.

You do that by specifying a passcode that must be typed before anyone can use the iPad. You can set either a simple four-digit passcode, or a longer, more complex one that uses any combination of numbers, letters, and symbols.

Note Yes, having a passcode hoop to jump through before using your iPad is a hassle. To minimize the bother, turn off the passcode when using your iPad at home, and only turn it on when you take your iPad out in public.

Follow these steps to set up your passcode:

1. **On the Home screen, tap Settings.** The Settings app appears.
2. **Tap General.** The General screen appears.
3. **Tap Passcode Lock.** The Passcode Lock screen appears.
4. **If you prefer to set a complex passcode, tap the Simple Passcode switch to Off.**

5. **Tap Turn Passcode On.** The Set Passcode screen appears.

6. **Tap your passcode.** For security, the characters appear in the passcode box as dots.

7. **If you're typing a complex passcode, tap Next.** Your iPad prompts you to reenter it.

8. **Tap your passcode again.**

9. **If you're typing a complex passcode, tap Done.**

Caution You really, really need to remember your iPad passcode. If you forget it, you're locked out of your own device and the only way to get back in is to use iTunes to restore the iPad data and settings from an existing backup (described in Chapter 14).

With your passcode now active, iPad displays the Passcode Lock screen, as shown in Figure 3.1. You can also get to this screen by tapping Settings in the Home screen, then General, then Passcode Lock, and then typing your passcode.

3.1 Use the Passcode Lock screen to configure the iPad passcode lock.

39

This screen offers six options:

- **Turn Passcode Off.** If you want to stop using your passcode, tap this button and then type the passcode (for security; otherwise an interloper could just shut off the passcode).

- **Change Passcode.** Tap this button to type a new passcode. Note that you first need to type your old passcode and then type the new one.

- **Require Passcode.** This setting determines how much time elapses before the iPad locks the device and requests the passcode.

  - The default setting is Immediately, which means you see the Enter Passcode screen as soon as you finish dragging Slide to Unlock.

  - The other options are After 1 minute, After 5 minutes, After 15 minutes, After 1 hour, and After 4 hours. Use one of these if you want to be able to work with your iPad for a bit before getting locked out. For example, the After 1 minute option is good if you need to quickly check e-mail without having to type your passcode.

- **Simple Passcode.** Use this switch to toggle between a simple four-digit passcode and a complex passcode.

- **Picture Frame.** Tap this setting to Off if you don't want your iPad used as a picture frame while it's locked.

- **Erase Data.** When this setting is On, your iPad will self-destruct, er, I mean erase all of its data when it detects ten incorrect passcode attempts. Ten failed passcodes almost always means that some nasty person has your device and is trying to guess the pass-code. If you have sensitive or private data on your device, having the data erased auto-matically is a good idea.

With the passcode activated, when you bring the iPad out of standby, you drag the Slide to Unlock slider as usual, and then the Enter Passcode screen appears, as shown in Figure 3.2. Then, type your passcode (and tap Return if it's a complex passcode) to unlock the iPad.

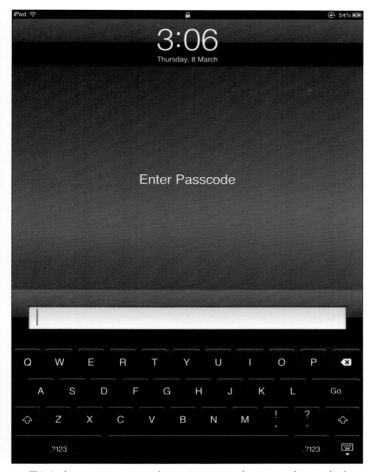

3.2 This is the screen you see when using a complex passcode to unlock your iPad.

Configuring Your iPad to Sleep Automatically

You can put your iPad into Standby mode at any time by tapping the Sleep/Wake button once. This drops the power consumption considerably (mostly because it shuts off the screen), but you can still receive incoming notifications and text messages. Also, if you have the iPod app running, it continues to play.

However, if your iPad is on but you're not using it, the device automatically goes into Standby mode after two minutes. This is called Auto-Lock and it's a handy feature because it saves battery power and prevents accidental taps when your iPad is just sitting there. It's also a crucial feature if you've protected your iPad with a passcode lock, as described earlier, because if your iPad never sleeps, it never locks either unless you shut it off manually.

To make sure your iPad sleeps automatically, or if you're not comfortable with the default two-minute Auto-Lock interval, you can make it shorter, longer, or turn it off altogether. Here are the steps to follow:

1. **On the Home screen, tap Settings.** The Settings app appears.

2. **Tap General.** The General screen appears.

3. **Tap Auto-Lock.** The Auto-Lock screen appears, as shown in Figure 3.3.

3.3 Use the Auto-Lock screen to set the Auto-Lock interval or to turn it off.

4. **Tap the interval you want to use.** You have five choices: 2 Minutes, 5 Minutes, 10 Minutes, 15 Minutes, or Never.

Backing Up Your iPad

When you sync your iPad with your computer (using either a USB or Wi-Fi connection), iTunes automatically creates a backup of your current iPad data before performing the sync. Note, however, that iTunes doesn't back up your entire iPad, which makes sense because most of what's on your device — music, photos, videos, apps, and so on — is already on your computer. Instead, iTunes only backs up data unique to the iPad, including your text messages, Web Clips, network and app settings and data, Safari history and cookies, and so on.

However, what if you've configured iTunes not to automatically sync your iPad? Is there a way to back up your iPad without performing a sync? You bet there is! To do so, follow these steps:

1. **Connect your iPad to your computer.**

2. **Open iTunes if it doesn't launch automatically.**

3. **In the Devices section, right-click your iPad, and then click Back Up.** iTunes backs up the iPad data.

If you have an iCloud account, you can use it to back up your iPad without having to connect it to a computer. To set it up, follow these steps:

1. **In the iPad Home screen, tap Settings.** The Settings app appears.

2. **Set up your iCloud account if you haven't already done so.** See Chapter 2 for the details.

3. **Tap iCloud.**

4. **Tap Storage & Backup.**

5. **Tap the iCloud Backup switch to On.** Your iPad warns you that you'll no longer be able to use iTunes for backups.

6. **Tap OK.**

7. **Tap Back Up Now.** Your iPad backs up its data to your iCloud account.

Configuring Parental Controls

If your children have access to your iPad, you probably don't want them installing or deleting apps, or editing your account settings. Similarly, if they have iPads of their own, you may be a bit worried about some of the content they might be exposed to on the web, YouTube, or in iTunes, or you might not want them giving away their current location.

For all those and similar parental worries, you can sleep better at night by activating the iPad parental controls. These controls restrict the content and activities kids can see and do.

Here's how to set them up:

1. **On the Home screen, tap Settings.** The Settings screen appears.

2. **Tap General.** The General screen appears.

3. **Tap Restrictions.** The Restrictions screen appears.

4. **Tap Enable Restrictions.** iPad displays the Set Passcode screen for you to specify a four-digit code that you can use to override the parental controls. (Note that this passcode is not the same as the passcode lock code you learned about earlier in the chapter.)

5. **Tap the four-digit restrictions passcode and then retype the code.** iPad returns you to the Restrictions screen and enables all the controls, as shown in Figure 3.4.

3.4 Use the Restrictions screen to configure the parental controls you want to use.

6. **In the Allow section for each app or task, tap the On/Off switch to enable or disable the restriction.**

7. **If you don't want your children to make changes to the current location services settings, tap Location under Allow Changes, and then tap Don't Allow Changes.**

8. **If you don't want your children to make changes to the current mail, calendar, or contacts account settings, tap Accounts under Allow Changes, and then tap Don't Allow Changes.**

9. **Under Allowed Content, tap Ratings For and then tap the country with the ratings you want to use.**

10. **For each of the content controls — Music & Podcasts, Movies, TV Shows, and Apps — tap the control, and then tap the highest rating you want your children to use.**

11. **If you don't want your children to be able to make purchases within apps, tap the In-App Purchases switch to Off.** If you leave this setting on, consider tapping Require Password and then tapping Immediately. This ensures that your children must type a password before they can make in-app purchases. If you leave the Require Password setting at 15 minutes, it means your kids can make in-app purchases without a password for up to 15 minutes after the initial purchase of the app.

12. **In the Game Center section (which appears at the bottom of the Restrictions screen), tap the On/Off switches to enable or disable multiplayer games, and to enable or disable adding friends.**

Locating and Protecting a Lost iPad

Depending on how you use your iPad, you can easily end up with a pretty large chunk of your life residing on it. That sounds like a good thing, I know, but if you happen to lose the iPad, you've also lost that chunk of your life. You've also opened up a gaping privacy hole because anyone can now delve into your data. (I'm assuming here you haven't configured your iPad with a passcode lock, as described earlier.)

If you've been syncing your iPad with your computer regularly, then you can probably recover most, or even all, of that data. However, I'm sure you'd probably rather find your iPad because it's expensive and there's just something creepy about the thought of some stranger flicking through your stuff.

The old way of finding your iPad consisted of scouring every nook and cranny that you visited before losing the iPad and calling up various lost-and-found departments to see if anyone's turned in your iPad. The new way to find your iPad is a great app (and it's also an iCloud feature) called Find My iPhone. Yes, it's called Find My *iPhone*, even on the iPad. Find My iPhone uses known Wi-Fi hotspots (as well as the GPS sensor and cellular antenna if you have a 3G or 4G iPad) to locate the device. You can also use Find My iPhone to send a message to the iPad, and remotely lock or delete your data. The next few sections provide the details.

Caution   The only drawback to Find My iPhone is that if someone else finds your iPad, that person can easily turn off the feature. To prevent this, turn on the passcode lock as described earlier in this chapter. If your iPad is already lost, use Find My iPhone on another iPad, an iPhone, or on iCloud to remotely lock the iPad, as described later in this chapter.

Activating Find My iPhone

Find My iPhone works by looking for a particular signal that your iPad beams out into the ether. This signal is turned off by default, so you need to turn it on if you ever plan to use Find My iPhone. Here are the steps to follow:

1. **Add your iCloud account as described in Chapter 6 if you haven't already done so.** When you add the account, be sure to tap OK when iCloud asks if it can use your location.

2. **On the Home screen, tap Settings**. The Settings app appears.

3. **Tap iCloud**. Your iCloud account settings appear.

4. **Tap the Find My iPad switch to On.** Your iPad asks you to confirm.

5. **Tap Allow.** Your iPad activates the Find My iPad feature, as shown in Figure 3.5.

6. **Tap Done.**

3.5 In your iCloud settings screen, tap the Find My iPad switch to On.

Locating your iPad on a map

With Find My iPad now active, you can use the Find My iPhone app or iCloud to locate it at any time. The next two sections show you how to do this using the app and iCloud.

Locating your iPad using the Find My iPhone app

Follow these steps to see your lost iPad on a map using the Find My iPhone app:

1. **On an iPad, iPhone, or iPod touch that has the Find My iPhone app installed, tap the app to launch it.** Find My iPhone prompts you to type your Apple ID.

2. **Tap your Apple e-mail address and password.** Note that you must use the same Apple ID as the one you used to activate the Find My iPad setting on your iPad.

3. **Tap Go.** The app signs in to your Apple account.

4. **If the app asks whether it can use your current location, tap OK.**

5. **If you're using Find My iPhone on an iPad, tap Devices.**

6. **In the list of devices, tap your lost iPad.** The Find My iPhone app locates the iPad on a map, as shown in Figure 3.6.

7. **To see if the location has changed, click the Refresh Location button (the circular arrow).** On the iPad version of the app, the Refresh Location button appears to the right of the Devices button; on the iPad and iPod touch, it appears in the lower-left corner of the screen.

3.6 In the list of devices, tap your iPad to locate it on a map.

Locating your iPad using iCloud

Follow these steps to see your lost iPad on a map using iCloud:

1. **Log in to your iCloud account.**

2. **Click the Switch Apps icon (the cloud).**

3. **Click Find My iPhone.** The iCloud Find My iPhone application appears.

4. **Click your iPad in the My Devices list.** iCloud locates your iPad on a map.

5. **To see if the location has changed, click the Refresh Location button (the circular arrow in the top right corner of the My Devices list).**

Sending a message to your iPad

If you think another person has your iPad, you can try to contact him by sending a message to the iPad using the Find My iPhone app or the iCloud Find My iPhone feature. Here's how it works:

1. **Tap or click your iPad in the My Devices list.** Find My iPhone locates your iPad on a map.

2. **Tap or click the blue More icon to the right of your iPad name.** Find My iPhone displays information about your iPad, as well as buttons for various actions you can take.

3. **Tap or click Display Message or Play Sound.** Find My iPhone displays the Display a Message dialog.

4. **Type your message.** Figure 3.7 shows an example.

5. **If you want to be sure the other person sees your message, leave the Play sound switch in the On position.**

6. **Tap or click Send.** iCloud sends the message, which then appears on the iPad screen, as shown in Figure 3.8.

3.7 You can send a message to your lost iPad.

3.8 The message appears on the iPad screen.

Remotely locking your iPad

While you're waiting for the other person to return your iPad, you probably don't want her rummaging around in your stuff. To prevent that, you can remotely lock the iPad by following these steps:

1. **Tap or click your iPad in the Devices list.** Find My iPhone locates your iPad on a map.

2. **Tap or click the blue More icon to the right of your iPad name.** Find My iPhone displays information about your iPad, as well as buttons for various actions you can take.

3. **Tap or click Remote Lock.** Find My iPhone displays the Remote Lock dialog, as shown in Figure 3.9.

4. **Tap or click the numbers in the keypad to enter a four-digit passcode.**

5. **Reenter a four-digit passcode.** Find My iPhone remotely locks the iPad.

3.9 To prevent anyone from messing with your lost iPad, you can remotely apply a passcode lock.

Remotely deleting the data on your iPad

If you can't get the other person to return your iPad, and it contains sensitive or confidential data (or just that big chunk of your life I mentioned earlier), you can use the Find My iPhone app or the iCloud Find My iPhone feature to take the drastic step of remotely wiping all of the data on the iPad. To erase all data from your missing iPad:

1. **Tap or click your iPad in the Devices list.** Find My iPhone locates your iPad on a map.

2. **Tap or click the blue More icon to the right of your iPad name.** Find My iPhone displays information about your iPad, as well as buttons for various actions you can take.

3. **Tap or click Remote Wipe.** Find My iPhone displays the warning shown in Figure 3.10.

4. **Tap or click Erase All Data.** Find My iPhone remotely wipes all the data from the iPad.

3.10 If you're certain your lost iPad is a lost cause, you can remotely erase all of its data.

How Do I Configure My iPad?

If you've made your way through the first three chapters of this book, then you're connected to a network, you have all your desktop data synced to your iPad, and that data is safe. What else could anyone need? You'd be surprised. Although the iPad works like a champ right out of the box, even champs can improve their game. You may find that the iPad default settings make sense for the average user, but you're far from average — after all, you bought this book! This chapter shows you how to configure your iPad to work the way you do.

Creating a Custom Home Screen

When you first start your iPad (and each time you press the Home button), the Home screen appears. You use this screen as the launching pad (so to speak) for all of your iPad adventures. Using the Home screen requires almost no training: just tap the icon you want and the app loads lickety-split. It's perfection itself.

Oh, but things are never as perfect as they appear, are they? In fact, the following are several Home screen features that make maneuvering it a bit cumbersome:

- When you hold your iPad, it is easy to accidently tap the icons in the left and right columns because they're easily reachable by your thumbs.

- If you have more than 20 icons, they extend to a second (or third, or fourth) Home screen. If the app you want isn't on the main Home screen, you must first flick to the screen that has the app icon (or tap the dot for the screen you want), and then tap the icon.

- If your icons extend onto multiple Home screens, the four icons in the iPad Dock area appear on every Home screen, so they're always available.

Note   How do you end up with more than 20 icons? Easy: the App Store. It's an online retailer devoted solely to apps designed to work with the iPad technologies: Multi-touch, GPS, the accelerometer, wireless, and more. You can download apps via Wi-Fi or a cellular connection if you have a cellular iPad (and the app is less than 20MB). On the Home screen, tap the App Store icon to see what's available.

You can make the Home screen more efficient by doing three things: Moving your four most-used icons to the iPad Dock; moving eight other commonly used icons to the left and right columns of the main Home screen; and making sure any icon you tap frequently appears somewhere on the main Home screen.

You can do all of this by rearranging the Home screen icons as follows:

1. **Display the Home screen.**

2. **Tap and hold any Home screen icon.** When you see the icons wiggling, release your finger.

3. **Tap and drag the icons into the positions you prefer.** To move an icon to a different screen, tap and drag it to the left edge of the current screen if you want to move it to a previous screen, or to the right edge if you want to move it to a later screen. Next, wait for the new screen to appear and then drop the icon where you want it. You can also include a maximum of six icons on the Dock.

4. **Rearrange the existing Dock icons by dragging them left or right to change the order.**

5. **To replace a Dock icon, first tap and drag the icon off the Dock to create some space.** Then, tap and drag any Home screen icon into the Dock.

6. **Press the Home button.** iPad saves the new icon arrangement.

Creating an app folder

The best way to make the main Home screen more manageable is to reduce the total number of icons with which you have to work. This isn't a problem when you're just starting out with your iPad because it comes with a limited number of apps. However, the addictive nature of the App Store almost always means that you end up with screen after screen of apps. The iPad lets you use a maximum of 11 screens. If you fill each screen to the brim — that's 20 apps per screen — you end up with 224 total icons (including the four Dock icons). That's a lot of icons.

Now, when I tell you to reduce the number of icons on the Home screens, I don't mean that you should delete apps. Too drastic! Instead, you can take advantage of a feature called app folders. Just like a folder on your hard drive in which you can store multiple files, an app folder can store multiple app icons — up to 20, in fact. This enables you to group related apps together under a single icon. This not only reduces your overall Home screen clutter, but it can also make individual apps easier to find.

Here are the steps to follow to create and populate an app folder:

1. **Navigate to the Home screen that contains at least one of the apps you want to include in your folder.**

2. **Tap and hold any icon until you see all the icons wiggling.**

3. **Tap and drag an icon that you want to include in the folder, and drop it on another icon that you want to include in the same folder.** Your iPad creates the folder and

displays a text box so that you can type a name for the folder. The default name is the underlying category used by the apps, as shown in Figure 4.1. If the apps are in different categories, your iPad uses the category of the app you dragged and dropped.

4.1 Drop one app icon on another to create an app folder.

4. **Tap inside the text box to edit the name if you feel like it and tap Done when you finish.**

5. **Press the Home button.** Your iPad saves your new icon arrangement.

Use the following techniques to work with your app folders:

- **Add another app to the folder.** Tap and drag the app icon and drop it on the folder.

- **Launch an app.** Tap the folder to open it (see Figure 4.2) and then tap the app.

- **Rename a folder or rearrange apps within a folder.** Tap the folder to open it, and then tap and hold any app icon within the folder. You can then edit the folder name, and drag and drop the apps within the folder.

- **Remove an app from a folder.** Tap the folder to open it, tap and hold any app icon within the folder, and then drag it out of the folder.

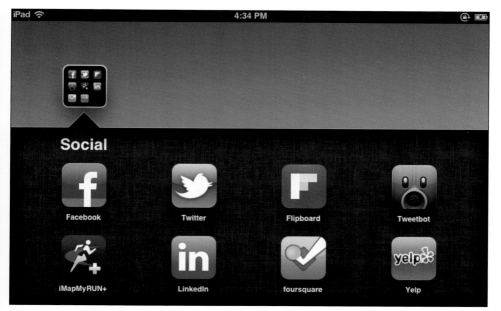

4.2 Tap an app folder to reveal its icons.

Adding a Safari Web Clip to the Home screen

Do you visit a certain web page all the time? You can set up a bookmark to that page in the iPad Safari browser, but an even faster way to access it is to add it to the Home screen as a Web Clip icon. A *Web Clip* is a link to a page that preserves the page's scroll position and zoom level. For example, suppose a page has a form at the bottom. To use that form, you have to navigate to the page, scroll to the bottom, and then zoom in to see it better. However, you can perform all three actions — navigate, scroll, and zoom — automatically with a Web Clip.

Follow these steps to save a page as a Web Clip icon on the Home screen:

1. **Use the iPad Safari browser to navigate to the page you want to save.**
2. **Scroll to the portion of the page you want to see.**
3. **Pinch and spread your fingers over the area on which you want to zoom in until you can comfortably read the text.**

4. **Tap the Actions button (the one with the arrow) at the top of the screen.** iPad displays a list of actions you can perform.

5. **Tap Add to Home Screen.** iPad prompts you to edit the Web Clip name.

6. **Edit the name as needed.** Names up to about 10-14 characters can be displayed on the Home screen without being broken. The fewer uppercase letters you use, the longer the name can be. For longer names, iPad displays the first and last few characters (depending on the locations of spaces in the name), separated by an ellipsis (...). For example, if the name is My Home Page, it appears in the Home screen as My Ho...Page.

7. **Tap Add.** iPad adds the Web Clip to the Home screen and displays the Home screen. If your main Home screen is already filled to the brim with icons, iPad adds the Web Clip to the first screen that has space available. Figure 4.3 shows a Home screen with a Web Clip.

4.3 The Web Clip has been added to the Home screen.

Note To delete a Web Clip from the Home screen, tap and hold any Home screen icon until the icon dance begins. Each Web Clip icon displays an X in the upper-left corner. Tap the X of the Web Clip you want to remove. When iPad asks you to confirm, tap Delete and press the Home button to save the configuration.

Resetting the default Home screen layout

If you make a bit of a mess of your Home screen, or if someone else is going to be using your iPad, you can reset the Home screen icons to their default layout. Follow these steps:

1. **On the Home screen, tap Settings.** The Settings screen appears.

2. **Tap General.** The General screen appears.

3. **Tap Reset.** The Reset screen appears.

4. **Tap Reset Home Screen Layout.** iPad warns you that the Home screen will be reset to the factory default layout.

5. **Tap Reset.** iPad resets the Home screen to the default layout, but it doesn't delete the icons for any apps you've added.

Working with App Notifications

Lots of apps take advantage of an iOS feature called *notifications*, which enables them to send messages and other data to your iPad. For example, the Facebook app displays an alert on your iPad when a friend sends you a message. Similarly, the Foursquare app, which lets you track where your friends are located, sends you a message when a friend checks in at a particular location.

If an app supports notifications, the first time you start it your iPad usually displays a message like the one shown in Figure 4.4, asking if you want to allow push notifications for the app. Tap OK if you're cool with that; if you're not, tap Don't Allow.

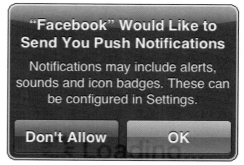

The following are the four kinds of push notifications:

- **Sound.** This is a sound effect that plays when some app-related event occurs.

4.4 Your iPad lets you allow or disallow push notifications for an app.

- **Alert.** This is a message that pops up on your iPad screen. You must then tap a button to dismiss the message before you can continue working with your current app.

- **Banner.** This is a message that appears at the top of the screen, as shown in Figure 4.5. Unlike an alert, a banner allows you to keep using your current app and disappears automatically after a few seconds. If you prefer to switch to the app to view the message, tap the banner. Banners are a new feature in iOS 5.

4.5 iOS 5 can display alert notifications as banners that appear at the top of the screen.

● **Badge.** This is a small red icon that appears in the upper-right corner of an app icon. The icon usually displays a number, which might be the number of messages you have waiting for you on the server.

Displaying the Notification Center

If you miss an alert or banner, or if you see a banner but ignore it, you can still eyeball your recent notification message by displaying the Notification Center. This is a new iOS 5 feature that combines all your recent alerts and banners in one handy location. So, not only can you see the most recent alert (as you could in previous versions of iOS), but you can also see the last few so you don't miss anything.

Even better, displaying the Notification Center is a snap — just swipe down from the top of the screen. As you can see in Figure 4.6, the Notification Center displays your recent messages sorted by app. From here, you can either tap an item to switch to that app, or you can tap elsewhere on the screen to hide the Notification Center.

4.6 Swipe down from the top of the screen to display the Notification Center.

Customizing notifications

For each app, your iPad also lets you toggle individual notification types (sounds, alerts, and badges), switch between banner and alert messages, or you can even remove an app from the Notification Center altogether. You can also configure app notifications to appear in the Lock screen, as shown in Figure 4.7. This is handy because you can see your notifications without having to unlock your iPad.

Here's how to configure app notifications:

1. **On the Home screen, tap Settings.** The Settings app appears.

2. **Tap Notifications.** The Notifications screen appears.

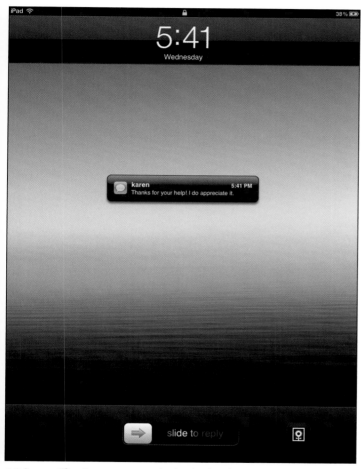

4.7 App notifications can appear in the iPad Lock screen.

3. **Tap the app you want to customize.** The app notification settings appear. Figure 4.8 shows the settings for the Game Center app. Note that not all apps support all possible settings.

4. **To remove the app from the Notification Center, tap the Notification Center switch to Off.**

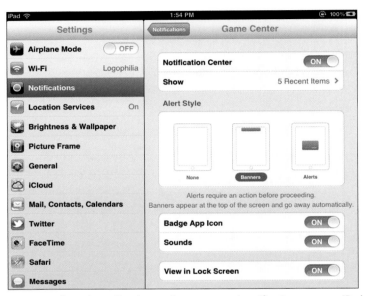

4.8 Use each app's notification settings to control notifications on your iPad.

5. **To set the maximum number of app messages that appear on the Notification Center, tap Show and then tap the number of messages.**

6. **In the Alert Style section, tap the style you prefer for message notifications.** Tap None to turn off alerts, or tap the style you want: Banners or Alerts.

7. **If the app supports badges, use the Badge App Icon switch to toggle this type of notification on or off.**

8. **If the app supports sounds, use the Sounds switch to toggle this type of notification on or off.**

9. **Use the View in Lock Screen to toggle whether the app notifications appear in the iPad Lock screen.**

10. **Tap Notifications to return to the Notifications screen.**

11. **Repeat Steps 3 to 10 to customize each app.**

Connecting Your iPad with a Bluetooth Device

Your iPad is configured to use a wireless technology called Bluetooth, which enables you to make wireless connections to other Bluetooth-friendly devices. For your iPad, this includes Bluetooth headsets, keyboards, speakers, and printers.

In theory, connecting Bluetooth devices should be criminally easy: You turn on the Bluetooth feature on each device — in Bluetooth jargon, you make the device *discoverable* — bring them within 33 feet of each other, and they connect without further ado. In practice, however, there's usually at least a bit of further ado (and sometimes plenty of it). This usually takes one or both of the following forms:

- **Making your device discoverable.** Unlike Wi-Fi devices that broadcast their signals constantly, most Bluetooth devices only broadcast their availability when you say so. This makes sense in many cases because you usually only want to connect a Bluetooth component such as a headset or keyboard with a single device. By controlling when the device is discoverable, you ensure that it works only with the device you want it to.

- **Pairing the iPad and the device.** As a security precaution, many Bluetooth devices need to be paired with another device before the connection is established. In most cases, the pairing is accomplished by entering a multidigit passkey — your iPad calls it a PIN — that you must then enter into the Bluetooth device (assuming, of course, that it has some kind of keypad). In the case of a headset, the device comes with a default passkey that you must type into your iPad to set up the pairing.

Making your iPad discoverable

So your first order of Bluetooth business is to ensure that your iPad is discoverable by activating the Bluetooth feature. To do so, follow these steps:

1. **On the Home screen, tap Settings.** The Settings screen appears.
2. **Tap General.** The General screen appears.
3. **Tap Bluetooth.** The Bluetooth screen appears.

4. **Tap the Bluetooth On/Off button to change the setting to On, as shown in Figure 4.9.** To remind you that Bluetooth is on, your iPad displays the Bluetooth icon in the status bar, as pointed out in Figure 4.9.

4.9 Use the Bluetooth screen to make your iPad discoverable.

Pairing your iPad with a device

Follow these general steps to pair your iPad with a Bluetooth device:

1. **On the Home screen, tap Settings.** The Settings screen appears.

2. **Tap General.** The General screen appears.

3. **Tap Bluetooth.** The Bluetooth screen appears.

4. **If the device has a separate switch or button that makes it discoverable, switch it on or press it.** Wait until you see the device name appear in the Bluetooth screen, as shown in Figure 4.10.

4.10 The device name appears in the Bluetooth screen when it becomes discoverable and Connected appears next to it when it's paired.

5. **Tap the name of the Bluetooth device.** If your iPad can pair with the headset automatically, you see Connected in the Bluetooth screen and you can skip the rest of these steps. Otherwise, your iPad displays a PIN that you must enter on the device.

6. **Type the device PIN.** Your iPad pairs with the device and returns you to the Bluetooth screen, where you now see Connected beside the device name (see Figure 4.10).

7. **Tap Quit, and the device is ready to use.**

Making a paired headset the audio output device

After you pair a Bluetooth headset, your iPad usually starts using the headset as the output device right away. If it doesn't or if you want to switch back to using the iPad as the output device, follow these steps to make it do so:

1. **Double tap the Home button.** Your iPad displays its multitasking controls.

2. **Swipe right to bring the audio control into view.**

3. **Tap the AirPlay button (it's to the right of the Next/Fast Forward button).** Your iPad displays a list of output devices, as shown in Figure 4.11.

4.11 Tap the AirPlay button to see a list of audio output devices.

4. **Tap the device you want to use for audio output.** Your iPad starts playing the song through the device.

Unpairing your iPad from a device

When you no longer plan to use a Bluetooth device for a long period of time, you should unpair it from your iPad. Follow these steps:

1. **On the Home screen, tap Settings.** The Settings screen appears.
2. **Tap General.** The General screen appears.
3. **Tap Bluetooth.** The Bluetooth screen appears.
4. **Tap the name of the Bluetooth device.**
5. **Tap Forget this Device.** Your iPad unpairs the device.

More Useful iPad Configuration Techniques

You've seen quite a few handy iPad customization tricks so far, but you're not done yet! Not by a long shot. The next few sections take you through a few more heartwarmingly useful iPad customization techniques.

Changing the name of your iPad

When you first configure your iPad, one of the chores you perform is giving it a custom name. This might sound frivolous, but there's a good reason to give your iPad a unique name. First, recall from Chapter 3 that when you sync your iPad, iTunes automatically creates a backup of the iPad data. Each backup is identified by the name of the iPad and the date the backup was performed. If you're in an environment where the same copy of iTunes is used to sync multiple iPads, giving each iPad its own name enables you to differentiate between multiple iPad backups.

Of course, feel free to rename your iPad for the sake of giving it a cool or snappy name if the mood strikes by following these steps

1. **In the iPad Home screen, tap Settings.** The Settings screen appears.
2. **Tap General.** The General settings appear.

3. **Tap About.** The About page appears.

4. **Tap Name.** The Settings app displays a text box with the current name of your iPad inside.

5. **Edit the name, as you see fit.**

Turning sounds on and off

Your iPad is often a noisy little thing that makes all manner of rings, beeps, and boops, seemingly at the slightest provocation. Consider the following short list of events that can give the iPad lungs a workout:

- **Incoming e-mail and text messages.**
- **Outgoing e-mail messages and tweets.**
- **Calendar and reminder alerts.**
- **Locking and unlocking the device.**
- **Tapping the keys on the on-screen keyboard.**

What a racket! None of this may bother you when you're on your own, but if you're in a meeting, a movie, or anywhere else where extraneous sounds are unwelcome, you may want to turn off some (or all) of the iPad sound effects.

If you want to go the total silence route, you can switch your iPad into silent mode, which means it doesn't play any alerts or sound effects. You switch the iPad between regular and silent modes using the Mute switch located beside the Volume rocker (if you have your iPad in portrait mode with the Home button at the bottom, it appears on the right edge of the device near the top). Use the following techniques to switch between silent and regular modes:

- **Put the device in silent mode.** Slide the Mute switch toward the Volume rocker. A red dot appears in the Mute switch, and on the iPad screen you see the Volume icon with a slash through it.

- **Resume regular mode.** Slide the Mute switch away from the Volume rocker. You no longer see the red dot in the Mute switch and on the iPad screen you see the Volume icon.

If silent mode is a bit too drastic, you can control exactly which sounds your iPad utters by follow-ing these steps:

1. **On the Home screen, tap Settings.** The Settings screen appears.

2. **Tap General.** The General screen appears.

3. **Tap Sounds.** The Sounds screen appears, as shown in Figure 4.12.

4.12 Use the Sounds screen to turn the iPad sounds on and off.

4. **In the Ringer and Alerts section, drag the volume slider to set the volume of the ringtone that plays when a message or alert comes in.**

5. **To lock the ringer volume, tap the Change with Buttons switch to the Off position.** This means that pressing the volume buttons on the side of the iPad has no effect on the ringer volume.

6. **To set a different default ringtone, tap Ringtone to open the Ringtone screen.** Tap the ringtone you want to use (your iPad plays a preview) and then tap Sounds to return to the Sounds screen.

7. **For each of the events in the list (from Ringtone to Reminder Alerts), tap the event and then tap the sound you want to hear.** You can also tap None to turn off the event sound.

8. **To turn off the sound that your iPad makes when you lock and unlock it, tap the Lock Sounds switch to Off.**

9. **To turn off the sound that your iPad makes each time you tap a key on the virtual keyboard, tap the Keyboard Clicks switch to Off.**

Configuring the side switch

When you hold your iPad in portrait mode with the Home button at the bottom, notice that the right side of the iPad contains two controls: The volume and, above it, a switch, which Apple simply refers to as the side switch. This switch doesn't have a name because you can configure it to perform one of two different tasks. By default, the side switch is a mute control that toggles the volume on and off. However, you can also use the side switch as a rotation lock control that, when activated, prevents your iPad from rotating when you change the orientation.

Follow these steps to configure the side switch:

1. **On the Home screen, tap Settings.** The Settings screen appears.

2. **Tap General.** The General screen appears.

3. **In the Use Side Switch to section, tap either Mute or Lock Rotation.**

Customizing the keyboard

If you've never been a big fan of on-screen keyboards (particularly, the stylus-activated keyboards on most tablet devices or the iPhone keyboard, which is a bit too small for rapid and accurate typing), then I think you'll love the iPad keyboard. In landscape mode, the keyboard runs along the long edge of the iPad, meaning that it takes up the full eight inches of available screen width. To put this into perspective, the landscape keyboard on the iPad is actually *wider* than the Apple Wireless Keyboard (if you measure just the letter keys, such as Q to P on the top row). In other words, your days of typing with a stylus or thumb are over. Unless you have basketball player-size hands, with the iPad keyboard you can type normally.

The iPad keyboard even changes depending on the app you use. For example, the regular keyboard features a spacebar at the bottom. However, if you're surfing the web with Safari, the keyboard that appears when you type in the address bar does away with the spacebar. In its place, you find a colon (:), a slash (/), an underscore (_), a hyphen (-), and a button that enters the characters *.com*. Web addresses don't use spaces so Apple replaced the spacebar with three things that commonly appear in a URL. Nice!

Another nice innovation you get with the iPad keyboard is a feature called Auto-Capitalization. If you type a punctuation mark that indicates the end of a sentence — for example, a period (.), a question mark (?), or an exclamation point (!) — or if you press Return to start a new paragraph, the iPad automatically activates the Shift key because it assumes you're starting a new sentence.

On a related note, double-tapping the spacebar activates a keyboard shortcut: Instead of entering two spaces, the iPad automatically enters a period (.) followed by a space. This is ever-so-slightly more efficient than tapping the period key and the spacebar separately.

Genius

Typing a number or punctuation mark normally requires three taps: Tapping Number (.?123), tapping the number or symbol, and then tapping ABC. Here's a faster way: Tap and hold the Number key to open the numeric keyboard, slide the same finger to the number or punctuation symbol you want, and then release the key. This types the number or symbol and redisplays the regular keyboard all in one touch.

For many people, one of the keys to quick iPad typing is to clear the mind and just tap away without worrying about accuracy. In many cases, you might be rather amazed at how accurate this willy-nilly approach can be. Why does it work? The secret is the iPad Auto-Correction feature, which watches what you're typing and automatically corrects any errors. For example, if you tap *hte*, your iPad automatically corrects this to *the*. Your iPad displays the suggested correction before you complete the word (say, by tapping a space or a comma) and you can reject the suggestion by tapping it.

If you do end up with spelling errors (for example, by rejecting a proper correction), your iPad lets you know by displaying the miscreant words underlined with red dots. Tap an underlined term to see a list of suggested corrections and then tap the one that works for you.

One thing the iPad keyboard doesn't seem to have is a Caps Lock feature that, when activated, enables you to type all uppercase letters. To do this, you need to tap and hold the Shift key, and then use a different finger to tap the uppercase letters. However, the iPad keyboard actually *does* have a Caps Lock feature; it's just that it's turned off by default.

To turn on Caps Lock and control Auto-Capitalization, Auto-Correction, the spell-checker, and the spacebar double-tap shortcut, follow these steps:

1. **On the Home screen, tap Settings.** The Settings screen appears.
2. **Tap General.** The General screen appears.

3. **Tap Keyboard.** The Keyboard screen appears.

4. **If you no longer want your iPad to automatically activate the Shift key at the beginning of sentences, tap the Auto-Capitalization setting to Off.**

5. **If you no longer want your iPad to suggest spelling corrections as you type, tap Auto-Correction to Off.**

6. **If you no longer want your iPad to underline misspelled words in your notes and messages, tap Check Spelling to Off.**

7. **If you want to use the Caps Lock feature, tap the Enable Caps Lock switch to On.**

8. **If you want to use the spacebar double-tap shortcut, tap the ". " Shortcut setting to On.**

9. **To add an international keyboard layout, tap International Keyboards to open the Keyboards screen, and then set the keyboard layout you want to add to On.**

Note

If you want to use the new Dictation feature (described in Chapter 6), be sure to tap the Keyboard screen's Dictation switch to the On position.

Undocking and splitting the keyboard

Earlier in this chapter I mentioned that when you're holding your iPad, it's slightly easier to tap the Home screen icons in the left and right columns because they're within thumb distance. This also applies to the on-screen keyboard, where left-side keys (such as Q, A, and Z), as well as right-side keys (such as Delete and Return) are within easy reach of the thumbs. For this reason, most people prefer to put their iPad down on a flat surface so that they can type with multiple fingers rather than just the thumbs.

Typing while holding your iPad got a whole lot easier in iOS 5 because it enables you to split the on-screen keyboard into two halves — one that appears on the left side of the screen and one that appears on the right. Because both halves are within reaching distance of all but the shortest thumbs, you can type on and hold your iPad simultaneously.

Another on-screen keyboard conundrum is that, in many apps, the keyboard always appears docked at the bottom of the screen, but the text you are typing appears at (or near) the top of the screen. This relatively huge distance between keyboard and text makes it more difficult to type accurately and quickly. Once again, however, iOS 5 rides to the rescue, enabling you to undock the keyboard and position it anywhere on the screen.

Splitting and undocking are controlled by a single setting. To turn this setting on, follow these steps:

1. **On the Home screen, tap Settings.** The Settings screen appears.

2. **Tap General.** The General screen appears.

3. **Tap Keyboard.** The Keyboard screen appears.

4. **Tap the Split Keyboard switch to On.**

The next time the on-screen keyboard comes up, tap and hold the Hide Keyboard button, which appears in the lower-right corner of the keyboard. After a couple of seconds, you see the options shown in Figure 4.13.

You have two choices:

- **Undock.** Tap this option to undock the keyboard and display it in the middle of the screen. To move the keyboard to the position you prefer, tap and drag the Hide Keyboard button.

- **Split.** Tap this option to undock the keyboard and split it in two halves, as shown in Figure 4.14. Again, you can move the split keyboard to a new position by tapping and dragging the Hide Keyboard button.

4.13 Tap and hold the Hide Keyboard button to see these options.

Genius

A slightly easier way to split and position the keyboard is to tap and drag the Hide Keyboard button.

When you're ready to return to the normal keyboard layout, tap and hold the Hide Keyboard button, and then tap Dock & Merge.

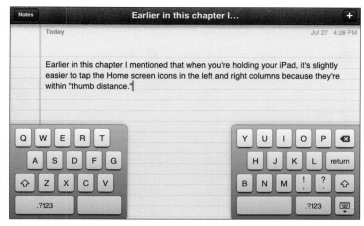

4.14 Tap Split to split the keyboard as shown for easier thumb typing.

Creating text shortcuts

The Auto-Correction keyboard feature that I mentioned earlier can speed up your typing chores a tad because it displays suggestions whenever it recognizes the word you're currently typing. When the suggestion appears, tap a word-ending character, such as a space, comma, or period, and your iPad automatically fills in the rest of the word.

Still, this is only marginally useful for speeding up typing because Auto-Correction plays it safe and usually waits until you have only a character or two left before it displays the suggested word. If you really want to shift your iPad typing into a higher gear, you need to take advantage of the text shortcuts feature in iOS 5.

If you've ever created a keyboard macro or used the AutoText feature in Microsoft Word, you'll know exactly what's happening here. A text shortcut is a short sequence of characters (usually just two or three) that represents a longer phrase. When you type the shortcut characters, your iPad displays the phrase (much the same way that Auto-Correction does) and you then type a word-ending character to replace the shortcut characters with the entire phrase.

Note

When your iPad displays the longer phrase, it also includes an X at the end, which you can tap to tell iPad not to enter the phrase. This is just like Auto-Correction, but remember that the two features aren't the same. If you turn off Auto-Correction, as I describe earlier in this chapter, you can still use text shortcuts.

These phrases can be dozens or even hundreds of characters long, so if you have phrases or boil-erplate that you use all the time, your iPad typing fingers will thank you for saving them a ton of wear and tear. Here are the steps to follow to create a text shortcut:

1. **If you have the phrase you want to use somewhere on your iPad, copy it.** This saves some time later when you create your shortcut.

2. **On the Home screen, tap Settings.** The Settings screen appears.

3. **Tap General.** The General screen appears.

4. **Tap Keyboard.** The Keyboard screen appears.

5. **Tap Add New Shortcut.** The Shortcut screen appears.

6. **If you copied the phrase earlier, paste it into the Phrase text box.** Otherwise, type the phrase.

7. **Use the Shortcut text box to type the characters you want to use to repre-sent the phrase.** The shortcut must be at least two characters long. Figure 4.15 shows an example.

8. **Tap Save.** Your iPad saves the text shortcut.

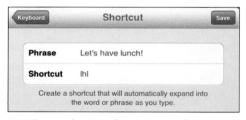

4.15 Type a phrase and two or more characters to represent the phrase.

Note

To remove a text shortcut, display the Keyboard screen, tap Edit, tap the red button to the left of the shortcut you want to remove, tap Delete, and then tap Done.

Activating and using multitasking gestures

With every new version of iOS (and even Mac OS X) there are new multitouch gestures to learn. iOS 5 was no exception, but the following new gestures are actually quite useful:

● **When you're running an app, pinch four or five fingers to return to the iPad Home screen.** This feels more natural than pressing an off-screen button to get back to the Home screen.

- **Swipe up with four or five fingers to reveal the multitasking bar.** Again, this feels more touch-friendly than having to double-click the Home button.

- **Swipe left or right with four or five fingers to switch between running apps**. This is often a better technique than using the multitasking bar to switch apps because you can see each app as you swipe.

These gestures are turned on by default, but here are the steps to follow to make sure that's the case:

1. **On the Home screen, tap Settings.** The Settings screen appears.

2. **Tap General.** The General screen appears.

3. **Tap the Multitasking Gestures switch to On.**

Signing in to your Twitter account

Twitter, that 140-characters-or-less phenomenon, started off by asking you the not-so-musical question, *What are you doing?* It's a question that seems crafted to elicit nothing but the most trivial of replies: I just woke up; I'm having toast for breakfast; I'm in a boring meeting; I just finished dinner; I'm going to bed.

But Twitter users took that original question and broadened it into a world of new questions: What are you reading? What great idea did you just come up with? What are you worried about? What interesting person did you just see or hear? What great information did you stumble upon on the web? What hilarious video would you like to share? Which is why, a couple of years ago, Twitter itself changed the original question from *What are you doing?* to *What's happening?*

Of course, what's most likely happening is that you're working or playing with your iPad, and you've got something to share with your Twitter followers: A link, a photo, a video, or what have you. In the past, sharing such things required jumping through a few too many hoops. However, iOS 5 gets rid of those hoops by baking Twitter right into the system. Once you sign in to your Twitter account using the Settings app, you can tweet stuff directly from apps, such as Safari and Photos.

Here's how to sign in:

1. **On the Home screen, tap Settings.** The Settings screen appears.

2. **Tap Twitter.** The Twitter screen appears.

3. **Type your Twitter account name in the User Name text box.**

4. **Type your account password in the Password text box.**

5. **Tap Sign In.** Your iPad connects to your Twitter account. It also prompts you to install the free Twitter iPad app, so click Later or Install, as you prefer.

Genius

If you have multiple Twitter accounts, you can add more by displaying the Twitter screen, tapping Add Account, typing the account username and password, and then tapping Sign In.

Resetting the iPad

If you've spent quite a bit of time in the iPad Settings screen, your device probably doesn't look much like it did fresh out of the box. That's okay, though, because your iPad should be as individual as you are. However, if you've gone a bit *too* far with your customizations, your iPad might feel a bit alien and uncomfortable. That's okay, too, because I know an easy solution to the problem: You can erase all of your customizations and revert to the iPad default settings.

A similar problem comes up when you want to sell or give your iPad to someone else. Chances are good that you don't want the new owner to see your data — contacts, appointments, e-mail, favorite websites, music, and so on — and it's unlikely the other person wants to wade through all that stuff anyway (no offense). To solve this problem, you can erase not only your custom settings, but also all the content you stored on the iPad.

The iPad Reset app handles these scenarios and a few more to boot. Here's how it works:

1. **On the Home screen, tap Settings.** The Settings screen appears.

2. **Tap General.** The General screen appears.

3. **Tap Reset.** The Reset screen appears.

4. **Tap one of the following reset options:**

   • **Reset All Settings.** Tap this option to reset your custom settings to the factory default settings.

   • **Erase All Content and Settings.** Tap this option to reset your custom settings and remove any data you stored on the iPad.

Caution

If you have any content on your iPad that isn't synced with iTunes — for example, iTunes music you've recently downloaded or an Apps Store program you've recently installed — you lose that content if you choose Erase All Content and Settings. First sync your iPad with your computer to save your content, and then run the reset.

- **Reset Network Settings.** Tap this option to delete your Wi-Fi network settings, which is often an effective way to solve Wi-Fi problems.

- **Reset Keyboard Dictionary.** Tap this option to reset your keyboard dictionary. This dictionary contains a list of the keyboard suggestions that you've rejected. Tap this option to clear the dictionary and start fresh.

- **Reset Home Screen Layout.** Tap this option to reset your Home screen icons to their default layout.

- **Reset Location Warnings.** Tap this option to wipe out the location preferences for your apps. A location warning is the dialog you see when you start a GPS-aware app for the first time, and your iPad asks if the app can use your current location. You tap either OK or Don't Allow, and these are the preferences you're resetting here.

5. **When the iPad asks you to confirm, tap Reset.**

Note

Remember that the keyboard dictionary contains rejected suggestions. For example, if you type *Viv*, iPad suggests *Big* instead. If you tap the *Big* suggestion to reject it and keep *Viv*, the word *Big* is added to the keyboard dictionary.

How Can I Get More Out of iPad Web Surfing?

When Apple first announced the iPad, one of the presenters demonstrated its Safari web browser and summarized the experience with a terrific line: "It just feels right to hold the Internet in your hands." That's a succinct description of web surfing on the iPad, not only because it's perfectly pithy, but also because the iPad might be the ultimate web surfing tool. It's portable, fast, intuitive, and offers *no* compromises — it shows web pages just as each designer intended. This chapter takes you through my favorite tools and techniques for getting more out of web surfing on your iPad.

Touchscreen Tips for Web Surfing

The case in favor of crowning the iPad the best web surfing appliance ever isn't hard to make: It's blazingly fast, it renders most sites perfectly, and the large screen means you almost always see a complete (horizontally, at least) view of the regular version of each page rather than a partial view, or an ugly, dumbed-down mobile version of it.

But what really sets iPad web surfing apart not only from other tablet devices, but also from desktop, notebook, and netbook computers, is the touchscreen. With other devices, although you can click links and fill in forms, the page is really a static entity that just sits there. However, with the iPad (as well as its smaller touchscreen cousin, the iPhone), you can zoom in and out of the page by spreading and pinching your fingers, and you can pan the page by flicking a finger in the direction you want to go. You really feel as though you're not just interacting with the web page, but *manipulating* it with your bare hands!

The touchscreen is the key to efficient and fun web surfing on the iPad, so here's a little collection of touchscreen tips that ought to make your web excursions even easier and more pleasurable:

- **Double tap.** A quick way to zoom in on a page that has various sections is to double tap the specific section — be it an image, a paragraph, a table, or a column of text — that you want magnified. Your iPad zooms the section to fill the width of the screen. Double tap again to return the page to the regular view.

Note

The double-tap-to-zoom trick works only on pages that have identifiable sections. If a page is just a wall of text, you can double tap until the cows come home (that's a long time) and nothing much happens.

- **Precision zooming.** Zooming on the iPad is straightforward: To zoom in, spread two fingers apart; to zoom out, pinch two fingers together. However, when you zoom in on a web page, it's almost always because you want to zoom in on something. It may be an image, a link, a text box, or just a section of text. To ensure that your target ends up in the middle of the zoomed page, place your thumb and forefinger together on the section of the screen you want to zoom, and then spread them apart to zoom in.

○ **The old pan-and-zoom.** Another useful technique for getting a target in the middle of a zoomed page is to zoom and pan at the same time. That is, as you spread (or pinch) your fingers, you also move them up, down, left, or right to pan the page at the same time. This takes a bit of practice, and often the iPad allows you to pan either horizontally or vertically (not both), but it's still a useful trick.

○ **One tap to the top.** If you're reading a particularly long-winded web page and you're near the bottom, you may have quite a long way to scroll if you need to head back to the top of the page. Save the wear and tear on your flicking finger! Instead, tap the page title, which appears just above the address box, and Safari immediately transports you to the top of the page.

○ **Tap and hold to see where a link takes you.** You click a link in a web page by tapping it with your finger. In a regular web browser, you can see where a link takes you by hovering the mouse pointer over the link and checking out the link address in the status bar. That doesn't work in your iPad, but you can still find the URL of a link before tapping it. Hold your finger on the link for a few seconds and Safari displays a pop-up screen that shows the link address, as shown in Figure 5.1. If the link looks legit, either tap Open to surf there in the current browser page, or tap Open in

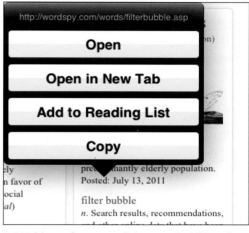

5.1 Hold your finger on a link to see the URL and several link options.

New Tab to start a fresh page (browser pages are covered later in this chapter). If you decide not to go there, tap anywhere outside of the pop-up screen.

○ **Tap and hold to make a copy of a link address.** If you want to include a link address in another app, such as a note or an e-mail message, you can copy it. Tap and hold your finger on the link for a few seconds, and Safari displays the pop-up screen (refer to Figure 5.1). Tap Copy to place the link address into memory, switch to the other app, tap the cursor, and then tap Paste.

- **Use the portrait view to navigate a long page.** When you rotate your iPad 90 degrees, the touchscreen switches to landscape view, which gives you a wider view of the page. Return the iPad to its upright position, and you return to portrait view. If you have a long way to scroll in a page, first use the portrait view to scroll down and then switch to the landscape view to increase the text size. Scrolling in the portrait view goes much faster than in landscape.

- **Two-fingered frame scrolling.** Some websites are organized using a technique called *frames* in which the overall site takes up the browser window, but some of the site pages appear in a separate rectangular area — called a frame — usually with its own scroll bar. In such sites, you may find that the usual one-fingered scroll technique scrolls only the entire browser window, not the content within the frame. To scroll the frame stuff, you must use two fingers. Weird!

- **Getting a larger keyboard.** The on-screen keyboard appears when you tap into a box that allows typing. I've noticed, however, that the keyboard you get in landscape view uses noticeably larger keys than the one you see in portrait view. For the fumble-fingered among us, larger keys are a must, so always rotate the iPad into landscape mode to type text.

Note
Remember that rotating the iPad changes the view only if your iPad is upright. The iPad uses gravity to sense the change in orientation, so if it's lying flat on a table, rotating it won't do anything — rotate it before you put it on the table.

- **Save typing with standard web addresses.** Most websites have addresses that start with http://www. and end with .com/. Safari on your iPad knows this and uses this otherwise unremarkable fact to save you tons of typing. If you type just a single block of text into the address bar — it could be a single word such as wiley, or two or more words combined into one, such as wordspy — and then tap Go, Safari automatically adds http://www. to the front and .com/ at the end. So wiley becomes http://www.wiley.com/ and wordspy becomes http://www.wordspy.com/.

Browsing Tips for Faster Surfing

If you're like me, the biggest problem you have with the web is that it's just so darned huge. We spend great big chunks of our day visiting sites and still never seem to get to everything on that day's To Surf list. The iPad helps lessen (but, alas, not eliminate) this problem by allowing you to surf wherever Wi-Fi can be found (or just wherever if you have a cellular iPad). Even so, the faster and more efficient your iPad surfing sessions are, the more sites you see. The touchscreen tips I covered earlier can help and in this section I take you through a few more useful tips for speedier surfing.

Browsing with tabs

These days, it's a rare web surfer who marches sequentially through a series of web pages. In your own surfing sessions, you probably leave a few web pages open full time (for things like Google searches and RSS feed monitoring). It's also likely that you come across a lot of links that you want to check out while leaving the original page open in the browser. In your computer's web browser, you probably handle these and similar surfing situations by launching a tab for each page you want to leave open in the browser window. It's an essential web browsing technique, but can it be done with the iPad Safari browser?

Caution Be careful if you have the full complement of nine browser tabs opened. If you click a link that automatically opens in a new browser tab, Safari automatically shuts down the next browser tab. This could be a problem if you had some important info in that window. To avoid this, consider opening a maximum of eight Safari tabs so you always have an extra one available if you need it.

Yes, indeed, and the even better news is that Safari in iOS 5 supports tabbed browsing instead of the slightly clunky pages it used in previous versions. And you're not restricted to a meager two tabs — no ma'am. Your iPad lets you open up to nine — count 'em, *nine* — tabs, so you can throw some wild web page parties.

Note Some web-based apps and web page links are configured to automatically open the tab in a new window, so you may see a new tab being created when you tap a link. Also, if you add a Web Clip to your Home screen (as I describe in Chapter 4) tapping the icon opens the Web Clip in a new Safari tab.

The following are the two methods you can use to open a page in a new tab:

● **In Safari, tap the New Tab icon (+) shown in Figure 5.2.** Safari creates the new tab. You can then either type the address or run a search to find the page you want.

● **On a web page, tap and hold a link to display the link options shown in Figure 5.2, and then tap Open in New Tab.**

Tabs →  ← New tab

5.2 You can start a new tab by tapping the New Tab icon (+), or by tapping and holding a link and then tapping Open in New Tab.

Genius

If you recently closed a tab, you can reopen it quickly by tapping and holding the New Tab icon. This displays the Recently Closed Tabs list, which shows the tabs you've closed during the current Safari session. You then tap the tab you want to reopen. Note, however, that this technique only works if you have less than nine tabs open.

Once you have multiple tabs on the go, you navigate them by tapping the tab you want to view. To close a tab that you no longer need, tap it and then tap the X that appears on the left side of the tab.

Opening a tab in the foreground

When you tap and hold a link and then tap Open in New Tab, Safari keeps the current page active and loads the new one in the background. That's often the behavior you want because it lets the new page take its sweet time loading while you continue to read the current one. However, you might find that most of the time you open the new tab and then switch to it immediately. In these situations, performing that extra tap to select the new tab gets old in a hurry. The solution is to configure Safari to always open new tabs in the foreground. To set it up, follow these steps:

1. **On the Home screen, tap Settings.** The Settings screen slides in.

2. **Tap Safari.** Your iPad displays the Safari screen.

3. **Tap the Open New Tabs in Background switch to Off.**

Viewing a page without distractions

It seems like only a few years ago that purse-lipped pundits and furrow-browed futurologists were lamenting that the Internet signaled the imminent demise of reading. With pursuits such as viral videos and online gaming a mere click or two away, who would ever sit down and actually *read* things? Well, a funny thing happened on the way to the future: people read more now than they ever did. Sure, there's some concern that we're no longer reading long articles and challenging books, but most of us spend much of the day reading online.

On the one hand, this isn't all that surprising because there's just so much text out there, most of it available free, and much of it professionally written and edited. On the other hand, this is actually quite surprising, because reading an article or essay online is no picnic. The problem is the sheer amount of distraction on almost any page: Background colors or images that clash with the text; ads above, to the side of, and within the text; site features such as search boxes, feed links, and content lists; and those ubiquitous icons for sharing the article with your friends on Facebook, Twitter, Digg, and on and on.

Figure 5.3 shows a typical example.

Reader icon

5.3 Today's web pages are all too often festooned with ads, icons, and other bric-a-brac.

Fortunately, Safari for iOS 5 can help solve this problem by offering the Reader feature. Reader removes all those extraneous page distractions that just get in the way of your reading pleasure. So, instead of a cacophony of text, icons, and images, you see pure, simple, large-enough-to-be-easily-read text. How do you arrive at this blissful state? By tapping the Reader icon, which appears on the right side of the address bar, as pointed out in Figure 5.3. Safari instantly transforms the page, and you see something similar to the one shown in Figure 5.4 (this is the Reader version of the page shown in Figure 5.3).

ROGERS 12:06 PM 100%

www.wired.com/magazine/2012/01/ff_a Reader Google

Let the Robot Drive: The Autonomous Car of the Future Is Here | Wired Magazine | Wired.com

A A Page 1

Let the Robot Drive: The Autonomous Car of the Future Is Here

Photo: Spencer Higgins

The object, vaguely pink, sits on the shoulder of the freeway, slowly shimmering into view. Is it roadkill? A weird kind of sagebrush? No, wait, it's … a puffy chunk of foam insulation! "The laser almost certainly got re- turns off of it," says Chris Urmson, sitting behind the wheel of the Prius he is not driving. A note is made (FOD: foreign object or debris, lane 1) as we drive past, to help our computerized car understand the curious flotsam it has just seen.

It's a Monday, midday, and we are heading north on California Highway 85 in a Google autonomous vehicle. In October 2010, when *The New York Times* reported that Google had built a fleet of self-driving cars that had

5.4 The Reader version of a web page is a simple and easy-to-read text affair.

Syncing your bookmarks

The Web era is into its third decade now, so you certainly don't need me to tell you that it is a mani- festly awesome resource that redefines the phrase *treasure trove*. No, at this stage of your web career, you're probably most concerned with finding great web treasures and returning to the best or most useful of them in subsequent surfing sessions. The Safari History list can help here (I talk about it later in this chapter), but the best way to ensure that you can easily return to a site a week, a month, or even a year from now is to save it as a bookmark.

By far, the easiest way to get bookmarks for your favorite sites into your iPad is to take advantage of your best bookmark resource: the Safari browser on your Mac (or your Windows PC), or the Internet Explorer browser on your PC (which calls them *favorites*). You've probably used those browsers for a while and have all kinds of useful and fun bookmarked sites at your metaphorical fingertips. To get those bookmarks at your literal fingertips — that is, on your iPad — you need to include bookmarks as part of the synchronization process between the iPad and iTunes (which I talk about in general terms in Chapter 2).

Genius

Having used Safari or Internet Explorer for a while means having lots of great sites bookmarked, but it likely also means that you have lots of digital dreck — that is, sites you no longer visit or that have gone belly-up. Before synchronizing your bookmarks with the iPad, consider taking some time to clean up your existing bookmarks. You'll thank yourself in the end.

Bookmark syncing is turned on by default but, to make sure, follow these steps:

1. **Connect your iPad to your computer.**
2. **In the iTunes sources list, click the iPad.**
3. **Click the Info tab.**
4. **Scroll down to the Web Browser section and use one of the following techniques:**
   - **Mac.** Select the Sync Safari bookmarks check box, as shown in Figure 5.5.

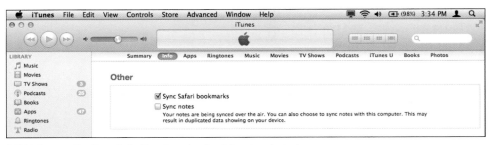

5.5 Make sure the Sync Safari bookmarks check box is selected.

   - **Windows.** Select the Sync Bookmarks With check box and then select your web browser from the drop-down list.

5. **Click Apply.** iTunes begins syncing the bookmarks from your computer to your iPad.

Genius

What's that? You've already synced your bookmarks to your iPad, and you now have a bunch of useless sites clogging up the Safari bookmark arteries? Not a problem! Return to your desktop Safari (or Internet Explorer), purge the bogus bookmarks, and then resync your iPad. Any bookmarks you blew away also get trashed from your iPad.

Adding bookmarks manually

Even if you get your iPad bookmarks off to a flying start by copying a bunch of them from your Mac or Windows PC and now have a large collection at your beck and call, that doesn't mean your iPad bookmark collection is complete. After all, you might (heck, you *will*) find some interesting sites while you're surfing with the iPad. If you think you might want to pay a site another visit down the road, you can create a new bookmark right on the iPad. Here are the steps to follow:

1. **On the iPad, use Safari to navigate to the site you want to save.**

2. **Tap the Actions button (pointed out in Figure 5.6) in the status bar.**

3. **Tap Add Bookmark.** This opens the Add Bookmark screen, as shown in Figure 5.6.

4. **Tap in the top box, and type a name for the site that helps you remember it.** This name is what you see when you scroll through your bookmarks.

5. **Tap Bookmarks.** This displays a list of your bookmark folders.

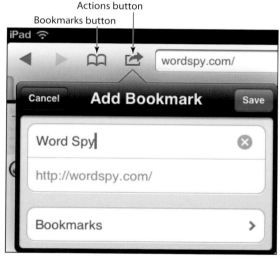

Actions button
Bookmarks button

5.6 Use the Add Bookmark screen to specify the bookmark name and location.

6. **Tap the folder you want to use to store the bookmark.** Safari returns you to the Add Bookmark screen.

7. **Tap Save.** Safari saves the bookmark.

Note Syncing bookmarks is a two-way street, which means that any site you bookmark in your iPad is added to your desktop version of Safari (or Internet Explorer) the next time you sync.

Managing your bookmarks

After you have a few bookmarks stashed away in the bookmarks list, you may need to perform a few housekeeping chores from time to time, including changing a name, address, or folder of a bookmark; reordering bookmarks or folders; or getting rid of bookmarks that have worn out their welcome.

Before you can do any of this, you need to get the Bookmarks list into Edit mode by following these steps:

1. **In Safari, tap the Bookmarks icon in the status bar (see Figure 5.6).** Safari opens the Bookmarks list.

2. **If the bookmark you want to mess with is located in a particular folder, tap to open that folder.** For example, if you've synced with Safari, you should have a folder named Bookmarks Bar that includes all the bookmarks and folders that you've added to the Bookmarks Bar in your desktop version of Safari.

3. **Tap Edit.** Your iPad switches the Bookmarks list to Edit mode, as shown in Figure 5.7. With Edit mode on the go, you're free to toil away at your bookmarks. Here are the techniques to master:

   - **Edit bookmark info.** Tap the bookmark to fire up the Edit Bookmark screen. From here, you can edit the bookmark name, or change its address or folder. When you finish, tap the name of the current bookmark folder in the top-left corner of the screen.

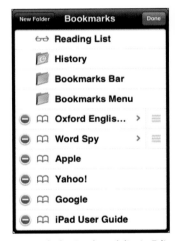

5.7 With the Bookmark list in Edit mode, you can edit, rearrange, and delete bookmarks to your heart's content.

   - **Change the bookmark order.** Use the drag icon (the three horizontal bars) on the right to tap and drag a bookmark to a new position in the list. Ideally, you should move your favorite bookmarks near the top of the list for easiest access.

- **Add a bookmark folder.** Tap New Folder to launch the Edit Folder screen, and then tap a folder title and select a location. Feel free to use bookmark folders at will because they're a great way to keep your bookmarks neat and tidy (if you're into that kind of thing).

- **Delete a bookmark.** No use for a particular bookmark? No problem. Tap the Delete icon to the left of the bookmark and then tap the Delete button that appears.

When the dust settles and your bookmark chores are finished, tap Done to get out of Edit mode.

Saving a page to read later

In your web travels, you'll often come upon a page with fascinating content that you can't wait to read. Unfortunately, a quick look at the length of the article tells you that you're going to need more time than what you currently have available. So what's a body to do? Quickly scan the article and move on with your life? No, when you come across good web content, you need to savor it. So, should you bookmark the article for future reference? That's not bad, but bookmarks are really for things you want to revisit often, not for pages that you might only read once.

The best solution is a new Safari 5 feature called the Reading List. As the name implies, this is a simple list of things to read. When you don't have time to read something now, add it to your Reading List and you can read it at your leisure.

There are a couple of techniques you can use to add a page to your Reading List:

- **Use Safari to navigate to the page that you want to read later, tap the Actions button, and then tap Add to Reading List.**

- **Tap and hold a link for the page that you want to read later and then tap Add to Reading List.**

When you're settled into your favorite easy chair and have the time (finally!) to read, open Safari, tap the Bookmarks icon, and then tap Reading List. Safari displays the Unread list (see Figure 5.8) and you just tap the article you want to read. Safari immediately removes the page from the Unread list, but if you need to see it again, tap All in the Reading List.

5.8 Load up the Reading List with your recent web finds for easy reading when it's convenient for you.

Retracing your steps with the History list

Bookmarking a website (as I described earlier in this chapter) is a good idea if that site contains interesting or fun content that you want to revisit. Sometimes, however, you may not realize that a site had useful data until a day or two later. Similarly, you may like a site's stuff but decide against bookmarking it, only to regret that decision down the road. You could waste a big chunk of your day trying to track down the site, or you may run into Murphy's Web Browsing Law: A cool site that you forget to bookmark is never found again.

Fortunately, your iPad has your back. As you navigate the nooks and crannies of the web, iPad keeps track of where you go, and stores the name and address of each page in the History list. The limited iPad memory means that it can't store tons of sites, but it might have what you're looking for. Here's how to use it:

1. **In Safari, tap the Bookmarks icon (see Figure 5.6) in the status bar.** Safari opens the Bookmarks list.

2. **If you see the Bookmarks screen (see Figure 5.7), skip to Step 3.** Otherwise, tap the folder names that appear in the upper-left corner of the screen until you get to the Bookmarks screen.

3. **Tap History.** Safari opens the History screen, as shown in Figure 5.9. It shows the sites you've visited today at the top, followed by a list of previous surfing dates.

4. **If you visited the site you're looking for on a previous day, tap that day.** Safari displays a list of the sites you visited on that day.

5. **Tap the site you want to revisit.** Safari loads the site.

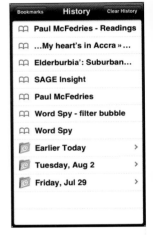

5.9 Safari stores your recent browsing past in the History list.

Filling in Online Forms

Many web pages include forms where you fill in some data and then submit the form, which sends the data off to some server for processing. Filling in these forms in the iPad Safari browser is mostly straightforward:

● **Text box.** Tap inside the text box to display the touchscreen keyboard, type your text, and then tap Done.

Text area. Tap inside the text area, and then use the keyboard to type your text. Most text areas allow multiline entries, so you can tap Return to start a new line. When you finish, tap Done.

Check box. Tap the check box to toggle the check mark on and off.

Radio button. Tap a radio button to activate it.

Command button. Tap the button to make it do its thing (usually, submit the form).

Many online forms consist of a bunch of text boxes or text areas. If the idea of performing the tap-type-Done cycle over and over isn't appealing to you, fear not. The iPad Safari browser offers an easier method:

1. **Tap inside the first text box or text area.** The keyboard appears.

2. **Type the text you want to enter.** Above the keyboard, notice the Previous and Next buttons, as shown in Figure 5.10.

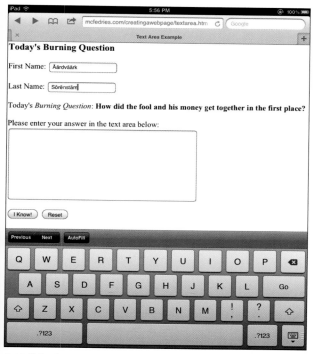

5.10 If the form contains multiple text boxes or text areas, you can use the Previous and Next buttons to navigate them.

3. **Tap Next to move to the next text box or text area.** If you need to return to a text box, tap Previous instead.

4. **Repeat Steps 2 and 3 to fill in the text boxes.**

5. **Tap Done.** Safari returns you to the page.

I haven't yet talked about selection lists, and that's because the iPad browser handles them in an interesting way. When you tap a list, Safari displays the list items in a separate box, as shown in Figure 5.11. In the list of items, the currently selected item appears with a check mark to its right. Tap the item you want to select.

Putting On Hairs: Reader Survey

Select your hair color:

Brunette ▼

Select your hair style:

Straight ▼

Bouffant	
Mohawk	
Page Boy	
Permed	
Shag	
Straight	✓
Style? What style?	

5.11 Tap a list to see its items in a separate box for easier selecting.

Turning on AutoFill

The iPad Safari browser makes it relatively easy to fill in online forms, but it can still be slow going, particularly if you have lots of text boxes or text areas. To help make forms less of a chore, the iPad Safari browser supports a welcome feature called AutoFill. Just as with the desktop version of Safari (or just about any other mainstream browser), AutoFill remembers the data you type into forms and then enables you to fill in similar forms with the simple tap of a button. You can also configure AutoFill to remember usernames and passwords.

To take advantage of this nifty new feature, you first have to turn it on by following these steps:

1. **On the Home screen, tap Settings.** Your iPad opens the Settings screen.

2. **Tap Safari.** The Safari screen appears.

3. **Tap AutoFill to open the AutoFill screen.**

4. **Tap the Use Contact Info switch to the On position.** This tells Safari to use your item in the Contacts app to grab data for a form. For example, if a form requires your name, Safari uses your contact name.

5. **The My Info field should show your name; if it doesn't, tap the field and then tap your item in the All Contacts list.**

6. **If you want Safari to remember the usernames and passwords you use to log in to sites, tap the Names & Passwords switch to the On position.**

Now when you visit an online form and access any text field in the form, the AutoFill button becomes enabled. Tap AutoFill to fill in those portions of the form that correspond to your contact data, as shown in Figure 5.12. Notice that the fields Safari is able to automatically fill in display with a yellow background.

Saving website login passwords

If you enabled the Names & Passwords option in the AutoFill screen, each time you fill in a username and password to log in to a site, Safari displays the dialog shown in Figure 5.13, asking if you want it to remember the login data. It gives you three choices:

- **Yes.** Tap this button to have Safari remember your username and password.

- **Never for this Website.** Tap this button to tell Safari not to remember the username and password, and to never again prompt you to save the login data.

- **Not Now.** Tap this button to tell Safari not to remember the username and password this time, but to prompt you again next time you log in to this site.

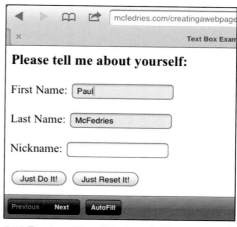

5.12 Tap AutoFill to fill in form fields with your contact data.

5.13 If you configure Safari to remember usernames and passwords, you see this dialog when you log in to a site.

Note

Your iPad is a cautious beast, so it doesn't offer to save all of the passwords you enter. In particular, if the login form is part of a secure site, then your iPad doesn't ask if you want to save the password. This means you won't be tempted to store the password for your online bank, corporate website, or any site where you saved your credit card data (such as Amazon and similar online shopping sites).

Getting Even More Out of Safari

You've seen lots of great Safari tips and techniques so far in this chapter, but I hope you're up for even more, because you have a ways to go. The rest of this chapter covers useful techniques such as using the History list, changing the default search engine, viewing RSS feeds, and configuring the Safari security options.

Protecting your privacy by deleting the History list

The iPad History list of sites you've recently surfed is a great feature when you need it and an innocuous one when you don't. However, at times the History list is just plain uncool. For example, suppose you shop online to get a nice gift for your spouse's birthday. If your significant other also uses your iPad, your surprise might be ruined if the purchase page accidentally shows up in the History list. Similarly, if you visit a private corporate site, a financial site, or any other site you wouldn't want others to see, the History list might betray you.

And sometimes unsavory sites can end up in your History list by accident. For example, you might tap a legitimate-looking link in a web page or e-mail message, only to end up in some dark, dank Net neighborhood. Of course, you high-tail it out of there right away with a quick tap of the Back button, but that nasty site is now lurking in your History.

Whether you have sites on the History list that you wouldn't want anyone to see or if you just find the idea of your iPad tracking your web movements to be a bit sinister, follow these steps to wipe out the History list:

1. **In Safari, tap the Bookmarks icon in the status bar.** Safari opens the Bookmarks list.

2. **Tap the folder names that appear in the upper-left corner of the screen until you get to the Bookmarks screen.**

3. **Tap History.** Safari opens the History screen.

4. **Tap Clear History.** Safari prompts you to confirm.

5. **Tap Clear History.** Safari deletes every site from the History list.

Genius
There's another way to clear the History and it may be faster if you're not currently working in Safari. In the Home screen, tap Settings, tap Safari, and then tap Clear History. When your iPad asks you to confirm, tap Clear History.

Deleting website data

As you wander around the web, Safari gathers and saves bits of information for each site. For example, it stores some site text and images so that it can display the page faster if you revisit the site in the near future. Similarly, if you activated AutoFill for names and passwords, Safari stores that data on your iPad. Finally, most major sites store small text files called cookies on your iPad that save information for things like site preferences and shopping carts.

Storing all this data on your iPad is generally a good thing because it can speed up your surfing. However, it's not always a safe or private thing. For example, if you elect to have Safari save a site password, you might change your mind later on, particularly if you share your iPad with other people. Similarly, cookies can sometimes be used to track your activities online, so they're not always benign.

In previous versions of iOS, you could use the Settings app to clear all of your stored cookies, saved passwords, or stored web page text and images (this is called the *cache*). However, those were awfully blunt instruments, particularly if you were only concerned about a site or two. Fortunately, iOS 5 introduces a more finely honed tool that enables you to delete the data for an individual website.

Here's how it works:

1. **On the Home screen, tap Settings.** Your iPad opens the Settings screen.

2. **Tap Safari.** The Safari screen appears.

3. **Tap Advanced to open the Advanced screen.**

4. **Tap Website Data.** Safari displays a list of the recent sites for which it has stored data, as well as the size of that data, as shown in Figure 5.14.

5. **If you don't see the site you want to remove, tap Show All Sites at the bottom of the list.**

6. **Tap Edit.**

7. **Tap the red Delete icon to the left of the site you want to clear.**

8. **Tap the Delete icon that appears to the right of the site's data size value.** Safari removes the site's data.

5.14 The Website Data screen shows you which sites have saved data on your iPad.

Browsing privately

If you find yourself constantly deleting your browsing history or website data, you can save your-self a bit of time by configuring Safari to do this automatically. This is called *private browsing* and it means that Safari doesn't save any data as you browse. More specifically, it means the following:

- **Sites aren't added to the history (although the Back and Forward buttons still work for navigating sites that you've visited in the current session).**
- **Web page text and images aren't saved.**
- **Search text isn't saved with the search box.**
- **AutoFill passwords aren't saved.**

To activate private browsing, follow these steps:

1. **On the Home screen, tap Settings.** The Settings screen appears.
2. **Tap Safari.** The Safari settings appear.
3. **Tap the Private Browsing switch to On.** The Settings app asks if you want to close your existing Safari tabs.
4. **To close the tabs, tap Close All.** If you prefer to keep the tabs open, tap Keep All, instead.

Tweeting a web page

If you have a Twitter account, there's a good chance that one of your favorite 140-characters-or-less pastimes is sharing interesting, useful, or funny websites with your followers. Using a client such as the official Twitter app or TweetDeck is fine for this, but it means you have to copy the site address, switch to the app, and then paste the address. For quick tweets, it's easier and faster just to stay in Safari, which now lets you send a tweet directly from a web page. Here's what you do:

1. **Use Safari to navigate to the page that you want to tweet.**
2. **Tap the Actions button.**
3. **Tap Tweet.** Safari displays the Tweet dialog.
4. **If you added more than one account to the iPad Twitter settings, tap the username in the From section, and then tap the name of the account you want to use to send the tweet.**

5. **Type your tweet text in the large text box.** As you can see in Figure 5.15, the Tweet dialog displays a number in the lower-right corner telling you how many characters you have left.

6. **If you want to include your present whereabouts as part of the tweet, tap Add Location.**

7. **Tap Send.** Your iPad posts the tweet.

Cancel	Tweet	Send

From: @paulmcf

Apple has cash. Lots and lots of cash.

Add Location   82

5.15 iOS 5 lets you tweet about a website directly from Safari.

Changing the default search engine

When you tap the Search box at the top of the Safari screen, your iPad loads the Google screen, places the cursor inside the Search box, and displays the keyboard so you can type your search text and then run the search. The screen is named Google because Google is the default iPad search engine. If you have something against Google, you can switch to using either Bing or Yahoo! as your search engine of choice. To do so, follow these steps:

1. **In the Home screen, tap Settings.** Your iPad opens the Settings screen.

2. **Tap Safari.** The Safari screen appears.

3. **Tap Search Engine.** Your iPad opens the Search Engine screen.

4. **Tap Bing or Yahoo!.** Your iPad now uses your choice as the default search engine.

Setting the web browser security options

It's a jungle out there in cyberspace, with nasty things lurking in the digital weeds. The folks at Apple are well aware of these dangers, of course, so they've clothed your iPad in protective gear to help keep the bad guys at bay. Safari, in particular, has the following four layers of security:

● **Phishing protection.** A *phishing* site is a website that, on the surface, appears to belong to a reputable company, such as an online bank or major corporation. In reality, some dark-side hackers have cobbled the site together to fool you into providing your precious login or credit card data, Social Security number, or other private information. Many of these sites are either well known or sport tell-tale signs that mark them as fraudulent. iPad Safari comes with a Fraud Warning setting that, when activated, displays a warning about such sites.

- **JavaScript.** This is a programming language that website developers commonly use to add features to their pages. However, programmers who have succumbed to the dark side of The Force can use JavaScript for nefarious ends. Your iPad comes with JavaScript support turned on, but you can turn it off if you're heading into an area of the web where you don't feel safe. However, many sites won't work without JavaScript, so I don't recommend turning it off full time.

- **Pop-up blocking.** Pop-up ads (and their sneakier cousins, the pop-under ads) are annoying at the best of times, but they really get in the way on the iPad because the pop-up not only creates a new Safari page, but it immediately switches to that page. So now you have to tap the Pages icon, delete the pop-up page, and then (if you already had two or more pages running) tap the page that generated the pop-up. Boo! You can thank your preferred deity that not only does your iPad come with a pop-up blocker that stops these pests, but it's also turned on by default. However, some sites use pop-ups for legitimate reasons: Media players, login pages, important site announcements, and so on. For those sites to work properly, you may need to temporarily turn off the pop-up blocker.

- **Cookies.** These are small text files that many sites store on the iPad and use to store information about your browsing session. The most common example is a shopping cart, where your selections and amounts are stored in a cookie. However, for every benign cookie, at least one not-so-nice cookie is used by a third-party advertiser to track your movements and display ads supposedly targeted to your tastes. Yuck. By default, your iPad doesn't accept third-party cookies, so that's a good thing. However, you can configure Safari to accept every cookie that comes its way or no cookies at all (neither of which I recommend).

Follow these steps to customize the iPad web security options:

1. **On the Home screen, tap Settings.** The Settings screen slides in.
2. **Tap Safari.** Your iPad displays the Safari screen, as shown in Figure 5.16.
3. **To configure the cookies that Safari allows, tap Accept Cookies.** Tap the setting you want — None, From visited, or Always — and then tap Safari. The From visited setting (the default) means that Safari accepts cookies directly only from the sites you visit and spits out any from third-party sites, such as advertisers.
4. **Tap the Fraud Warning setting in the Security section to toggle phishing protection On and Off.**

5.16 Use the Safari screen to set the iPad web security settings.

5. **Tap the JavaScript setting to toggle JavaScript support On and Off.**

6. **Tap the Block Pop-ups setting to toggle pop-up blocking On and Off.**

7. **If you want to get rid of all the cookies that have been stored on your iPad, tap Clear Cookies and Data and, when you're asked to confirm, tap Clear.** It's a good idea to clear cookies if you're having trouble accessing a site or if you suspect some unwanted cookies have been stored on your iPad (for example, if you surfed for a while with Accept Cookies set to Always).

Searching web page text

When you're perusing a page on the web, it's not unusual to be looking for specific information. In those situations, rather than reading through the entire page to find the info you seek, it would be a lot easier to search for the data. You can easily do this in the desktop version of Safari or any other computer browser, but, at first glance, the Safari app doesn't seem to have a Find feature anywhere. It's there all right, but you need to know where to look. To use the Find feature, follow these steps:

1. **Use the Safari app to navigate to the web page that contains the information you seek.**

2. **Tap inside the Search box in the top right of the Safari window.**

3. **Tap the search text you want to use.** Safari displays the usual web page matches, but it also displays On This Page (*X* matches), where *X* is the number of times your search text appears on the web page, as shown in Figure 5.17.

4. **Tap Find *search* (where *search* is the search text you entered).** Safari highlights the first instance of the search term, as shown in Figure 5.18.

5. **Tap the right-pointing arrow to cycle through the instances of the search term that appear on the page.** Note that you can also cycle backward through the results by tapping the left-pointing arrow. Also, when you tap the right-pointing arrow after the last result appears, Safari returns you to the first result.

6. **When you're finished with the search, tap Done.**

5.17 The On This Page message tells you the number of matches that appear on the current web page.

What is introversion? In its modern sense, the concept goes back to the 1920s and the psychologist Carl Jung. Today it is a mainstay of personality tests, including the widely used Myers-Briggs Type Indicator. Introverts are not necessarily shy. Shy people are anxious or frightened or self-excoriating in social settings; introverts generally are not. Introverts are also not misanthropic, though some of us do go along with Sartre as far as to say "Hell is other people at breakfast." Rather, introverts are people who find other people tiring.

Extroverts are energized by people, and wilt or fade when alone. They often seem bored by themselves, in both senses of the expression. Leave an extrovert alone for two minutes and he will reach for his cell phone. In contrast, after an hour or two of being socially "on," we introverts need to turn off and recharge. My own formula is roughly two hours alone for every hour of socializing. This isn't antisocial. It isn't a sign of depression. It does not call for medication. For introverts, to be alone with our thoughts is as restorative as sleeping, as nourishing as eating. Our motto: "I'm okay, you're okay—in small doses."

How many people are introverts? I performed exhaustive research on this question, in the form of a quick Google search. The answer: About 25 percent. Or: Just under half. Or—my favorite—"a minority in the regular population but a majority in the gifted population."

Are introverts misunderstood? Wildly. That, it appears, is our lot in life. "It is very difficult for an extrovert to understand an introvert," write the education experts Jill D. Burruss and Lisa Kaenzig. (They are also the source of the quotation in the previous paragraph.) Extroverts are easy for introverts to

5.18 Safari highlights the first instance of the search term that appears on the current web page.

Printing a web page with AirPrint

If you have a printer that supports the AirPrint standard for wireless printing, then you can send documents, such as web pages, directly to your printer.

Here's how it works:

1. **Use the Safari app to navigate to the web page you want to print.**

2. **Tap Actions.** A menu of web page actions appears.

3. **Tap Print.** The Printer Options screen appears.

4. **Tap Printer.** If the Printer field already shows the printer you want to use, you can skip to Step 6. Your iPad looks for wireless printers on your network and then displays a list of those available, as shown in Figure 5.19.

5.19 Your iPad displays a list of available printers.

5. **Tap the printer you want to use.** Your iPad adds the printer to the Printer Options screen and then enables the other controls, as shown in Figure 5.20.

6. **In the Copy field, tap the plus sign (+) to set the number of copies you want to print.**

7. **Configure the other printer options as needed.** Note that the options you see vary from printer to printer.

8. **Tap Print.** Your iPad sends the web page to the printer.

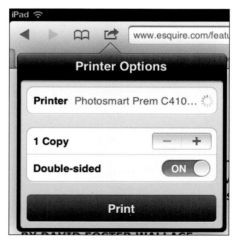

5.20 Use the Printer Options screen to configure the print job and then print the web page.

Note   It took a while, but there are now quite a few printers that support the AirPrint standard, including some from Brother, Canon, EPSON, Hewlett Packard, and Lexmark. To find out more, and to see a list of AirPrint-ready printers, visit: www.apple.com/ipad/features/airprint.html.

Viewing an RSS feed

Some websites remain relatively static over time, so you only need to check in every once in a while to see if anything's new. Other sites change content regularly — once a week or even once a day — so you know in advance when to check for new material. However, on the more verbose sites — particularly blogs — the content changes frequently, but not regularly. For these sites, keeping up with new content can be time consuming and it's criminally easy to miss new information. (Murphy's Blog Reading Law: You always miss the post that everyone's talking about.)

To solve this problem, tons of websites now maintain RSS (Real Simple Syndication) feeds. A *feed* is a special file that contains the most recent information added to the site. The bad news is that your iPad's Safari browser doesn't give you any way to subscribe to a site's feed like you can with desktop Safari or Internet Explorer. The good news, though, is that your iPad can use a web-based RSS reader application (http://reader.mac.com) that can interpret a site's RSS feed. It then displays the feed in the comfy confines of Safari.

Follow these steps to set up your iPad to view an RSS feed:

1. **In Safari, navigate to a web page that you know has an RSS feed.**

2. **Pan and zoom the page until you find the link to the RSS feed.** The link is often accompanied by (or consists entirely of) an icon that identifies it as leading to a feed. Look for an XML icon, an RSS icon, or an orange feed icon.

3. **Tap the link.** Safari loads the RSS file into the reader.mac.com feed reader application.

Note

You can bookmark RSS feed links and save them to the Home screen just as you would a link to a web page.

How Do I Make the Most of E-mail on My iPad?

As more and more people start sending status updates on social networking sites, and texting, Tweeting, and Skyping, the more old-fashioned e-mail seems. Yes, reading and composing e-mail is dishwater-dull, but do you know what else it is? It's *universal*. Almost everyone who's online has an e-mail account, and it remains the best way to get in touch and exchange information (at least digitally). Your iPad comes with a decent e-mail app that's easy to use, but there are still plenty of tricks and techniques you should know to help you get the most out of Mail on your iPad.

Managing Your iPad E-mail Accounts

The Mail app that comes with your iPad is a nice e-mail program that makes the most of the two iPad orientations. In portrait mode, you see a big version of the current message, complete with embedded photos and other media. In landscape mode, you get a two-pane view that shows your Inbox messages in one and the current message in the other. Landscape mode is great for composing messages because you get the huge keyboard and a nice, big compose window.

The Mail app also has a few features and settings that make it ideal for doing e-mail away from your desk. First, however, you have to set up your iPad with one or more e-mail accounts.

Syncing your e-mail accounts

The Mail app on your iPad is most useful when it's set up to use an e-mail account that you also use on your computer. That way, when you're on the road or out on the town, you can check your messages and rest assured that you won't miss anything important (or even anything unimportant, for that matter). This is most easily done by syncing an existing e-mail account between your computer and your iPad. If you already have an existing account up and running — whether it's a Mail account on your Mac, or an Outlook or Windows Mail account on your Windows PC (not, however, Windows Live Mail, which isn't supported by iTunes) — you can convince iTunes to gather all the account details and pass them along to your iPad.

Note For some accounts, you need to be careful that your iPad doesn't delete incoming messages from the server before you have a chance to download them to your computer. I show you how to set that up later in this chapter.

Here's how it works:

1. **Connect your iPad to your computer.**
2. **In the iTunes Devices list, click the iPad.**
3. **Click the Info tab.**
4. **In the Mail Accounts section, use one of the following techniques:**
   - **Mac.** Select the Sync Mail Accounts check box, and then select the check box beside each account you want to add to iPad, as shown in Figure 6.1.

6.1 Make sure you select the Sync Mail Accounts check box and at least one account in the list.

- **Windows.** Select the Sync Mail Accounts From check box, select your e-mail program from the drop-down list, and then select the check box beside each account you want to add to iPad.

5. **Click Apply.** You may see a message asking if AppleMobileSync can be allowed access to your keychain (your Mac's master password list).

6. **If you see that message, click Allow.** iTunes begins syncing the selected e-mail account settings from your computer to your iPad.

Note

Remember that iPad syncs only your e-mail account *settings* (username, password, mail servers, and so on), not your e-mail account *messages*.

Adding an account manually

Syncing e-mail accounts as I describe in the previous section is useful when you want to do the e-mail thing on multiple devices. However, you may also prefer to have an e-mail account that's

109

exclusively for the iPad. For example, if you join an iPad mailing list, you may prefer to have those messages sent only to your iPad. That's a darn good idea, but it means that you have to set up the account on the iPad itself, which requires a fair amount of tapping.

Note   You may think you can avoid the often excessive tapping required to enter a new e-mail account into your iPad by creating the account in your computer's e-mail program and then syncing with your iPad. That works, but there's a hitch: You *must* leave the new account in your e-mail program. If you delete or disable it, iTunes also deletes the account from the iPad.

How you create an account on your iPad with the sweat of your own brow depends on the type of account you have. First, the following are the six e-mail services that your iPad recognizes (a seventh is MobileMe, which I'm ignoring here because Apple is shuttering that service in 2012):

- **iCloud.** This is the Apple web-based e-mail service (that also comes with applications for calendars, contacts, storage, and more).

- **Microsoft Exchange.** Your iPad supports accounts on Exchange servers, which are common in large organizations. Exchange uses a central server to store messages and you usually work with your messages on the server, not your iPad. However, one of the great features in iPad is support for Exchange ActiveSync, which automatically keeps your iPad and your account on the server synchronized. I discuss the ActiveSync settings later in this chapter.

- **Google Gmail.** This is a web-based e-mail service run by Google.

- **Yahoo!.** This is a web-based e-mail service run by Yahoo!.

- **AOL.** This is a web-based e-mail service run by AOL.

- **Window Live Hotmail.** This is a web-based e-mail service run by Microsoft.

Your iPad knows how to connect to these services, so to set up any of these e-mail accounts, you only need to know the address and the account password.

Otherwise, your iPad Mail app supports the following e-mail account types:

- **POP (Post Office Protocol).** This is the most popular type of account. Its main characteristic for your purposes is that incoming messages are stored only temporarily on the provider's mail server. When you connect to the server, the messages are downloaded to iPad and removed from the server. In other words, your messages (including copies of messages you send) are stored locally on your iPad. The advantage here is that you don't need to be online to read your e-mail. After it's downloaded to your iPad, you can read it (or delete it, or whatever) at your leisure.

● **IMAP (Internet Message Access Protocol).** This type of account is most often used with web-based e-mail services. It's the opposite of POP (sort of) because all of your incoming messages, as well as copies of messages you send, remain on the server. In this case, when Mail works with an IMAP account, it connects to the server and works with the messages on the server itself, not on your iPad (although it *looks* like you're working with the messages locally). The advantage here is that you can access the messages from multiple devices and multiple locations, but you must be connected to the Internet to work with your messages.

Your network administrator or your e-mail service provider can let you know what type of e-mail account you have. Your administrator or provider can also give you the information you need to set up the account. This includes your e-mail address, the username and password you use to check for new messages, any security information you need to specify to send messages, the host name of the incoming mail server (typically something like mail.*provider*.com or pop.*provider*.com, where *provider*.com is the domain name of the provider), and the host name of the outgoing mail server (typically either mail.*provider*.com or smtp.*provider*.com).

With your account information clutched in your fist, follow these steps to forge a brand new account on your iPad:

1. **On the Home screen, tap Settings.** Your iPad opens the Settings screen.
2. **Tap Mail, Contacts, Calendars.** The Mail, Contacts, Calendars screen appears.
3. **Tap Add Account.** This opens the Add Account screen, as shown in Figure 6.2.
4. **You have two ways to proceed:**
   ● If you're adding an account for iCloud, Microsoft Exchange, Gmail, Yahoo!, AOL, or Windows Live Hotmail, tap the corresponding logo. In the account information screen that appears, type your name, e-mail address, password, and an account description. Tap Save and you're done!
   ● If you're adding another account type, tap Other and continue with Step 5.

6.2 Use the Add Account screen to choose the type of e-mail account you want to add.

5. **Tap Add Mail Account to open the New Account screen.**

6. **Use the Name, Address, Password, and Description text boxes to type the corresponding account information, and then tap Next.**

7. **Tap the type of account you're adding: IMAP or POP.**

8. **In the Incoming Mail Server section, use the Host Name text box to type the host name of your provider's incoming mail server as well as your username and password.**

9. **In the Outgoing Mail Server section, use the Host Name text box to type the host name of your provider's outgoing (SMTP) mail server.** If your provider requires a username and password to send messages, type those as well.

10. **Tap Save.** Your iPad verifies the account info (which might take a minute or three) and then returns you to the Mail settings screen with the account added to the Accounts list.

Specifying the default account

If you've added two or more e-mail accounts to your iPad, Mail specifies one of them as the default account. This means that Mail uses this account when you send a new message, when you reply to a message, and when you forward a message. The default account is usually the first account you add to your iPad. However, you can change this by following these steps:

1. **On the Home screen, tap Settings.** The Settings screen appears.

2. **Tap Mail, Contacts, Calendars.** Your iPad displays the Mail, Contacts, Calendars screen.

3. **In the Mail section of the screen, tap Default Account.** This opens the Default Account screen, which displays a list of your accounts. The current default account is shown with a check mark beside it, as shown in Figure 6.3.

4. **Tap the account you want to use as the default.** Your iPad places a check mark beside it.

6.3 Use the Default Account screen to set the default account you want Mail to use when sending messages.

Switching to another account

When you open the Mail app (by tapping Mail in the Dock in the iPad Home screen), you usually see the Inbox folder of your default account. If you have multiple accounts set up on your iPad and you want to see what's going on with a different one, follow these steps to make the switch:

1. **On the Home screen, tap Mail to open the Mail app.**

2. **In landscape mode, tap the mailbox button in the top-left corner of the screen (but below the status bar).** If you're in portrait mode, tap Inbox and then tap the mailbox button. The Mail app displays the Mailboxes screen, as shown in Figure 6.4.

3. **Tap the account with which you want to work:**

   ● If you only want to see the account's Inbox folder, tap the account name in the Inboxes section of the Mailboxes screen.

   ● If you want to see all of the account's available folders, tap the account name in the Accounts section of the Mailboxes screen. Mail displays a list of the account's folders and you then tap the folder with which you want to work.

6.4 Use the Mailboxes screen to choose the e-mail Inbox or account to which you want to switch.

Temporarily disabling an account

The Mail app checks for new messages at a regular interval (I show you how to configure this interval a bit later in this chapter). If you have several accounts configured in Mail, this incessant checking can put quite a strain on your iPad battery. To ease up on the juice, you can disable an account temporarily to prevent Mail from checking it for new messages. To do so, follow these steps:

1. **On the Home screen, tap Settings.** Your iPad displays the Settings screen.

2. **Tap Mail, Contacts, Calendars to see the Mail settings.**

3. **Tap the account you want to disable.** Your iPad displays the account settings.

4. **Depending on the type of account, you can use one of the following techniques to temporarily disable it:**

   ● **iCloud, Exchange, Gmail, Yahoo!, AOL, or Hotmail.** Tap the Mail switch to Off. If the account syncs other types of data, such as contacts and calendars, you can also turn those switches off.

   ● **POP or IMAP.** Tap the Account switch to Off, as shown in Figure 6.5.

5. **Tap Done to return to the Mail settings screen.**

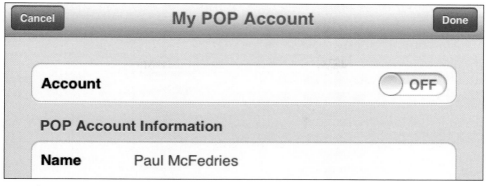

6.5 In the account settings screen, tap the Account switch to Off.

When you're ready to work with the account again, repeat these steps to turn the Mail or Account switch back to On.

Deleting an account

If an e-mail account has grown tiresome and boring (or you just don't use it anymore), you should delete it to save storage space, speed up sync times, and save battery power. Follow these steps to delete an account:

1. **On the Home screen, tap Settings.** The Settings screen appears.

2. **Tap Mail, Contacts, Calendars to get to the Mail settings.**

3. **Tap the account you want to delete.** This opens the account settings.

4. **Tap Delete Account.** Your iPad asks you to confirm.

5. **Tap Delete.** Your iPad returns you to the Mail settings screen and the account no longer graces the Accounts list.

Configuring E-mail Accounts

Setting up an e-mail account on your iPad is one thing, but making that account do useful things — or sometimes, anything at all — is quite another. The next few sections take you through a few useful settings that help you get more out of e-mail and troubleshoot e-mail problems.

Leaving messages on the server

In today's increasingly mobile world, it's not unusual to find you need to check the same e-mail account from multiple devices. For example, you may want to check your business account using not only your work computer but also your home computer, or your iPad while commuting or traveling.

If you need to check e-mail on multiple devices, you can take advantage of how POP e-mail messages are delivered over the Internet. When someone sends you a message, it doesn't come directly to your computer. Instead, it goes to the server that your ISP (or your company) has set up to handle incoming messages. When you ask your e-mail client to check for new messages, it communicates with the POP server to see if any messages are waiting in your account. If so, the client downloads those messages to your computer and then instructs the server to delete the copies of the messages that are stored on the server.

The trick, then, is to configure the e-mail program so that it leaves a copy of the messages on the POP server after you download them. This way, the messages are still available when you check messages using another device. Fortunately, the intuitive folks who designed the version of Mail on your iPad must have understood this because the program automatically sets up POP accounts to do just that. Specifically, after you download any messages from the POP server to your iPad, the Mail app leaves the messages on the server.

Here's a good overall strategy that ensures you can download messages on all your devices, but prevents messages from piling up on the server:

- **Let your main computer be the computer that controls deleting the messages from the server.** In Mac OS X, the default Mail setting is to delete messages from the server after one week and that's fine.

- **Set all of your other devices — particularly your iPad — not to delete messages from the server.**

Genius

To leave messages on the server in Outlook, choose Tools ➪ Account Settings, click the account, click Change, and then click More Settings. Click the Advanced tab and select the Leave a Copy of Messages on the Server check box. In Outlook Express or Windows Live Mail, choose File ➪ Options ➪ Email Accounts, click your e-mail account, and click Properties. Click the Advanced tab and then select the Leave a Copy of Messages on Server check box.

It's a good idea to check your iPad POP accounts to ensure they're not deleting messages from the server. To do that (or to use a different setting, such as deleting messages after a week or when you delete them from your Inbox), follow these steps:

1. **On the Home screen, tap Settings.** The Settings screen appears.

2. **Tap Mail, Contacts, Calendars.** Your iPad opens the Mail, Contacts, Calendars settings screen.

3. **Tap the POP account with which you want to work.** The account settings screen appears.

4. **Tap Advanced.** Your iPad displays the Advanced screen.

5. **Tap Remove.** The Remove screen appears, as shown in Figure 6.6.

6.6 Use the Remove screen to ensure your iPad is leaving messages on your POP server.

6. **Tap Never.** If you prefer that your iPad delete messages from the server after a set period of time, tap After one day, After one week, or After one month.

Using a different server port

For security reasons, some Internet service providers (ISPs) insist on routing all of their customers' outgoing mail through their Simple Mail Transfer Protocol (SMTP) servers.

This usually isn't a big deal if you're using an e-mail account maintained by the ISP, but it can lead to the following problems if you're using an account provided by a third party (such as your web-site host):

- **Your ISP might block messages sent using the third-party account because it thinks you're trying to relay the message through the ISP server (a technique often used by spammers).**

- **You might incur extra charges if your ISP allows only a certain amount of SMTP bandwidth per month or a certain number of sent messages, whereas the third-party account offers higher limits or no restrictions at all.**

- **You might have performance problems such as the ISP server taking much longer to route messages than the third-party host.**

You may think that you can solve the problem by specifying the third-party host's SMTP server in the account settings. However, this usually doesn't work because outgoing e-mail is sent by default through port 25. When you use this port, the outgoing mail goes through the ISP's SMTP server.

To work around this problem, many third-party hosts offer access to their SMTP servers via a port other than the standard port 25. For example, the iCloud SMTP server (smtp.icloud.com) also accepts connections on ports 465 and 587.

Here's how to configure an e-mail account to use a nonstandard SMTP port:

1. **On the Home screen, tap Settings.** You see the Settings screen.

2. **Tap Mail, Contacts, Calendars.** The Mail, Contacts, Calendars settings screen appears.

3. **Tap the POP account with which you want to work.** The account settings screen appears.

4. **Tap SMTP.** Your iPad displays the SMTP screen.

5. **In the Primary Server section, tap the name of your server.** Your iPad displays the server settings.

6. **Tap Server Port.** Your iPad displays a keypad so you can type the port number, as shown in Figure 6.7.

6.7 Tap Server Port to type the new port number for outgoing messages.

Configuring authentication for outgoing mail

Because spam is such a big problem these days, many ISPs now require SMTP authentication for outgoing mail. This means that you must log on to the SMTP server to confirm that you're the person sending the mail (as opposed to some spammer spoofing your address). If your ISP requires authentication on outgoing messages, you need to configure your e-mail account to provide the proper credentials.

If you're not sure about any of this, check with your ISP. If that doesn't work out, by far the most common type of authentication is to specify a username and password (this happens behind the scenes when you send messages).

Follow these steps to configure your iPad e-mail account with this kind of authentication:

1. **On the Home screen, tap Settings.** Your iPad displays the Settings screen.

2. **Tap Mail, Contacts, Calendars.** The Mail, Contacts, Calendars settings screen appears.

3. **Tap the POP account with which you want to work.** The account settings screen appears.

4. **Tap SMTP.** Your iPad displays the SMTP screen.

5. **In the Primary Server section, tap the server name.** Your iPad displays the server settings.

6. **In the Outgoing Mail Server section, tap Authentication.** Your iPad displays the Authentication screen.

7. **Tap Password.**

8. **Tap the server address to return to the server settings screen.**

9. **In the Outgoing Mail Server section, type your account username in the User Name box and the account password in the Password box.**

10. **Tap Done.**

Configuring E-mail Messages

The rest of this chapter takes you through a few useful and timesaving techniques for handling e-mail messages on your iPad.

Setting the number of messages to display

By default, the Mail app displays the 50 most recent messages in an e-mail account Inbox. If you want to see more messages, you must scroll to the bottom of the message list and then tap Load More Messages. That's not a big deal if you just have a few more messages to display, but if you have hundreds of messages on the server and you need to see them, constantly loading a new batch of 50 can get old in a hurry.

The iOS 5 version of Mail solves that problem by letting you set a higher default number of messages to display. You can display 100, 200, 500, or even 1,000 recent messages. To set up how many messages you want displayed, follow these steps:

1. **On the Home screen, tap Settings.** You see the Settings screen.

2. **Tap Mail, Contacts, Calendars.** The Mail, Contacts, Calendars settings screen appears.

3. **Tap Show.** The Show screen appears, as displayed in Figure 6.8.

6.8 Use this screen to set the default number of recent messages that you see in your Inbox.

4. **Tap the number of recent messages you want to display.** Your iPad puts the new setting into effect.

Identifying messages sent to you

In the iPad Mail app, the Inbox folder tells you who sent you each message, but it doesn't tell you to whom the message was sent (that is, which addresses appeared on the To line or the Cc line). No big deal, right? Maybe, maybe not.

You see, bulk mailers — I'm talking newsletters, mailing lists, and, notoriously, spammers — often don't send messages directly to each person on their subscriber lists. Instead, they use a generic bulk address, which means, significantly, that your e-mail address doesn't appear on the To or Cc lines. That's significant because most newsletters and mailing lists — and all spam — are low-priority messages that you can ignore when you process a stuffed Inbox.

Okay, great, but what good does all of this do if Mail doesn't show the To and Cc lines? You can configure Mail to show a little icon for messages that were sent directly to you:

● **If the message includes your address in the To field, you see a *To* icon to the left of it.**

● **If the message includes your address in the Cc field, you see a *Cc* icon to the left of it.**

Neat! Here's how to make this happen:

1. **On the Home screen, tap Settings.**
   The Settings screen appears.

2. **Tap Mail, Contacts, Calendars.** The
   Mail, Contacts, Calendars screen
   appears.

3. **In the Mail section, tap the Show To/
   Cc Label switch to the On position.**

When you examine your Inbox, you see the
To and Cc icons on messages addressed to
you, as shown in Figure 6.9. You don't see
either icon on bulk messages.

6.9 With the Show To/Cc Label switch turned on,
Mail shows you which messages were addressed
directly to you.

E-mailing a link

The web is all about finding content that's interesting, educational, and, of course, fun. If you
stumble across a page that meets one or more of these criteria, the only sensible thing to do is
share your good fortune with someone else, right? So, how do you do that? Some web pages are
kind enough to include an E-mail This Page link or something similar, but you can't count on having one of those around. Instead, the usual method is to copy the page address, switch to your
e-mail program, paste the address into the message, choose a recipient, and then send it.

And, yes, with the iPad copy-and-paste feature, you can do all that, but boy, it sure seems like a ton
of work. So are you stuck using this unwieldy method? Not a chance (you probably knew that).
Your iPad includes a great little feature that enables you to plop the address of the current Safari
page into an e-mail message with just a couple of taps. You then ship out the message and make
the world a better place.

Here's how it works:

1. **Use Safari to navigate to the page you want to share.**

2. **Tap the Actions button (the one with the arrow) in the status bar.** Safari displays a
   dialog with several options.

3. **Tap Mail Link to this Page.** This opens a new e-mail message. As you can see in Figure 6.10, the new message already includes the page title as the Subject and the page address in the message body.

6.10 Your iPad can create a new e-mail message with a web page title and address already inserted.

4. **Choose a recipient for the message.**

5. **Edit the message text as you see fit.**

6. **Tap Send.** Your iPad fires off the message and returns you to Safari.

Creating iCloud message folders

In your e-mail program on your computer, you've no doubt created lots of folders to hold different types of messages that you want or need to save: Projects, people, mailing list gems, and so on. This is a great way to reduce Inbox clutter and organize the e-mail portion of your life.

Of course, these days the e-mail portion of your life extends beyond your computer and probably includes lots of time spent on your iPad. Wouldn't it be great to have that same folder convenience and organization on your favorite tablet? Happily, you can. If you have an iCloud account, any folders (technically, Apple calls them *mailboxes*) that you create on your iCloud account — either on your computer or on the iCloud site — are automatically mirrored on the iPad Mail app.

Even better, you can create new iCloud message folders right from the comfort of your iPad. To do so, follow these steps:

1. **On the Home screen, tap Mail to open the Mail app.**

2. **In landscape mode, tap the mailbox button in the top-left corner of the screen (but below the status bar).** If you're in portrait mode, tap Inbox and then tap the mailbox button. The Mail app displays the Mailboxes screen.

3. **In the Accounts section, tap your iCloud account.** Mail displays the iCloud folders list.

4. **Tap Edit.** Mail opens the iCloud folders list for editing.

5. **Tap new Mailbox.** The Edit Mailbox screen appears, as shown in Figure 6.11.

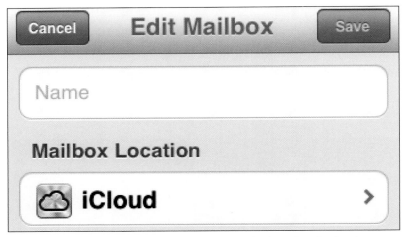

6.11 Use the Edit Mailbox screen to type a name and select a location for the message folder.

6. **Type a name for the new folder.**

7. **Tap the Mailbox Location and then tap the folder in which you want to store your new folder.**

8. **Tap Save.** Mail adds the folder, and iCloud propagates the change to the cloud.

9. **Tap Done.**

Note

To move a message to your new folder, display the iCloud Inbox folder, tap the message, tap the Move icon (the folder), and then tap the new folder.

Formatting an e-mail

We're all used to rich text e-mail messages by now, where formatting such as bold and italics is used to add pizzazz or emphasis to our e-musings. Until iOS 5 came along, the Mail app was having none of that. Oh, sure, it could *display* rich text formatting, but the missives you composed in the Mail app were as plain as plain text could get.

The iOS 5 version of Mail changes all that by giving you a limited set of formatting options for text: Bold, italics, and underline. It's not much, but it's a start. Here are the steps to follow to format text in the Mail app:

1. **In your e-mail message, tap within the word or phrase you want to format.** The Mail app displays the cursor.

2. **Tap the cursor.** Mail displays a set of options.

3. **Tap Select.** Mail selects the word closest to the cursor.

4. **If needed, drag the selection handles to select the entire phrase you want to format.** Mail displays a set of options for the selected text.

5. **Tap the arrow on the right side of the options.** Mail displays more options.

6. **Tap the B/U button.** Mail displays the Bold, Italics, and Underline buttons, as shown in Figure 6.12.

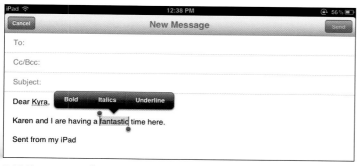

6.12 You can now format e-mail text.

7. **Tap the formatting you want to apply.** Mail leaves the formatting options on the screen, so feel free to apply multiple formats, if needed.

8. **Tap another part of the screen to hide the formatting options.**

Genius

If you're composing a message on your computer and decide to work on it later, your mail program stores the message as a draft that you can reopen any time. The Mail app doesn't *appear* to have that option, but it does. In the message window, tap Cancel (unintuitive, I know!) and then tap Save Draft. When you're ready to resume editing, open the account in the Mailboxes screen, tap Drafts, and then tap your saved message.

Setting a minimum font size

Some people who send e-mails must have terrific eyesight because the font they use for the message text is positively microscopic. Such text is tough to read even on a big screen, but when it's crammed into the iPad touchscreen, you'll be reaching for the nearest magnifying glass. Of course, that same touchscreen can also solve this problem: A quick finger spread magnifies the text accordingly.

That's easy enough if you just get the occasional message with nanoscale text, but if a regular correspondent does this, or if your eyesight isn't quite what it used to be (so *all* of your messages appear ridiculously teensy), then a more permanent solution might be in order. Your iPad rides to the rescue once again by letting you configure a minimum font size for your messages. This means that if the message font size is larger than what you specify, your iPad displays the message as is; however, if the font size is smaller than your specification, your iPad scales up the text to your minimum size. Your tired eyes will be forever grateful.

Follow these steps to set your minimum font size:

1. **On the Home screen, tap Settings.** The Settings screen appears.

2. **Tap Mail, Contacts, Calendars.** Your iPad displays the Mail, Contacts, Calendars settings screen.

3. **In the Mail section, tap Minimum Font Size.** The Minimum Font Size screen appears.

4. **Tap the minimum font size you want to use: Small, Medium, Large, Extra Large, or Giant.** Mail uses the font size you select (or larger) when displaying your messages.

Creating a custom iPad signature

E-mail signatures can range from the simple — a signoff such as "Cheers," or "All the best," followed by the sender's name — to baroque masterpieces filled with contact information, snappy quotations, or even some text-based artwork! On your iPad, the Mail app takes the simple route by adding the following signature to all of your outgoing messages (new messages, replies, and forwards):

Sent from my iPad

I really like this signature because it's short, simple, and kinda cool (and I, *of course*, want my recipients to know that I'm using my iPad). If that default signature doesn't rock your world, you can create a custom one that does. To do so, follow these steps:

1. **On the Home screen, tap Settings.** Your iPad opens the Settings screen.

2. **Tap Mail, Contacts, Calendars.** You see the Mail, Contacts, Calendars settings screen.

3. **In the Mail section, tap Signature.** The Signature screen appears.

4. **Type the signature you want to use.**

5. **Tap Mail, Contacts, Calendars.** Mail saves your new signature and uses it on all outgoing messages.

Caution

Mail doesn't give any way to cancel your edits and return to the original signature, so type your text carefully. If you make a real hash of things, tap Clear to get a fresh start.

Disabling remote images

Lots of messages nowadays come not just as plain text, but also with fonts, colors, images, and other flourishes. This fancy formatting, called either *rich text* or *HTML*, makes for a more pleasant e-mail experience, particularly when using images in messages. Who doesn't like a bit of eye candy to brighten his day?

Note

HTML stands for Hypertext Markup Language and is a set of codes that folks use to put together web pages.

Unfortunately, however, getting images in your e-mail messages can sometimes be problematic because:

● **A cellular connection may cause trouble.** It may take a long time to load the images or, if your data plan has an upper limit, you may not want a bunch of e-mail images taking a big bite out of that limit.

● **Not all e-mail images are benign.** A web bug is an image that resides on a remote server and is added to an HTML-formatted e-mail message by referencing an address on the remote server. When you open the message, Mail uses the address to download the image for display within the message. That sounds harmless enough, but if the message is junk e-mail, it's likely that the address also contains either your e-mail address or a code that points to it. When the remote server gets a request to load the image, it knows not only that you've opened the message, but also that your e-mail address is legitimate. So, not surprisingly, spammers use web bugs all the time because, for them, valid e-mail addresses are like gold.

The iPad Mail app displays remote images by default. To disable remote images, follow these steps:

1. **On the Home screen, tap Settings.** Your iPad opens the Settings screen.

2. **Tap Mail, Contacts, Calendars.** You see the Mail, Contacts, Calendars settings screen.

3. **In the Mail section, tap the Load Remote Images switch to the Off position.** Mail saves the setting and no longer displays remote images in your e-mail messages.

Preventing Mail from organizing messages by thread

The Mail app groups your messages by thread, which means the original message and all of the replies you receive are grouped together in the account Inbox folder. This is usually remarkably handy, because it means you don't have to scroll through a million messages to locate the reply you want to read.

Mail indicates a thread by displaying the number of messages it contains on the right side of the latest message. Tap the message to see a list of the messages in the thread and then tap the one you want to read.

Organizing messages by thread is not always convenient. As you view and scroll through your messages (by tapping the Next and Previous buttons), Mail jumps into a thread when you come to one. You then scroll through each message in the thread, which can be a real hassle if there are a large number of replies.

If you find that threads are more of a hassle than they're worth, you can follow these steps to configure Mail not to organize messages by thread:

1. **On the Home screen, tap Settings.** Your iPhone opens the Settings screen.

2. **Tap Mail, Contacts, Calendars.** You see the Mail, Contacts, Calendars settings screen.

3. **Tap the Organize By Thread switch to the Off position.** Your iPhone saves the setting and no longer organizes your images by thread.

Deleting Gmail messages

With most e-mail accounts, you can tidy up the Inbox folder by tapping Edit, choosing one or more messages you no longer need, and then tapping Delete. Not so in your Google Gmail account, however. When you open your Gmail Inbox, tap Edit, and then select one or more messages, you see an Archive button instead of a Delete button, as shown in Figure 6.13. Tapping Archive moves the selected messages to the All Mail folder.

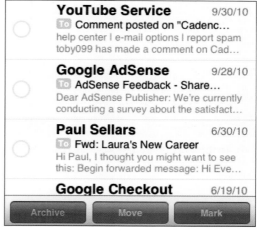

6.13 By default, Mail archives Gmail messages instead of deleting them.

If you really prefer to delete your Gmail messages instead of archiving them, follow these steps to knock some sense into the Mail app:

1. **On the Home screen, tap Settings.** Your iPad opens the Settings screen.

2. **Tap Mail, Contacts, Calendars.** You see the Mail, Contacts, Calendars settings screen.

3. **Tap your Gmail account.** Your iPad opens the Gmail settings.

4. **Tap the Archive Messages switch to the Off position.** Your iPad saves the setting and no longer archives your Gmail messages.

Configuring the Exchange ActiveSync settings

If you have an account on a Microsoft Exchange Server 2003 or 2007 network, and that server has deployed Exchange ActiveSync, you're all set to have your iPad and Exchange account synchronized automatically. That's because ActiveSync supports wireless push technology. This means that if there is a change to any of the following on your Exchange server account, that change is immediately synced with your iPad:

- **E-mail.** If you receive a new message on your Exchange account, ActiveSync immediately displays it in the iPad Mail app.

- **Contacts.** If someone at work adds or edits data in the server address book, those changes are immediately synced to your iPad Contacts list.

- **Calendar.** If someone at work adds or edits an appointment in your calendar, or if someone requests a meeting with you, that data is immediately synced with the iPad Calendar application.

- **Reminder.** If someone at work adds or edits a reminder, that data is immediately synced with the Reminders app on your iPad.

ActiveSync works both ways, too. If you send e-mail messages, add contacts or appointments, or accept meeting requests, your server account is immediately updated with the changes. And all this data whizzing back and forth is safe, because it's sent over a secure connection.

Your iPad also gives you a few options for controlling ActiveSync. The following steps show you how to set them:

1. **On the Home screen, tap Settings.** Your iPad opens the Settings screen.

2. **Tap Mail, Contacts, Calendars to open the Mail, Contacts, Calendars settings.**

3. **Tap your Exchange account.** The Exchange account settings screen appears, as shown in Figure 6.14.

6.14 Use the Exchange account settings screen to customize the iPad ActiveSync support.

4. **To sync your Exchange e-mail account, tap the Mail On/Off switch to the On position.**

5. **To sync your Exchange address book, calendars, and reminders, tap the Contacts, Calendars, and Reminders On/Off switches, respectively, to the On position.**

6. **To control the amount of time that gets synced on your e-mail account, tap Mail Days to Sync and then tap the number of days, weeks, or months you want to sync.**

7. **To set the mail folders that get pushed to your iPad, tap Mail Folders to Push, and then tap each folder that you want pushed.**

Dictating e-mail messages

Most people predicted that the third-generation iPad would come with the Siri voice-activated assistant that was such a hit with the iPhone 4S. Apple didn't add Siri to the new iPad, but they did add the Dictation feature. This enables you to dictate text instead of typing. Dictation supports American, British, and Australian English, as well as French, German, and Japanese.

Before you can use Dictation, you must activate it. On the iPad Home screen, tap Settings and tap General. Next, tap Keyboard, tap the Dictation switch to On, and then tap Enable when your iPad asks you to confirm.

When you tap inside the body of a new message, the keyboard that appears shows a Mic icon beside the spacebar. Tap the Mic icon and then start dictating. Here are some notes:

- For punctuation, you can say the name of the mark you need, such as "comma" (,), "semi-colon" (;), "colon" (:), "period" or "full stop" (.), "question mark" (?), "exclamation point" (!), "dash" (-), or "at sign" (@).

- You can enclose text in parentheses by saying "open parenthesis," then the text, and then "close parenthesis."

- To surround text with quotation marks, say "open quote," then the text, and then "close quote."

- To render a word in all uppercase letters, say "all caps," and then say the word.

- To start a new paragraph, say "new line."

- You can have some fun by saying "smiley face" for :-), "wink face" for ;-), and "frown face" for :-(.

When you're finished, tap the mic icon to let the Dictation feature know that you're done. Dictation then processes your speech and converts it to text within the message window.

Configuring iPad to automatically check for new messages

By default, your iPad checks for new messages only when you tell it to. To set it up, follow these steps:

1. **On the Home screen, tap Mail to open the Mail app.**

2. **In landscape mode, tap the mailbox button in the top-left corner of the screen (but below the status bar).** If you're in portrait mode, tap Inbox and then tap the mailbox button. The Mail app displays the Mailboxes screen.

3. **In the Inboxes section, tap the account that you want.** Mail opens the folder and checks for messages.

Note

While you have an account's Inbox mailbox open, you can check for messages again by tapping the Refresh icon on the left side of the Inbox menu bar.

This is usually the behavior you want because it limits bandwidth if you're using the cellular network and saves battery life. However, if you're busy with something else and you're expecting an important message, you may prefer to have your iPad check for new messages automatically. Easy money! The Auto-Check feature is happy to handle everything for you. Follow these steps to set it up:

1. **On the Home screen, tap Settings to display the Settings screen.**

2. **Tap Mail, Contacts, Calendars.** The Mail, Contacts, Calendars settings screen appears.

3. **Tap Fetch New Data.** Your iPad opens the Fetch New Data screen.

4. **In the Fetch section, tap the interval you want to use, such as Every 15 minutes.**

5. **Tap Advanced to open the Advanced screen.**

6. **Tap each account you want your iPad to check automatically and then tap Fetch.**
   If you don't want your iPad to check a particular account for messages automatically, tap the account and then tap Manual.

When you're ready to return to checking for new messages on your own, repeat these steps and when you get to the Fetch New Data screen, tap Manual.

The large, high-resolution iPad display makes it the perfect portable photo album. No more whipping out wallet shots of your kids: Just show people your iPad photo albums. The iPad also comes with some great features that make it a breeze to browse photos and run slide shows. However, your third-generation iPad or iPad 2 is capable of more than just viewing photos. It's actually loaded with cool features that enable you to manipulate and take photos, and use them to enhance other parts of your digital life. This chapter is your guide to these features.

Preparing Your Photos for iPad with iPhoto

I mentioned in this chapter's introduction that your iPad comes with features that make it almost ridiculously easy to browse photos, no matter how large your collection. That's true, as far as it goes, but I should really have added a caveat: The iPad makes it easy to browse your photos *if* your photos have at least some semblance of organization.

To understand what I mean and to get a sense of how much (or how little) prep work you have to do, here's a quick look at the six viewing modes offered by the iPad Photos app:

- **Photos.** Tap this button at the top of the Photos app screen to see a list of all the photos stored on your iPad. The good news here is that the Photos app does *not* show the name of each photo, so you don't have to spend time fixing all those oddball names that your digital camera supplies to your images.

- **Photo Stream.** Tap this button to see the photos that you've synced through the cloud using the Photo Stream feature of iCloud.

- **Albums.** Tap this button to see your photos organized by album, where an *album* is a collection of photos that are related in some way. On a Windows PC, the Photos app uses your photo folders as albums, so be sure to organize your photos in their proper folders and give the folders descriptive names. On a Mac, you also can use folders to organize your photos but if you have iPhoto, you can create your own albums right in the program, as I describe in the next section.

- **Events.** Tap this button to see stacks of your photos organized by event. In iPhoto on a Mac, an *event* is a collection of photos taken during a particular time period, such as an afternoon outing or a day trip. To get the most out of the Events view, make sure your iPhoto events have descriptive names (click the current name, type the new name, and then press Return). If iPhoto created multiple events for the same time period, hold down ⌘, click each event, and then choose Events ➪ Merge Events.

- **Faces.** Tap this button to see stacks of your photos organized by the people in each photo. To take advantage of this cool feature, you need to have iPhoto '09 (or later) on a Mac and you need to use the program to add names to the faces in your photos, as described later in this chapter.

● **Places.** Tap this button to see a world map that shows pushpins for each location where you took at least one photo. To map your photos, you need to have iPhoto '09 (or later) on a Mac and you need to use the program to add locations to your photos, as described later in this chapter.

Organizing your photos

As I mentioned earlier, an album is a collection of photos that are related in some way. If you have iPhoto on your Mac, you can create customized albums that include only the photos you want to view. To create a customized album, follow these steps:

1. **Choose File ➪ New Album (or press ⌘+N).** iPhoto prompts you for an album name.

2. **Type a name for the new album and then press Enter.** iPhoto adds a new album to the Albums section of the sidebar.

3. **Click Photos.**

4. **For each photo you want to add to the new album, click, drag, and drop it on the album.**

Genius

For a faster way to create and populate an album, first open the Photos section of the iPhoto library or open an event with which you want to work. Press and hold the ⌘ key, and click each photo you want to include in your album. When you finish, choose File ➪ New Album (or press ⌘+N). iPhoto creates the new album and automatically populates it with the selected photos. Type the new album name and press Enter.

Adding names to faces

One of the awesome iPhoto features is that you can annotate your photos by adding names to the faces that appear in them. This enables you to navigate your photos by name in iPhoto. Even better, the iPad Photos app picks up these names and enables you to view all of the photos in which a certain person appears.

Follow these steps to add names to the faces in your photos:

1. **Double-click the photo that you want to annotate.**

2. **Click Info.** iPhoto displays its naming tools, adds boxes around each face in the photo, and displays Unnamed for each unrecognized face.

3. **For the face you want to name, click Unnamed.** iPhoto displays a text box below the face.

4. **Type the person's name or select it from the list of contacts that appears as you type, as shown in Figure 7.1, and press Return.**

7.1 Type the person's name or select it from your Address Book contacts.

5. **Repeat Steps 3 and 4 to name each person in the photo.** If iPhoto didn't mark a face, click Add a Face, size and position the box over the face, click Done, and then follow Steps 3 and 4.

6. **Click Info.** iPhoto exits naming mode.

Note

To add names to the faces in your photos, you must be using iPhoto '09 or later. To check this, click iPhoto in the menu bar and then click About iPhoto.

138

Mapping your photos

You can tell iPhoto the locations where your photos were taken. When you sync your photos to your iPad, this location data goes along with the photos, and you can use the Photos app to display a map that shows those locations. This enables you to view all of the photos taken in a particular place.

Note

To map your photos, you must be using iPhoto '09 or later. To check this, click iPhoto in the menu bar and then click About iPhoto.

Follow these steps to add a location to a photo:

1. **Click the event that you want to map.** If you want to map a single photo instead, open the event and click the photo.

2. **Click the Info icon.**

3. **Click Assign a Place.**

4. **Use the text box to type the location and then press Return, or choose a matching location from the list.** iPhoto opens a Google map and adds a pushpin to mark the location, as shown in Figure 7.2.

5. **Click and drag the pin to the correct location, if necessary.**

6. **Click Info.** iPhoto closes the Information window.

Genius

If you have a GPS-enabled camera phone — such as an iPhone — iPhoto automatically picks up location data from the photos, so you don't need to set the location yourself. However, for this to work, you must make sure this feature is activated. Choose iPhoto ⇨ Preferences to open the iPhoto preferences and click the Advanced tab. In the Look up Places list, choose Automatically. Note that you may still have to add or edit location names for your photos.

7.2 After you specify the location, iPhoto marks it on a map with a pushpin.

Syncing Photos

No iPad media collection is complete without a few choice photos to show off around the water cooler. If you have some good pics on your computer, you can use iTunes to send those images to the iPad. Note that Apple supports a number of image file types — the usual TIFF and JPEG formats that you normally use for your photos as well as BMP, GIF, JPG2000 or JP2, PICT, PNG, PSD, and SGI.

Syncing computer photos to your iPad

If you use your computer to process lots of photos and you want to take copies of some (or all) of those photos with you on your iPad, then follow these steps to get synced:

1. **Connect your iPad to your computer.**

2. **In iTunes, click your iPad in the Devices list.**

3. **Click the Photos tab.**

4. **Select the Sync Photos From check box.**

Note

If you have another photo-editing application installed on your computer, chances are good that it also appears in the Sync photos from list.

5. **Choose an option from the drop-down menu:**

   - **iPhoto (Mac only).** Choose this item to sync the photos, albums, and events you've set up in iPhoto.

   - **Choose Folder.** Choose this command to sync the images contained in a folder you specify.

   - **My Pictures (or Pictures on Windows Vista).** Choose this item to sync the images in the My Pictures (or Pictures) folder.

6. **Select the photos you want to sync.** The controls you see depend on what you chose in Step 5:

   - **My Pictures or Choose folder.** If you chose either of these, select either the All photos option or the Selected Folders option. If you select the latter, select the check box beside each subfolder you want to sync.

   - **iPhoto.** If this is what you chose you get two additional options: Select the All photos, albums, Events, and Faces option to sync your entire iPhoto library. Select the Selected albums, Events, and Faces, and automatically include option, and then select the check box beside each item you want to sync, as shown in Figure 7.3. Choose the number of events from the pop-up menu you want automatically synced.

7. **Click Apply.** iTunes syncs the iPad using your new settings.

Note

iTunes doesn't sync exact copies of your photos to the iPad. Instead, it creates what Apple calls TV-quality versions of each image. These are copies of the images that have been reduced in size to match the iPad screen size. This makes syncing faster and the photos take up much less room on your iPad.

| Summary | Info | Apps | Ringtones | Music | Movies | TV Shows | Podcasts | iTunes U | Books | Photos |

☑ **Sync Photos from** [iPhoto ⬦]   **361 photos**

    ○ All photos, albums, Events, and Faces
    ● Selected albums, Events, and Faces, and automatically include [no Events ⬦]
    ☐ Include videos

Albums

- ☐ Last Import
- ☐ Last 12 Months
- ☐ Photo Stream
- ☑ Dogs, Dogs, Dogs! 36
- ☑ Vacations 248
- ☐ iPhone Pics
- ☑ iPad Pics 44
- ☐ Weddings

Events

- ☑ Gypsy 36
- ☐ Wedding Pics
- ☑ Flowers 21
- ☑ Bahamas 169
- ☐ Dickie Lake 2006
- ☑ Flat Coat Calender 2009 12
- ☐ Brickworks Pics
- ☐ St. Maarten
- ☑ iPhonography 36

7.3 If you have iPhoto '09 or later on your Mac, you can sync specific albums and events to your iPad.

Syncing iPad photos to your computer

If you create a Safari bookmark on your iPad and then sync with your computer, that bookmark is transferred from the iPad to the default web browser on your computer. That's a sweet deal that also applies to contacts and appointments. Unfortunately, it doesn't apply to media files which, with two exceptions, travel along a one-way street from your computer to your iPad.

Ah, but then there are those two exceptions, and they're good ones. If you take any photos using the built-in cameras in your third-generation iPad or iPad 2, or if you receive any photos on your iPad (via, say, an e-mail message or text message), the sync process reverses itself and enables you to send some (or all) of those images to your computer. Sign me up!

The iPad-to-computer sync process bypasses iTunes entirely. Instead, your computer deals directly with iPad and treats it just as though it's some garden-variety media storage device. How this works depends on whether your computer is a Mac or a Windows PC, so I'll use separate sets of steps.

To sync your iPad photos to your Mac, follow these steps:

1. **Connect your iPad to your Mac.** iPhoto opens, adds your iPad to the Devices list, and displays the photos from your iPad Camera Roll album, as shown in Figure 7.4.

7.4 When you connect your iPad to your Mac, iPhoto shows up to handle importing photos.

2. Use the Event Name text box to name the event that these photos represent.

Genius

If you've imported some of your iPad photos in the past, you probably don't want to import them again. That's very sensible of you, and you can prevent that by hiding those photos. Select the Hide Photos Already Imported check box.

3. Choose how you want to import the photos:

- If you want to import every photo, click Import All.
- If you want to import only some of the photos, select the ones you want to import and click Import Selected.

4. Using the dialog that appears after the import is complete, choose what you want iPhoto to do with the photos on your iPad:

- If you want to leave the photos on your iPad, click Keep Photos.
- If you prefer to clear the photos from your iPad, click Delete Photos.

143

Here's how things work if you're syncing with a Windows 7 PC (these steps assume you've installed Windows Live Photo Gallery from the Windows Live Essentials site):

1. **Connect your iPad to your Windows 7 PC.** If you see the AutoPlay dialog box, click Import pictures and videos using Windows Live Photo Gallery, and skip to Step 5.

2. **Open Windows Live Photo Gallery.**

Genius

If you don't have Windows Live Photo Gallery installed, you can still access your iPad photos in Windows 7. Choose Start ⇨ Computer, and then double-click your iPad in the Portable Devices group. Open the Internal Storage folder, then the DCIM folder, and then the folder that appears (which will have a name such as 800AAAAA). Your iPad photos appear and you can then copy them to your computer.

3. **Choose Home ⇨ Import.** The Import Photos and Videos dialog box appears.

4. **Click the icon for your iPad and then click Import.** Windows Live Photo Gallery connects to your iPad to gather the photo information.

5. **Select the Import all new Items now option.** If you'd prefer to select the photos you want to Import, select the Review, organize, and group Items to import option. Then click Next, use the dialog box to choose the photos you want, and skip to Step 7.

6. **Type a tag for the photos.** A tag is a word or short phrase that identifies the photos.

7. **Click Import.** Windows Live Photo Gallery imports the photos.

Here's how things work if you're syncing with a Windows Vista PC:

1. **Connect your iPad to your Windows Vista PC.** The AutoPlay dialog box appears.

2. **Click Import Pictures Using Windows.** The rest of these steps assume you selected this option. However, if you have another photo-management application installed, it should appear in the AutoPlay list and you can click it to import the photos using that program.

3. **Type a tag for the photos.** A tag is a word or short phrase that identifies the photos.

4. **Click Import.** Windows imports the photos and opens Windows Photo Gallery to display them.

Preventing your iPad from sending photos to your computer

Each and every time you connect your iPad to your computer, you see iPhoto (on your Mac) or the AutoPlay dialog box (in Windows 7 or Windows Vista without iTunes installed). This is certainly convenient if you actually want to send photos to your computer, but you may find that you do that only once in a blue moon. In that case, having to deal with iPhoto or a dialog every time could cause even the most mild-mannered among us to start pulling out her hair. If you prefer to keep your hair, you can configure your computer not to pester you about getting photos from your iPad.

Here's how you set this up on your Mac:

1. **Connect your iPad to your Mac.**

2. **Choose Finder ➪ Applications to open the Applications folder.**

3. **Double-click Image Capture.** The Image Capture application opens.

4. **Click your iPad in the Devices list.**

5. **Click the Connecting this iPad opens menu and then click No application, as shown in Figure 7.5.**

6. **Choose Image Capture ➪ Quit Image Capture.** Image Capture saves the new setting and shuts down. The next time you connect your iPad, iPhoto ignores it.

7.5 Choose No application to prevent iPhoto from starting when you connect your iPad.

Note

Configuring your computer not to download photos from your iPad means that in the future you either need to reverse the setting or manually import your photos.

Follow these steps to convince Windows 7 and Windows Vista not to open the AutoPlay dialog box each time you connect your iPad:

1. **Choose Start ➪ Default Programs to open the Default Programs window.**

2. **Click Change AutoPlay Settings.** The AutoPlay dialog box appears.

145

3. **In the Devices section, open the Apple iPad list and choose Take No Action.**

4. **Click Save.** Windows saves the new setting.

Syncing photos via iCloud

Syncing photos from your computer isn't difficult, but it seems more than a little old-fashioned in this increasingly wireless age. Fortunately, if you have an iCloud account you can place your feet firmly in the modern era by using the Photo Stream feature to sync photos without even looking at a USB cable. Photo Stream automatically syncs photos you take using your third-generation iPad or iPad 2 cameras to your iCloud account, which then downloads them to your computer, your iPhone, or any other device associated with your account. Similarly, if you upload photos to iCloud using another device, those photos are synced automatically to your iPad.

Follow these steps to activate Photo Stream on your iPad:

1. **In the iPad Home screen, tap Settings to open the Settings app.**

2. **Tap Photos.**

3. **Tap the Photo Stream switch to On.**

Importing photos from a camera

If you have a stack of photos on a digital camera or iPhone, you may think the only way to get them onto your iPad is to first sync the photos to your Mac or PC, and then sync them from your computer to your iPad. And you'd be right — *most* of the time. However, Apple offers a way to avoid this time-consuming route: the Camera Connection Kit. This is an iPad accessory designed to get photos directly from a camera to an iPad. The kit comes with the following two adapters:

- **Camera Connector.** Connect this adapter's 30-pin connector to the 30-pin port on the iPad and then connect the USB cable to the USB port on the digital camera.

- **SD Card Reader.** Connect this adapter's 30-pin connector to the 30-pin port on the iPad, and then insert the digital camera's SD (Secure Digital) card. Actually, if you have photos on another SD card — for example, one from another camera, one someone else has given you, or one you've used to copy photos from a computer — you can also insert that SD card into the reader.

The Photos app recognizes the connection and you can then import some (or all) of the photos to the iPad.

Getting More Out of iPad Photos

After you dump a bucketful of photos onto your iPad, you can start messing around with them by tapping the Photos icon on the Home screen. In the Photos app, you use the five tabs at the top of the screen — Photos, Albums, Events, Faces, and Places, described earlier — to view your photos from different angles, so to speak. The next few sections take you through a few of the more interesting features of the Photos app.

Scrolling, rotating, zooming, and panning

You can do so much with your photos after they're on your iPad and it isn't your normal photo-browsing experience. You aren't just a passive viewer because you can actually take some control over what you see and how the pictures are presented.

You can use the following techniques to navigate and manipulate your photos:

- **Scroll.** You view your photos by flicking. If you're in landscape mode, flick left to view the next photo and right to view the previous shot. If you're in portrait mode, flick up to see the next image and down to display the previous image. Alternatively, tap the screen to display a sequence of thumbnails at the bottom of the Photos app window and run your finger along those thumbnails to quickly peruse the photos.

- **Rotate.** When a landscape shot shows up on your iPad, it is letterboxed at the top (that is, you see black space above and below the image). To get a better view, rotate the screen into the landscape position and the photo rotates right along with it, filling the entire screen. When you come upon a photo with a portrait orientation, rotate the iPad back to the upright position for best viewing.

- **Flip.** To show a photo to another person, flip the iPad so the back is toward you and the bottom is now the top. The iPad automatically flips the photo right-side up.

- **Zoom.** Zooming magnifies the shot that's on the screen. You can use two methods to do this:
  - **Double tap the area of the photo on which you want to zoom in.** The iPad doubles the size of the portion you tapped. Double tap again to return the photo to its original size.
  - **Spread and pinch.** To zoom in, spread two fingers apart over the area you want magnified. To zoom back out, pinch two fingers together.

- **Pan.** After you zoom in on the photo, drag your finger across the screen to move it along with your finger.

Note

You can scroll to another photo if you're zoomed in, but it takes much more work to get there because the iPad thinks you're trying to pan. For faster scrolling, return the photo to its normal size and then scroll.

Adding an existing photo to a contact

You can assign a photo to a contact in two ways: Straight from a photo album or through the Contacts app.

First, here's how you assign a photo from a photo album:

1. **Tap Photos in the Home screen.** The Photos app appears.

2. **Locate the image you want to use and tap it.** The Photos app opens the photo and reveals the photo controls.

3. **Tap the Actions button.** The Actions button is the arrow that appears on the right side of the menu bar. If you don't see it, tap the screen to reveal the controls. The Photos app displays a list of actions you can perform.

4. **Tap Assign to Contact.** A list of all of your contacts appears.

5. **Tap the contact you want to associate with the photo.** The Move and Scale screen appears.

6. **Drag the image so it's positioned on the screen the way you want.**

7. **Pinch or spread your fingers over the image to set the zoom level you want.**

8. **Tap Use.** iPad assigns the photo to the contact and returns you to your photo album.

To assign a photo using the Contacts app, follow these steps:

1. **On the Home screen, tap the Contacts icon to open the Contacts app.**

2. **Tap the contact to which you want to add a photo.** Your iPad displays the contact's Info screen.

3. **Tap Edit to put the contact into Edit mode.**

4. **Tap Add Photo and then, if you have a third-generation iPad or an iPad 2, tap Choose Photo.** Your iPad displays a list of photo albums, events, and faces.

5. **Tap the album, event, or face that contains the photo you want to use.**

6. **Tap the photo you want.** The Move and Scale screen appears.

7. **Drag the image so it's positioned on the screen the way you want.**

8. **Pinch or spread your fingers over the image to set the zoom level you want.**

9. **Tap Use.** iPad assigns the photo to the contact and returns you to the Info screen.

10. **Tap Done.** Your iPad exits Edit mode.

Saving a photo from an e-mail message

If someone sends you a nice photo in an e-mail message, you might want to save it to your iPad so you can check it out whenever you want, assign it to a contact, sync it to your computer, and so on. Follow these steps to save a photo from an e-mail message:

1. **On the Home screen, tap Mail.** The Mail app appears,

2. **Tap the mailbox that contains the photo message.** The Mail app opens the mailbox.

3. **Tap the message that contains the photo.** Your iPad opens the message for viewing.

4. **Tap and hold the image.** Mail displays a list of actions you can perform for the image.

5. **Tap Save Image.** If the message contains multiple images and you want to save them all, tap Save X Images (where X is the number of images in the message). Your iPad saves the image (or images) to the Photo app's Saved Photos album.

Creating a custom photo slide show

In the Photos app, you can open the Camera Roll or an album, tap Slideshow, and then tap Start Slideshow to run through the album images automatically. The basic slide show is pretty cool, but your iPad also offers a few settings for creating custom slide shows. For example, you can set how long each photo lingers on-screen and you can configure the slide show to display your photos randomly.

To customize your slide show settings, tap the Settings icon in the Home screen. When the Settings screen opens, tap the Photos icon to display the Photos screen.

You get the following three settings to configure your custom slide show:

- **Play Each Slide For.** You use this setting to set the amount of time that each photo appears on-screen. Tap Play Each Slide For, and then tap a time: 2 Seconds, 3 Seconds (this is the default), 5 Seconds, 10 Seconds, or 20 Seconds.

- **Repeat.** This setting determines whether the slide show repeats from the beginning after the last photo is displayed. To turn on this setting, tap the Repeat switch to the On position.

- **Shuffle.** You use this setting to display the album photos in random order. To turn on this setting, tap the Shuffle switch to the On position.

Using your iPad as a digital photo frame

Digital photo frames are devices that look like slightly bulked-up versions of regular photo frames, but they display a series of digital photos instead of just a single photo. A digital photo frame is a great idea in theory, but in practice they're a bit unwieldy, mostly because you have to somehow get your digital photos into the device (using a memory card, wireless network connection, USB cable, or whatever).

Why bother with that when your iPad not only already has your photos, but also sits up nice and pretty when it's moored in the optional dock accessory, or propped up by the Apple iPad Case? Just insert the iPad into the dock or case, and launch your slide show as described earlier.

Before getting to all that, you may want to take a second and configure a few iPad settings related to using the device as a picture frame. On the Home screen, tap Settings and the Settings app appears. Next, tap Picture Frame to open the Picture Frame screen.

You then get the following eight settings to configure your picture frame:

- **Transition.** Use this setting to specify the type of transition that your iPad uses between each photo. Tap the type of transition you prefer: Dissolve or Origami.

- **Show Each Photo For.** You use this setting to set the amount of time that each photo appears on-screen. Tap Play Each Slide For, and then tap a time: 2 Seconds, 3 Seconds (this is the default), 5 Seconds, 10 Seconds, or 20 Seconds.

- **Zoom in on Faces.** Leave this setting on to have your iPad zoom in on a recognizable face.

- **Shuffle.** You use this setting to display the album photos in random order. To turn on this setting, tap the Shuffle switch to the On position.
- **All Photos.** Tap this option to have your iPad include all of your photos in the frame display.
- **Albums.** Tap this option to include only your album photos in the show.
- **Faces.** Tap this option to include only your faces photos in the show.
- **Events.** Tap this option to include only your event photos in the show.

Creating a photo album

Earlier in this chapter, I covered how you can use your computer to organize your photos into albums prior to syncing them to your iPad. However, if you have been taking a lot of pictures on your iPad and your computer is nowhere in sight, you don't have to wait to organize your pics. The iOS 5 version of the Photos app enables you to create your own photo albums right on your iPad. These albums aren't transferred to your computer when you sync, but they're handy if you need to organize your photos quickly. Here's what you do to organize your photos:

1. **In the Photos app, tap Albums.**
2. **Tap Edit.** The Photos app opens the Albums section for editing.
3. **Tap New Album.** The Photos app prompts you for an album name.
4. **Type the name and then tap Save.** The Photos app displays a list of all your iPad images.
5. **Tap each image that you want to include in your new album.** The Photos app adds a check mark to each selected photo.
6. **Tap Done.** The Photos app creates the new album and adds it to the Albums.

Note

To remove an album you no longer need, tap Albums, tap Edit, and then tap the X icon in the upper-left corner of the album.

Taking iPad screenshots

You might come across a situation where you need to take a picture of your iPad screen. For example, you might see an error message while using an app. Instead of writing down the error message, it's easier to take a screenshot of it and then send it to the app's technical support department. Similarly, if you're playing a game and achieve a high score or pull off some spectacular feat, take a screenshot to show off to your friends and fellow gamers.

To take a screenshot, press and hold the On/Off button, press the Home button, and then release On/Off. Your iPad captures the screen and saves it as a PNG file in the Photos app Camera Roll.

Deleting a photo

If you mess up a photo using one of the iPad cameras, you should delete it before people think you have shoddy camera skills (we all know it was the iPad's fault, right?).

You might think that deleting a photo would be a straightforward proposition. Nope, not even close. That's because your iPad differentiates between the following two types of photos:

- **Photos that you add to the iPad via syncing with iTunes.**
- **Photos that you create directly by using the cameras in the third-generation iPad or iPad 2, taking a screenshot, saving a photo from an e-mail or web page, and so on.**

Synced photos *can't* be deleted directly via the iPad, but photos you create on the iPad *can* be deleted. Clear as mud, I know.

To delete a photo, follow these steps:

1. **Tap Photos in the Home screen.** The Photos app appears.
2. **Locate the image you want to blow away.** For example, if you know the photo is part of a particular event, open that event stack.
3. **Tap the doomed photo.** The Photos app opens the photo.
4. **Tap the screen to reveal the controls.**
5. **Tap the Delete button (the Trash icon).** The Photos app asks you to confirm the deletion.
6. **Tap Delete Photo.** The Photos app tosses the photo into the trash, wipes its hands, and returns you to the photos.

Genius

If you have duplicate synced photos on your iPad and can't delete the copies, connect the iPad to your computer. Click the iPad in iTunes, click the Photos tab, uncheck Sync Photos, and then click Apply. This removes all of the synced photos from the iPad. You then recheck Sync Photos and click Apply. You should end up with no duplicates on the iPad.

Streaming photos to Apple TV

If you have an Apple TV that supports AirPlay, you can use AirPlay to stream your photos or a photo slide show from your iPad to your TV.

Follow these steps to stream photos to Apple TV:

1. **Make sure Apple TV is turned on.**

2. **Using the iPad Photos app, display the album, event, face, or place you want to stream.**

3. **Open the first photo you want to stream.**

4. **Tap the screen to display the controls.**

5. **Tap the AirPlay button, which appears on the right side of the menu bar.** Your iPad displays a menu of output choices, as shown in Figure 7.6.

7.6 In the Photos app, tap the AirPlay button to stream photos to your Apple TV.

153

6. **Tap the name of your Apple TV device.** iPhone streams the video to that device and, hence, to your TV.

To stream a slide show, make sure your Apple TV is on and then tap Slideshow. In the Slideshow Options dialog that appears, shown in Figure 7.7, tap Apple TV in the list of output devices, and then configure and start the slide show.

Printing a photo with AirPrint

How do you print an iPad photo? The obvious answer would be to sync the photo to your Mac or Windows PC, and then print it from there. That works, of course, but it seems like a lot of extra work, and what if you don't have a Mac or PC handy? The better answer is that if you have a printer that supports the AirPrint standard for wireless printing, you can send a photo directly from your iPad to that printer. To set one up, follow these steps:

7.7 To stream a photo slide show, tap Slideshow, tap Apple TV, choose your show options, and then start the show.

1. **Use the Photos app to display the photo you want to print.**

2. **Tap the screen to display the controls.**

3. **Tap Actions.** A menu of web page actions appears.

4. **Tap Print.** The Printer Options dialog appears. If the Printer field already shows the printer you want to use, you can skip to Step 7.

5. **Tap Printer.** Your iPad looks for wireless printers on your network and then displays a list of the available printers.

6. **Tap the printer you want to use.** Your iPad adds the printer to the Printer Options dialog and then enables the other controls, as shown in Figure 7.8.

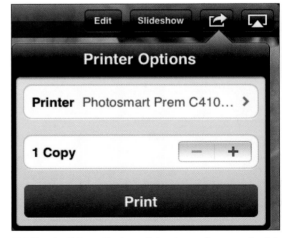

7.8 Use the Printer Options dialog to configure and print a photo.

7. **In the Copy field, tap the plus sign (+) to set the number of copies you want to print.**

8. **Configure the other printer options as needed.** Note that the options you see vary from printer to printer.

9. **Tap Print.** Your iPad sends the photo to the printer.

Editing Photos

The iPad isn't the easiest device in the world to use as a camera — it's a bit too big and unwieldy to hold steady. As a result, you might end up with a few less-than-perfect shots. There's not much you can do to fix blurry images (the biggest iPad photo faux pas), but other problems can be fixed by enhancing the color or brightness, removing red eye, and cropping out extraneous elements.

In the old days, you had to first sync your photos to your computer, make the fixes by using iPhoto or Windows Live Photo Gallery, and then sync the fixed photos back to your iPad. Now, however, iOS 5 lets you make these kinds of adjustments right on your iPad. The next three sections provide the details.

Enhancing a photo

If you have a photo that's too bright in some spots or if the color is washed out in others, the Photos app comes with an Enhance tool that can automatically adjust the color and brightness. Here's how to use it:

1. **In the Photos app, open the photo you want to fix.**

2. **Tap the photo to display the controls.**

3. **Tap Edit.** The Photos app displays its editing tools at the bottom of the screen.

4. **Tap Enhance.** The Photos app adjusts the color and brightness.

5. **Tap Save.** The Photos app saves your changes.

Removing red eye

When you use a flash to take a picture of one or more people, in some cases the flash may reflect off the subjects' retinas. The result is the common phenomenon of red eye, where each person's pupils appear red instead of black. Some cameras come with a Red-eye Reduction feature, which is usually a double flash: one to make the pupils contract before the shot and then another for the actual picture.

If you have a photo on your iPad where one or more people have red eye because of the camera flash, you can use the Photos app to remove it and give your subjects a more natural look. To eliminate red eye, follow these steps:

1. **In the Photos app, open the photo that contains the red eye you want to remove.**

2. **Tap the photo to display the controls.**

3. **Tap Edit.** The Photos app displays its editing tools.

4. **Tap Red-Eye.**

5. **Tap the red eye that you want to remove.** The Photos app removes the red eye.

6. **Repeat Step 5 until you've removed all of the red eye in the photo.**

7. **Tap Apply.** The Photos app applies the changes to the photo.

Cropping and straightening

If you have a photo containing elements that you do not want or need to see, you can often cut them out. This is called *cropping* and you can use the Photos app to do this. When you crop a photo, you specify a rectangular area of it that you want to keep. The Photos app then discards everything outside of the rectangle. Cropping is a useful skill because it can help you give focus to the true subject of a photo. Cropping is also useful for removing extraneous elements that appear on or near the edges of a photo.

As you probably know from hard-won experience, getting your iPad camera perfectly level when you take a shot is very difficult. It requires lots of practice and a steady hand. Despite your best efforts, you might still end up with a photo that is not quite level. To fix this problem, you can also use the Photos app to rotate the photo clockwise or counterclockwise so that the subject appears straight.

Follow these steps to crop and straighten a photo:

1. **In the Photos app, open the photo that you want to edit.**

2. **Tap the photo to display the controls.**

3. **Tap Edit.** The Photos app displays its editing tools.

4. **Tap Crop.** The Photos app displays a grid for cropping and straightening, as shown in Figure 7.9.

5. **Tap-and-drag a corner of the grid to set the area you want to keep.**

6. **To straighten the photo, place two fingers on the screen and rotate them clockwise or counterclockwise until the image is level.**

7. **Tap Crop.** The Photos app applies the changes to the photo.

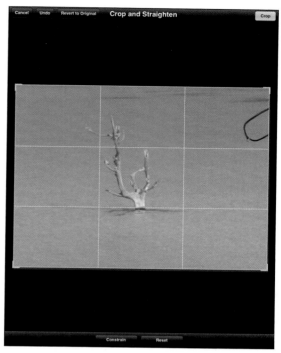

7.9 Tap Crop to display the cropping and straightening tools.

Genius

The fastest way to crop some photos is to tell the Photos app the dimensions you want to use for the resulting photo. Tap Constrain, and then tap either a specific shape (Original or Square), or a specific ratio (such as 5 × 7 inches or 8 × 10 inches). You then drag the photo (not the grid!) so that the portion you want to keep is within the grid.

Sharing Photos

You probably use the Photos app most often for personal trips down Memory Lane and there's nothing wrong with that. However, photos are for sharing, right? Of course! And with the big, bright iPad screen, it's easy to gather 'round a few nearby folks to show off your digital masterpieces by flicking left and right, or up and down. That's fine for nearby victims, uh, people, you can cajole into huddling around your iPad, but far-flung folks are another matter. How can you share your photo goodness with people across town or across the country? There are lots of ways, actually: You can send a photo via e-mail, include one in a text message, or tweet it.

Sending a photo via e-mail

More often than you'd think, being able to send photos from your iPad to someone's e-mail is a handy trick. This is particularly true if it's a photo you've just taken with one of the iPad cameras, or a photo you just received on your iPad (say, via an e-mail message), because then you can share the photo pronto without having to trudge back to your computer. You can e-mail any existing photo from one of your iPad photo albums.

Follow these steps to send one or more photos from your iPad via e-mail:

1. **In the Photos app, locate the image you want to use.** For example, if you know the photo is part of a particular album, open that album stack.

2. **Tap the screen to reveal the controls.**

3. **Tap the Actions button.** The Actions button is the arrow that appears on the right side of the menu bar. The Photos app displays the Select Items screen.

4. **Tap each photo you want to send.** The Photos app selects each photo.

5. **Tap Share and then tap Email.** In the New Message screen that appears, the photo appears in the body of the message.

Note If you're just sending a single photo, a quicker way to attach it to an e-mail message is to open the photo using the Photos app, tap the Actions button, and then tap Email Photo.

6. **Choose your message recipient, and type a Subject line.**

7. **Tap Send.** Your iPad sends the message and returns you to the photo.

Tweeting a photo

If you set up your Twitter account (or accounts) on your iPad, you can use it to tweet a sweet photo to your followers.

Here's how it works:

1. **In the Photos app, open the photo you want to tweet.**

2. **Tap the Actions button.**

3. **Tap Tweet.** The Photos app displays the Tweet dialog.

4. **If you added more than one account to the iPad Twitter settings, tap the username in the From section and then tap the name of the account you want to use to send the tweet.**

5. **Type your tweet text in the large text box.**

6. **If you want to include your present whereabouts as part of the tweet, tap Add Location.**

7. **Tap Send.** Your iPad posts the photo as a tweet.

Texting a photo

The new Messages app sends text messages outside of a cellular provider's messaging system. This means that you can use the Messages app to send unlimited (yes, that's right: *unlimited*) text messages via Wi-Fi or cellular. Your messages can be sent to other people using iPads, but also to those using other iOS devices, including iPhones, iPod touches, and Macs running OS X Mountain Lion. You can also send a photo in a text message. To do so, follow these steps:

1. **On the Home screen, tap Messages.** The Messages screen appears.

2. **Tap New Message.**

3. **Select your recipient.**

4. **Tap the Photo icon that appears to the left of the text box.**

5. **Select or take a photo.**

   - **If you want to send a photo already on your iPad, tap Choose Existing.** Locate and tap the photo and then tap Use.

   - **If you want to take a new photo, tap Take Photo or Video.** Take the shot and then tap Use.

6. **Type your message text.**

7. **Tap Send.** Messages sends the message with the photo attached.

Saving a photo from a text message

If someone sends you a nice photo in a text message, you might want to save it to your iPad so you can check it out whenever you want, assign it to a contact, sync it to your computer, and so on. Follow these steps to save a photo from a text message:

1. **On the Home screen, tap Messages.** The Messages screen appears.

2. **Tap the conversation that contains the photo message.** The Messages app opens the conversation screen.

3. **Tap the photo.** Your iPad opens it for viewing.

4. **Tap the Actions icon.** The Actions options appear.

5. **Tap Save Image.** Your iPad saves the image to the Camera Roll.

Using the iPad Cameras

Your third-generation iPad or iPad 2 comes with a couple of built-in digital cameras that you can use to take pictures while you're running around town. Taking a picture is straightforward. First, on the Home screen, tap Camera. If this is the first time you've opened the Camera app, it asks if it can use your current location. This is an excellent idea because it tags your photos with your present whereabouts, so be sure to tap OK. When the Camera app appears, make sure the Mode switch (see Figure 7.10) is set to Camera (to the left) instead of Video (to the right). Next, just line up your shot and tap either the Camera button (pointed out in Figure 7.10) or the Volume Up switch, which is located on the top edge of the iPad when you hold it in the landscape position with the Home button on the left. To view your photo, tap the Camera Roll button, which appears in the lower-left corner of the Camera app screen.

Understanding the iPad camera features

While using the camera itself may be simple, what you can do with photos on your iPad is pretty cool. For example, you can take a photo to use as the iPad wallpaper, or you can shoot a portrait of a friend or family member and use it as that person's contact photo. Before getting to those tasks, though, let's take a second to go over the following iPad camera features:

- **Rear- and front-facing cameras.** The third-generation iPad comes with two cameras: A 5-megapixel iSight camera on the back for regular shots, and a 0.3-megapixel camera on the front for taking self-portraits. In the Camera app, tap the Switch camera icon (pointed out in Figure 7.10) to switch between the front and rear cameras.

Camera button

Zoom slider

Camera roll

Options button

Switch camera icon

Mode switch

7.10 Tap the screen, and then drag the slider to zoom in and out.

- **Autofocus.** The iPad cameras automatically focus on whatever subject is in the middle of the frame.

- **Tap to focus.** If the subject you want to focus on is not in the middle of the frame, you can tap the subject and the iPad automatically moves the focus to that object. It also automatically adjusts the white balance and exposure.

- **Face detection.** This feature balances focus and exposure across any face it detects in the frame.

- **5X digital zoom.** You can zoom using the rear iPad camera. Pinch two fingers together on the screen to display the zoom slider, as shown in Figure 7.10. Then, drag the slider right to zoom in, or left to zoom out.

- **Geotagging.** The iPhone can use its built-in GPS sensor to add location data to each photo, a process called *geotagging*. This means you can organize your photos by location, which is great for vacation snaps and other trip-related photos.

Genius When you first launch the Camera app, it asks whether it can use your current location. You can control this — that is, you can toggle geotagging on and off — by launching the Settings app, tapping Location Services, and then tapping the Camera switch On or Off.

Taking a wallpaper photo

You can create an on-the-fly wallpaper image using the iPad 2 camera. Here are the steps to follow:

1. **On the Home screen, tap Camera.** The Camera app appears.
2. **Line up your subject and tap the Camera button to take the picture.**
3. **Tap the Camera Roll button in the lower-left corner.** Your iPad opens the Camera Roll photo album and displays a preview of the photo.
4. **Tap the Actions button.** The Actions button is the button to the right of the Slideshow button in the menu bar (if you don't see the menu bar, tap the screen). Your iPad displays a list of actions you can perform.
5. **Tap Use as Wallpaper.** Your iPad prompts you to choose the screen on which you want the wallpaper to appear.
6. **Tap either Set Lock Screen or Set Home Screen.** If you prefer to see the photo on both screens, tap Set Both, instead.
7. **Tap Done.** Your iPad returns you to the Camera app.

Taking a contact's photo

If you don't have a picture of a contact handy, that's not a problem. You can take advantage of the rear camera on your iPad and snap his image the next time you get together.

To take and assign a photo from the Camera app, follow these steps:

1. **In the Home screen, tap the Camera icon to enter the Camera app.** A shutter appears on the screen.

2. **If necessary, tap the Switch Camera icon to activate the rear camera.**

3. **Frame the person on your screen.**

4. **Tap the Camera button at the bottom of the screen (or the Volume Up button, if that's easier) to snap the picture.**

5. **Tap the Camera Roll icon in the bottom-left corner.** This opens the Camera Roll screen.

6. **Tap the photo you just took.** Your iPad opens the photo and reveals the photo controls.

7. **Tap the Actions button.** Your iPad displays a list of actions you can perform.

8. **Tap Assign to Contact.** A list of all of your contacts is displayed.

9. **Tap the contact you want to associate with the photo.** The Move and Scale screen appears.

10. **Drag the image so that it's positioned on the screen the way you want.**

11. **Pinch or spread your fingers over the image to set the zoom level you want.**

12. **Tap Use.** Your iPad assigns the photo to the contact and returns you to the photo.

13. **Tap Done.** Your iPad returns you to the Camera app.

How Do I Manage My eBook Library on My iPad?

Chances are good that, as you read these words, you're holding a physical book in your hands. Physical books are an awesome invention: They're portable and fully showoffable. Books aren't going away anytime soon, but the age of eBooks is upon us. The Amazon Kindle lit a fire under the eBook category, but it's clunky and tied to Amazon. The iPhone and iPod touch are actually the most popular eReaders, but they're a bit too small. The iPad fills in these gaps by supporting an open eBook format and by having a screen that's tailor made for reading.

stress right off the bat that you're not restricted to using iBooks for reading eBooks on your iPad. Tons of great eBook apps are available (I mention a few of them at the end of this chapter), so feel free to use any or all of them in addition to (or even instead of) iBooks.

Unlike the other apps I talk about in this book, iBooks isn't part of the default iPad app collection. Instead, you have to install it (it's free) from the App Store. When you first launch the App Store, it might ask if you want to download iBooks automatically. If so, go ahead and download it, and then feel free to skip the steps that follow. If not, or if you chose earlier not to download iBooks, then follow these steps to get the app onto your iPad:

1. **On the Home screen, tap App Store.** Your iPad opens the App Store.

2. **Tap Featured.** You can also tap any of the other sections that display the Search box: Genius, Top Charts, or Categories.

3. **Tap inside the Search box to display the keyboard, type iBooks, and then tap Search.** The search results appear.

4. **Beside the iBooks app, tap Install.** The App Store asks for your iTunes account password.

5. **Type your password and tap OK.** The App Store downloads and installs the app, and an iBooks icon appears on the Home screen.

6. **When the installation is complete, tap the iBooks icon to launch the app.** iBooks asks if you want to sync your eBook bookmarks, notes, and collections with your iTunes account. Syncing is a good idea if you plan on using iBooks on other devices, such as another iPad, an iPhone, or an iPod touch.

7. **Tap Sync.** Alternatively, tap Don't Sync if you don't need this functionality. Figure 8.1 shows the empty iBooks Bookshelf.

8.1 The iBooks Bookshelf mimics a real bookcase.

Understanding eBook Formats

One of the major reasons why it took eBooks a long time to become successful (in the same way that, say, digital music now rules the planet) is because the eBook world started out hopelessly and head-achingly confusing. At its worst, at least two dozen (yes, two *dozen*!) eBook formats were available and new formats jumped on the eBook bandwagon with distressing frequency.

That was bad enough, but it got worse when you considered that some of these formats required a specific eReading device or program. For example, the Kindle eBook format required either the Kindle eReader or the Kindle app. Similarly, the Microsoft LIT format required the Microsoft Reader program. Finally, things turned positively chaotic when you realized that some formats came with built-in restrictions that prevented you from reading eBooks on other devices or programs, or sharing them with other people.

What the eBook world needed was the simplicity and clarity that comes with having a near-universal eBook format (such as the MP3 format in music). Well, I'm happy to report that one format has emerged from the fray: EPUB. This is a free and open eBook standard created by the International Digital Publishing Forum (IDPF; see www.idpf.org). EPUB files (which use the .epub extension) are supported by most eReader programs and by most eReader devices (with the Amazon Kindle being the very noticeable exception). EPUB is leading the way not only because it's free and non-proprietary, but also because it offers the following cool features:

- **Text is resizable, so you can select the size that's most comfortable for you.**
- **The layout and formatting of the text are handled by Cascading Style Sheets (CSS).** This is an open and well-known standard that makes it easy to alter the look of the text, including changing the font.
- **Text is *reflowable*.** When you change the text size or the font, the text wraps naturally on the screen to accommodate the new character sizes (as opposed to some eBook formats that simply zoom in or out of the text).
- **A single eBook can have alternative versions of the book in the same file.**
- **eBooks can include high-resolution images right on the page.**
- **Publishers can protect book content by adding digital rights management (DRM) support.** DRM refers to any technology that restricts the usage of content to prevent piracy. Of course, depending on where you fall in the "information wants to be free" spectrum, DRM may not be cool and may not even be considered a feature.

So the first bit of good news is that the iBooks app supports the EPUB format, so all of the features in the previous list are available in the iBooks app.

Note

For the record, I should also mention that you can use the iBooks app to read books in three other formats: Plain text, HTML, and PDF.

The next bit of good news is that iBooks' support for EPUB means that a vast universe of public domain books is available to you. On its own, the Google eBookStore (http://books.google.com/ebooks) offers more than a *million* public domain eBooks. Several other excellent EPUB sites exist on the web, and I tell you about them, as well as how to get them onto your iPad, a bit later in this chapter.

By definition, public-domain eBooks are DRM-free, and you can use them any way you see fit. However, lots of the EPUB books you find come with DRM restrictions. In the case of iBooks, the DRM scheme of choice is called FairPlay. This is the DRM technology that Apple used on iTunes for many years. Apple phased out DRM on music a while ago, but still uses it for other content, such as movies, TV shows, and audiobooks.

FairPlay means that many of the eBooks you download through iBooks face the following restrictions:

- **You can access your books on a maximum of five computers, each of which must be authorized with your iTunes Store account info.**
- **You can read your eBooks only on your iPhone, iPad, iPod touch, or a computer that has iTunes installed.**

It's crucial to note the following two restrictions you trip over with DRM-encrusted eBooks:

- **FairPlay eBooks do not work on other eReader devices that support the EPUB format, including the Sony Reader and the Barnes & Noble Nook.**
- **EPUB-format books that come wrapped in some other DRM scheme do not work on iPad.**

However, remember that DRM is an optional add-on to the EPUB format. Although it's expected that most publishers will bolt FairPlay DRM onto books they sell in the iBookstore, it's not required. So, you should be able to find DRM-free eBooks in the iBookstore (and elsewhere).

Note

If you have an Amazon Kindle, I'm afraid it uses a proprietary eBook format, so Kindle eBooks won't transfer to the iBooks app (or any other eReader). However, Amazon does offer a Kindle app for the iPhone that you can use to download and read any Kindle books, even those you purchased earlier.

169

Managing Your iBooks Library

The iBooks app comes with a virtual wooden bookcase. It's a nice bit of eye candy, for sure, but it's certainly no more than that because the real point is to fill it with your favorite digital reading material. So, your first task is to add a few titles to the bookcase and the next few sections show you how to do just that.

Browsing books in the iBookstore

What if you're out and about with your iPad, you have a bit of time to kill, and you decide to start a book? That's no problem, because iBooks has a direct link to the Apple book marketplace, the iBookstore. Your iPad can establish a wireless connection to the iBookstore anywhere that you have Wi-Fi access or a cellular signal (ideally 3G or better for faster downloads, assuming you have a cellular version of the iPad).

You can browse or search for books, read reviews, and purchase any book you want (or grab a title from the large collection of free books). The eBook downloads to your iPad and adds itself to the iBooks bookcase. You can start reading within seconds!

What about the selection? When Apple announced the iPad and the iBooks app, it also announced that five major publishers would be stocking the iBookstore: Hachette, HarperCollins, Macmillan, Penguin, and Simon & Schuster. Since then, a number of other publishers have been added, including Random House, the last of the major publishers to sign on. So, along with all those free eBooks, you can rest assured that the iBookstore has an impressive selection.

To access the iBookstore, display the iBooks Bookshelf. If you haven't yet loaded the app, tap the iBooks icon to open it. If you're in the iBooks app reading a book, tap the screen to display the controls, tap Bookshelf, and then tap the Store icon.

As you can see in Figure 8.2, your iPad organizes the iBookstore similar to the App Store. That is, you get five browse buttons in the menu bar — Featured, Top Charts, Categories, Browse, and Purchased. You use these buttons to navigate the iBookstore.

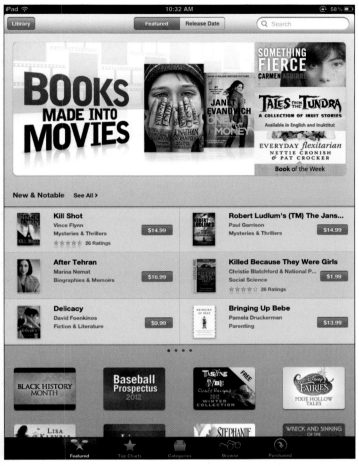

8.2 Use the browse buttons in the iBookstore menu bar to locate and manage apps for your iPad.

Here's a summary of what each browse button does for you:

- **Featured.** Tap this button to display a list of books picked by the iBookstore editors. The list shows each book's cover, title, author, category, star rating, number of reviews, and price. Tap Release Date to see the latest books and tap Featured to see the most popular books.

- **Top Charts.** Tap this button to see two charts: Top Paid books and Top Free books.

- **Categories.** Tap this button to browse books by category, such as History or Non-Fiction.

- **Browse.** Tap this button to browse through the bookstore using an alphabetical list of author names, also divided into the Paid and Free lists.

- **Purchased.** Tap this button to see a list of the books you've downloaded.

The iBookstore also includes a Search box in the upper-right corner so you can search for the book you want.

Note

Tap a book to get more detailed information about it. The Info screen that appears is divided into two sections. The left section shows standard book data, such as the title, author, cover, publisher, and number of pages. The right section is a scrollable window that gives you a description of the book, as well as user ratings and reviews.

Adding a PDF attachment to your library

If you receive an e-mail with an attached PDF file, you can open the attachment right from the Mail app. However, the iBooks app now supports PDFs, so if you'd prefer to read the file in the friendly confines of iBooks (where you can search the PDF and bookmark your current location), you need to transfer it to your iBooks Library. Here's how it's done:

1. **In the Mail app, open the message that contains the PDF attachment.**
2. **Tap and hold the PDF attachment.** Mail displays a menu of commands.
3. **Tap Open in "iBooks".** Your iPad opens the iBooks app and displays the PDF.

Working with collections

The latest version of iBooks now supports both eBooks and PDF documents. In a welcome burst of common sense, the iBooks programmers decided not to combine eBooks and PDFs on the same part of the Bookshelf. Instead, iBooks now supports separate library sections called *collections*. It comes with two default collections: One for eBooks (called Books) and one for PDF documents (called PDFs).

You can use the following techniques to work with your iBooks collections:

- **Switch to another collection.** Tap the Collections button and then tap the name of the collection you want to use.

- **Create a new collection.** Tap the Collections button, tap New, type the name of your collection (such as Fiction or Nonfiction), and then tap Done.

- **Move an item to a different collection.** Tap the Edit button, tap the item you want to move, and then tap the Move button. In the list of collections that appears, tap the collection you want to use as the item's new iBooks home.

- **Delete a collection.** Tap the Collections button, tap Edit, tap the red Delete button beside the collection you want to remove, and then tap Delete. If the collection isn't currently empty, tap Remove when iBooks asks you to confirm. For a nonempty collection, iBooks returns the items to their original locations (for example, eBooks to the Books collection).

Adding other EPUB eBooks to your library

With the apparent ascendance of the EPUB format, publishers and book packagers are tripping over each other to make their titles EPUB friendly. As a result, the web is awash in EPUB books, so you don't have to get all of your iPad eBook content from the iBookstore. Here's a short list of some sites where you can download EPUB files to your computer:

- **BooksOnBoard: www.booksonboard.com.** This site offers a variety of eBooks, although most aren't compatible with iBooks, thanks to DRM. To find non-DRM titles, go to the Advanced Search page and select the Adobe EPUB check box.

- **epubBooks: www.epubbooks.com.** This is a terrific site for all things related to the EPUB format. It offers a wide selection of public-domain EPUB books.

- **eBooks.com: www.ebooks.com.** This site has a variety of books in various eBook formats. However, most won't work in the iBooks app because most of the EPUB books use the DRM scheme from Adobe. You can go to the Search Options page and search for the "Unencrypted EPUB" file format to see the iBooks-friendly titles it offers.

- **Feedbooks: www.feedbooks.com.** This site offers public domain titles in several formats, including EPUB.

- **Google eBookstore: http://books.google.com/ebooks.** This site offers more than a million public-domain titles (many of which are free), plus lots of current releases that you can buy.

- **ManyBooks: http://manybooks.net.** This site offers a nice collection of free eBooks in a huge variety of formats. When you download a book, be sure to choose the EPUB (.epub) format in the Select Format drop-down list.

- **Smashwords: www.smashwords.com.** This intriguing site offers titles by independent and self-published authors. All eBooks are DRM-free and available in the EPUB format.

- **Snee: www.snee.com/epubkidsbooks.** This site offers lots of children's picture books in the EPUB format.

After you download an EPUB title to your computer, follow these steps to import it into iTunes on your Mac or Windows PC:

1. **In iTunes for the Mac, choose File ⇨ Add to Bookshelf or press ⌘+O.** In iTunes for Windows, choose File ⇨ Add File to Bookshelf or press Ctrl+O. The Add to Bookshelf dialog box appears.

2. **Locate and click the EPUB file you downloaded.**

3. **In iTunes for the Mac, click Choose.** In iTunes for Windows, click Open. iTunes adds the eBooks to the Books section of the library.

Editing the Bookshelf

When you add a book to the iBooks Bookshelf, the app clears a space for the new title on the left side of the top shelf of the bookcase. The rest of the books are shuffled to the right and down.

This is a sensible way to go about things if you read each book as you download it because it means the iBooks Bookshelf displays your books in the order you read them. Of course, life isn't always that orderly and you might end up reading your eBooks more haphazardly, which means the order the books appear in the Bookshelf won't reflect the order you read them.

Similarly, you may have one or more books in your iBooks Bookshelf that you refer to frequently for reference or because you're reading them piecemeal (such as a book of poetry, for example, or a collection of short stories). In that case, it would be better to have such books near the top of the bookcase where they're slightly easier to find and open.

For these and similar Bookshelf maintenance chores, iBooks lets you shuffle the books around to get them into the order you prefer. Here's how it works:

1. **Display the iBooks Bookshelf.**
   - If you haven't yet loaded the app, tap the iBooks icon to open the iBooks app.
   - If you're in the iBooks app and reading a book, tap the screen to display the controls and then tap Bookshelf.

2. **Tap Edit.** iBooks opens the Bookshelf for editing.

3. **Tap and drag the book covers to the bookcase positions you prefer.**

4. **If you want to remove a book from your library, tap Edit, tap the book cover, click the Delete button, and then click Delete when iBooks asks you to confirm.**

5. **Tap Done.** iBooks closes the Bookshelf for editing.

Note

You can also organize your books by list. In the Bookshelf screen, tap the Lists icon (the three horizontal lines to the right of the Search box). You can then tap the buttons on the bottom of the screen to organize your books by Titles, Authors, or Categories. Tap Bookshelf to view your books in the order they appear on the Bookshelf. Tap the Bookshelf icon (the four squares to the right of the Search box) when you're ready to return to the Bookshelf view.

Creating a custom eBook cover

If you've obtained any free books from the iBookstore or if you've downloaded public-domain books to iTunes, you have no doubt noticed that many (or really, most) of these books use generic covers. That's no big deal for a book or two, but it can get monotonous if you have many such books in your iBooks library (as well as making it hard to find the book you want). To work around this, you can create custom book covers from your own photos.

Your first task is to convert a photo (or any image) to something that's usable as a book cover. This involves loading the image into your favorite image-editing program and then doing the following three things:

- **Crop the image so that it's 420 pixels wide and 600 pixels tall.**
- **Use the text tool in the image-editing program to add the book title to the image.**
- **Save the image as a JPEG file.** If the image is already a JPEG, be sure to save it under a different name so you don't overwrite the original.

Now you're ready to use the new image as a book cover, which you do by importing the cover image into iTunes on your computer. To import the image into iTunes, follow these steps:

1. **In iTunes, click the Books category.** iTunes displays your eBooks.

2. **Right-click the book you want to customize and then click Get Info.** iTunes displays the book Info dialog.

3. **Click the Artwork tab.** This tab includes a large box for the book cover image.

4. **Use Finder (on a Mac) or Explorer (on a Windows PC) to locate the new cover image.** On a Mac, you can also locate the image in iPhoto.

5. **Click the new image and drop it inside the large box in the Artwork tab.**

6. **Click OK.** iTunes applies the new image as the book cover.

Syncing your iBooks library

If you've used your computer to grab an eBook from the iBookstore or to add a downloaded eBook to the iTunes library, you probably want to get that book onto your iPad as soon as possible. Similarly, if you've downloaded a few eBooks on your iPad, it's a good idea to back them up on your computer.

You can do both by following the steps below to sync eBooks between your computer and your iPad:

1. **Connect your iPad to your computer.** iTunes opens and accesses the iPad. If you added eBooks to your iPad, be sure to wait until iTunes syncs them to your computer.

2. **In iTunes, click your iPad in the Devices list.**

3. **Click the Books tab.**

4. **Select the Sync Books check box.**

5. **To sync only some of your books, select the Selected books option.**

6. **In the book list, select the check box beside each book that you want to sync, as shown in Figure 8.3.**

7. **Click Apply.** iTunes syncs the iPad using the settings for your new book.

8.3 You can sync selected books with your iPad.

Syncing eBooks via iCloud

If you purchase an eBook on your iPhone, a Mac, or a PC, getting it onto your iPad requires a lot of connecting and syncing. This all seems a tad primitive in this modern age. However, if you have an iCloud account, you can configure it to automatically download any new eBook purchases directly to your iPad, without a cable or your computer's iTunes application in sight.

To set this up, follow these steps:

1. **On your iPad, tap Settings in the Home screen to open the Settings app.**

2. **Tap Store.**

3. **If you haven't signed in to the iTunes Store, tap Sign In, and then type your iCloud username and password.**

4. **Tap the Books switch to On.** If this is the first time you've set up automatic downloads, your iPad asks you to confirm that you want data automatically downloaded to your iPad.

5. **If you have a cellular iPad and you want iCloud to sync eBooks even when you have a cellular-only connection, tap the Use Cellular Data switch to On.**

177

Now, each time you purchase an eBook via iTunes on another device, that book is automatically sent to the iBooks library on your iPad — usually within a few seconds.

Reading with iBooks

If you're a book-lover like me, when you have your iBooks Bookshelf groaning under the weight of all your eBooks, you may want to spend some time just looking at all the covers sitting prettily in that beautiful bookcase. Or not. If it's the latter, then it's time to get some reading done. The next few sections show you how to control eBooks and modify the display for the best reading experience.

Controlling eBooks on the reading screen

When you're ready to start reading a book using iBooks, getting started couldn't be simpler. First, you just need to display the iBooks Bookshelf. If you haven't loaded the app yet, tap the iBooks icon to open it. If you're in the iBooks app and reading a book, tap the screen to display the controls and then tap Bookshelf. Next, tap the book you want to read and iBooks opens it.

Here's a list of techniques you can use to control an eBook while reading it:

- **View one page at a time.** Orient the iPad in portrait mode.
- **View two pages at a time.** Orient the iPad in landscape mode.
- **Flip to the next page.** Tap the right side of the screen.
- **Flip to the previous page.** Tap the left side of the screen.
- **Manually turn a page.** Flick the page with your finger. Flick left to turn to the next page; flick right to turn to the previous page.
- **Access the iBooks controls.** Tap the middle of the screen. To hide the controls, tap the middle of the screen again.
- **Access the Table of Contents.** Display the controls and tap the Contents icon, pointed out in Figure 8.4. You can then tap an item in the Table of Contents to jump to that section of the book.
- **Go to a different page in the book.** Display the controls and tap a dot at the bottom of the screen.

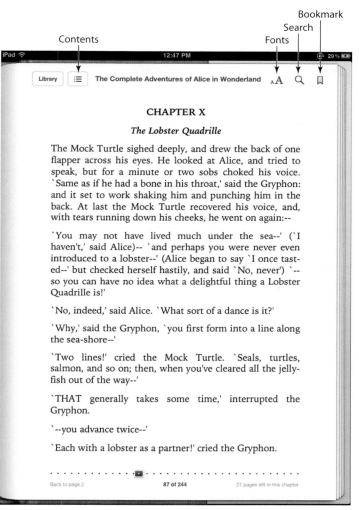

8.4 Tap the middle of the screen to display the controls.

- **Search the book.** Display the controls, tap the Search icon in the upper-right corner, type your search text, and tap Search. In the search results that appear, tap a result to display that part of the book.

- **Return to the iBooks Bookshelf.** Display the controls and tap Library in the upper-left corner.

Formatting eBook text

I mentioned near the top of the show that the EPUB format supports multiple text sizes and multiple fonts, and that the text reflows seamlessly to accommodate the new text size. The iBooks app takes advantage of these EPUB features, as shown here:

1. **While reading an eBook, tap the middle of the screen to display the controls.**

2. **Tap the Fonts icon (see Figure 8.4).** iBooks displays the Font options.

3. **Drag the slider, shown in Figure 8.5, to decrease or increase the screen brightness.**

4. **Tap the larger A to increase the text size or the smaller one to reduce it.**

5. **Tap Fonts.** iBooks displays a list of typefaces, as shown in Figure 8.5.

6. **Tap the typeface you want to use.** iBooks reformats the eBook for the new typeface.

7. **Tap Theme and then tap the color scheme you want to use.** For example, tap Sepia to switch to a sepia-colored background, or tap Night to switch to white text on a black background for easier reading in the dark.

8. **To remove the book interface elements that appear on the top, right, and bottom edges of the iBooks app, tap the Full Screen switch to On.**

9. **Tap the middle of the screen to hide the controls.**

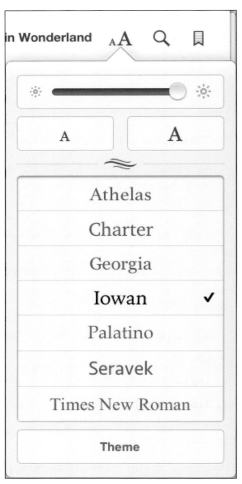

8.5 Tap the Fonts icon and then tap Fonts to display the iBooks typefaces.

Adding a bookmark

Reading an eBook with the iBooks app is so pleasurable you may not want to stop! However, you have to eat at some point. So, when it's time to set your book aside, mark your spot with a book-mark like this:

1. **Navigate to the spot you want to mark.**

2. **Tap the screen to display the controls.**

3. **Tap Bookmark (see Figure 8.4).** iBooks saves your spot by creating a bookmark at the current page.

To return to your place, follow these steps:

1. **Tap the page.** iBooks displays the reading controls.

2. **Tap the Contents icon (see Figure 8.4).** iBooks displays the Table of Contents.

3. **Tap the Bookmarks tab.** iBooks offers a list of the saved bookmarks.

4. **Tap the bookmark.** iBooks returns you to the bookmarked page.

Looking up a word in the dictionary

As you peruse an eBook, you may come across an unfamiliar word. You can look it up using any of the umpteen online dictionaries, but there's no need for that with iBooks. To look up a definition, follow these steps:

1. **Tap and hold the word that has you furrowing your brow.** iBooks displays a set of options.

2. **Tap Define.** iBooks looks up the word and then displays its definition.

3. **Tap outside of the definition to close it.**

Highlighting text

If you come across a word, phrase, sentence, paragraph, or section of text that strikes your fancy, you might want to return to it later on. The easiest way to do that is to highlight the text. This not only makes it stick out from the surrounding prose by displaying it with a yellow background, but iBooks also bookmarks it, so you can quickly find it again by using the same steps I described ear-lier to return to a regular bookmark.

Follow these steps to highlight text with iBooks:

1. **Tap and hold a word in the text you want to highlight.** iBooks selects the word and displays a set of options. If the word is all you want to highlight, skip to Step 3.

2. **Use the selection controls to expand the selection to include all the text you want to highlight.**

3. **Tap Highlight.** iBooks adds a yellow background to the text and creates a note for it.

4. **Tap the highlight color you want to use, or tap the Note icon to enter a note for the text.**

Genius

If you change your mind about the highlight background color, you can change it. Simply tap the highlight and then tap the color that you prefer.

Adding a note

Sometimes when you're reading a book you feel an irresistible urge to provide your own two cents. With a paper book, you can grab the nearest writing implement and jot a margin note, but that's not going to work too well with an eBook! Fortunately, the iBooks programmers have taken pity on inveterate margin writers and provided a Note feature. This allows you to add your own comments and asides. Even better, iBooks also creates a bookmark for each note, so you can quickly find your additions.

Follow these steps to create a note with iBooks:

1. **Tap and hold a word in the text on which you want to comment.** iBooks selects the word and displays a set of options. If the word is all you want to work with, skip to Step 3.

2. **Use the selection controls to expand the selection to include all of the text you want to use.**

3. **Tap Note.** iBooks displays a text box that looks like a sticky note.

4. **Type your note.**

5. **Tap outside the note.** iBooks adds a yellow background to the text, displays a note icon in the margin (with today's date shown on it), and creates a bookmark for the text.

Reading Other eBooks

In this chapter, I focus on the iBooks app. This is mostly because it's an excellent app that is optimized for the iPad and integrates seamlessly with iTunes. But the iPad is arguably the best eReader available today, so it seems a shame to ignore the massive universe of eBooks that aren't iBooks-compatible. If you want to turn your iPad into an ultimate eReader — capable of reading practically *any* eBook in practically *any* format — then just head for the App Store and install the appropriate eReader apps.

A complete list of eReader apps would extend for pages, so I just hit the highlights here:

- **Barnes & Noble NOOK for iPad.** If you don't have the NOOK (the Barnes & Noble eReading device), you can still read Barnes & Noble eBooks by installing the company's NOOK for iPad app. It supports the EPUB format protected by the Adobe DRM scheme.

- **eReader.** This app supports the eReader format.

- **iSilo.** This app (which costs $9.99) supports the iSilo and Palm Doc formats.

- **Kindle.** Amazon's Kindle app is the way to go if you want to read Kindle eBooks on your iPad.

- **Kobo.** This app is supplied by the same folks who make the Kobo eReader, and it supports both EPUB books and PDF documents.

- **Stanza.** This powerful app supports an amazing variety of eBook formats, including EPUB (protected by Adobe DRM), eReader, and Mobipocket.

Reading Magazines with Newsstand

The iPad just might be the perfect medium for reading magazines. It's just a bit smaller than a regular print magazine, so the pages look natural and uncluttered on the iPad screen. Plus magazine publishers have been coming up with all kinds of innovative new tools and techniques that make reading a digital version of a magazine a more interactive and media-rich experience than reading the print version.

If there's a problem with iPad-based magazines, it's that you have to manage a different app for each magazine, which gets clumsy once you have more than a half dozen or so magazine apps scattered around your Home screens. You can try plopping all your magazine apps into a single folder, but then it makes it hard to see the icon badges that tell you a new issue is available.

To solve these kinds of problems, iOS 5 introduced Newsstand, an app specifically designed to manage magazines. Newsstand is really a special folder, and when you tap it you see a replica of a magazine shelf, as shown in Figure 8.6. Magazine apps that know how to work with Newsstand (in the App Store, open the Newsstand category) load the most recent issue in Newsstand after you install them. This allows you to browse all of your available issues in a single spot. As I write this, a number of magazine publishers have signed on to support Newsstand, including Condé Nast (*Wired*, *The New Yorker*, *Vanity Fair*, and many more), National Geographic, Hearst, Bloomberg, and Disney. Newsstand also supports newspaper subscriptions, so you'll also see *The New York Times* and others.

8.6 Use the Newsstand app to organize your iPad magazine subscriptions.

How Can I Get More Out of the iPad Audio Features?

The Music app on your iPad is built with audio in mind. It lets you crank music, music videos, audiobooks, and podcasts. If you have a fast Wi-Fi (or even a cellular) connection, you can use your iPad to purchase music from the iTunes Store (tap the iTunes icon in the Home screen). Playing a track is a snap on your iPad: Tap Music, tap a browse button, and then tap the song. However, your iPad is more than a simple tap-and-play device. This chapter shows you how to take advantage of some of the more useful iPad audio features.

Getting iTunes Audio Ready for Your iPad

Although you can purchase and download songs directly from the iTunes Store on your iPad, I'm going to assume that the vast majority of your music library is cooped up on your Mac or PC, and that you're going to want to transfer that music to your iPad. Or perhaps I should say that you're going to want to transfer *some* of that music to the iPad. Most of us now have multigigabyte music collections, so depending on the storage capacity of your iPad (and the amount of other content you've stuffed into it, particularly videos and movies) it's likely that you want to copy only a subset of your music library.

If that's the case, then iTunes gives you four choices when it comes to selecting which tunes to transfer: Artists, genres, albums, and playlists. The first three are self-explanatory (and, in any case, I give you the audio syncing details a bit later in this chapter), but it's the last one that allows you to take control of syncing music to your iPad.

A *playlist* is a collection of songs that are related in some way. You can use your iTunes library to create customized playlists that include only the songs that you want to hear. For example, you might want to create a playlist of upbeat or festive songs to play during a party or celebration. Similarly, you might want to create a playlist of your current favorite songs.

Playlists are the perfect way to control music syncing for the iPad, so before you start transferring tunes, consider creating a playlist or three in iTunes. As the next three sections show, you can create three types of playlists: standard, Smart, and Genius.

Building a standard playlist

A standard playlist is one where you manually control which songs are in the playlist (as opposed to the automatic Smart and Genius playlists that I talk about in the next two sections). A standard playlist is a bit more work to maintain, but it gives you complete control over the contents.

Follow these steps to build a standard playlist:

1. **Choose File ⇨ New Playlist.** You can also press ⌘+N (Ctrl+N in Windows) or click the Create a Playlist button, which is the plus sign (+). iTunes adds a new item to the Playlists section and adds an edit box around the item.

2. **Type the name you want to give the playlist and then press Return (Enter in Windows).**

3. **In the iTunes Music library, display the song, album, artist, or genre that you want to include in the playlist.**

4. **Drag the song, album, artist, or genre, and drop it on the playlist.**

5. **Repeat Steps 3 and 4 to populate the playlist.**

Building a Smart Playlist

A standard playlist gives you a satisfying amount of control over the contents, but it can often be a hassle. For example, if you've created a playlist for a particular genre, then every time you add new music from that genre you must then drag the new tunes to the playlist. Similarly, if you assign a particular album or artist to a genre that's different than the one in your playlist, you have to manually remove the album or artist from the playlist.

Genius

If you're looking for a faster way to create and populate a standard playlist, iTunes offers another technique that lets you select some or all of the songs in advance. Press and hold the ⌘ key (the Ctrl key in Windows) and then click each song that you want to include in your playlist. When you're done, choose File ⇨ New Playlist from Selection or press ⌘+Shift+N (Ctrl+Shift+N in Windows).

To avoid this kind of digital music drudgery, you can create a *Smart Playlist* where the songs that appear in the list have one or more properties in common, such as the genre, rating, artist, or text in the song title. The key here is iTunes populates and maintains a Smart Playlist automatically. For example, if you build a Smart Playlist based on a particular genre, then every time you add new music from that genre, iTunes automatically includes it in the playlist. Similarly, if you change the genre of some music in your playlist, iTunes automatically removes it from the playlist.

Here are the steps to follow to build a Smart Playlist:

1. **Choose File ⇨ New Smart Playlist.** You can also press ⌘+Option+N (Ctrl+Alt+N in Windows) or hold down Option (Shift in Windows) and click the Create a Playlist button, which is the plus sign (+). iTunes displays the Smart Playlist dialog.

2. **Set up the conditions for the playlist by following these steps:**

   - **Use the first pop-up menu to choose the field you want to use for the first condition.**

   - **Use the second pop-up menu to choose an operator for the condition.** Your choices here depend on the field you selected in the first pop-up menu. For example, if you chose a text field, the available operators include: contains, is, and starts with. For a numeric field, the operators include: is greater than, is less than, and is in the range.

- **Use the third control (or set of controls) to enter the details of the condition.** Again, the controls you see depend on the type of field, although in most cases you see a single text box. If you chose *is in the range* as the operator, you see two text boxes so that you can enter the beginning and end values for the range.

3. **If you want to add another condition, click the Add button (+) to the right of the controls.** iTunes adds another set of condition controls to the dialog.

4. **Repeat Step 2 to specify the settings for the new condition.**

5. **Repeat Steps 3 and 4 to add as many conditions as you need.** Figure 9.1 shows an example of the Smart Playlist dialog with four conditions added.

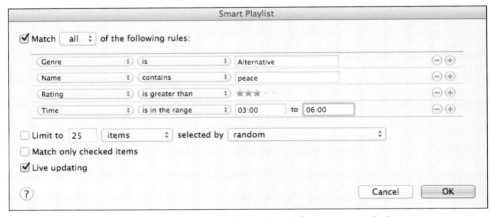

9.1 Use the Smart Playlist dialog to add the conditions that define your new playlist.

6. **If you want to limit the playlist to a certain length or number of songs, select the Limit to check box and specify the limit like this:**

   - Type the number in the first box, and then choose minutes, hours, MB, GB, or items in the first pop-up menu.

   - In the second pop-up menu, choose how to select the songs — for example, by least often played, by highest rating, or at random.

7. **Select the Match only checked items check box if you want to include only songs with check boxes you've selected.** This setting lets you clear a song's check box and make sure it won't show up in your Smart Playlists.

8. **Select the Live updating check box if you want iTunes to automatically update the Smart Playlist for you.**

9. **Click OK.** iTunes creates the playlist and displays an edit box around the name.

10. **Type the name you want to give the playlist, and then press Return (or Enter).**

Building a Genius playlist

You may be familiar with the iTunes Genius sidebar that shows you songs from the iTunes Store that are similar to a particular song in your library. A closely related feature is the Genius playlist. The idea here is that you pick a song in your music library and iTunes creates a playlist of other similar songs in your library. It's a ridiculously easy way to ride a particular sonic groove.

Follow these steps to set up a Genius playlist:

1. **In your music library or in a playlist, select the song you want to use as the starting point for the Genius playlist.**

2. **Click the Start Genius button (which looks like an atom surrounded by several electrons) in the lower-right corner of the iTunes window.**

3. **iTunes creates the Genius playlist.**

4. **To change the number of songs in the playlist, open the Limit To pop-up menu and choose a different number: 25, 50, 75, or 100.**

5. **Click Save Playlist.** iTunes adds the playlist to the Genius section of the sidebar.

Syncing Music and Other Audio Content

The brainy iBooks app and the sleek Safari browser may get the lion's share of kudos for the iPad, but many people reserve their rave reviews for its Music app (called the iPod app in previous versions of iOS). The darn thing is just so versatile: It can play music, of course, but it also happily cranks out audiobooks and podcasts on the audio side, and music videos, movies, and TV shows on the video side. Ear and eye candy in one package!

If there's a problem with this digital largesse, it's that the iPad player might be too versatile. Even if you have a big 64GB iPad, you may still find its confines a bit cramped, particularly if you're also loading it up with photos, contacts, and calendars, and you just can't seem to keep your hands out of the iBookstore and App Store cookie jars.

All this means that you probably have to pay a bit more attention when it comes to syncing audio to your iPad. The following sections show you how to do just that.

Syncing music and music videos

The iPad is a digital music player at heart, so you've probably loaded it up with lots of audio content and lots of music videos. To get the most out of the iPad music and video capabilities, you need to know all the different ways you can synchronize these items. For example, if you use the Music app primarily as a music player and the iPad has more hard drive capacity than you need for all your digital audio, feel free to throw all your music onto your iPad. On the other hand, your iPad may not have much free space, or you may want only certain songs and videos on the player to make it easier to navigate. Not a problem! You can configure iTunes to sync only the songs or playlists that you select.

Genius

Something I like about syncing playlists is that you can estimate in advance how much space your selected playlists will usurp on the iPad. In iTunes, click the playlist and examine the status bar, which tells you the number of songs in the playlist, the total duration, and, most significantly for your purposes, the total size of the playlist.

Before getting to the specific sync steps, you need to know the three ways to manually sync music and music videos. They are:

- **Playlists.** With this method, you specify the playlists you want iTunes to sync. Those playlists also appear on the Music app. This is by far the easiest way to manually sync music and music videos, because you usually just have a few playlists to select. The downside is that if you have large playlists and you run out of space on your iPad, the only way to fix the problem is to remove an entire playlist. Another bummer: with this method, you can only sync *all* or *none* of your music videos.

- **Check boxes.** With this method, you specify which songs and music videos get synced by selecting the little check boxes that appear beside every song and video in iTunes. This is fine-grained syncing for sure, but because your iPad can hold thousands of songs, it's also lots of work.

192

- **Drag and drop.** With this method, you click and drag individual songs and music videos, and drop them on the iPad icon in the iTunes Devices list. This is an easy way to get a bunch of tracks on your iPad quickly, but iTunes doesn't give you any way of tracking which tracks you've added.

Genius

What do you do if you want to select only a few tracks from a large playlist? Waste a big chunk of your life deselecting a few hundred check boxes? Pass. Here's a better way: Press ⌘+A (Mac) or Ctrl+A (Windows) to select every track, right-click (or Control+click) any track, and then click Uncheck Selection. Voila! iTunes deselects every track in seconds flat. Now you can select only the tracks you want. You're welcome.

Follow these steps to sync music and music videos using playlists:

1. **Connect your iPad to your computer.**

2. **In iTunes, click your iPad in the Devices list.**

3. **Click the Music tab.**

4. **Select the Sync Music check box.**

5. **If iTunes asks you to confirm that you want to sync music, click Sync Music.**

6. **Select the Selected playlists, artists, albums, and genres option.**

7. **Select the check box beside each playlist, artist, album, and genre you want to sync, as shown in Figure 9.2.**

8. **Select the Include music videos check box if you also want to add your music videos into the sync mix.**

9. **Select the Include voice memos check box if you also want to sync voice memos that you recorded on your iPhone or other device.**

10. **If you want iTunes to fill any remaining free space on your iPad with a selection of related music from your library, select the Automatically fill free space with songs check box.**

11. **Click Apply.** iTunes syncs your iPad using the new settings.

9.2 Select the Selected playlists, artists, albums, and genres option, and then select the items you want to sync.

Follow these steps to sync using the check boxes that appear beside each track in your iTunes Music library:

1. **Click your iPad in the Devices list.**

2. **Click the Summary tab.**

3. **Select the Sync only checked songs and videos check box.**

4. **Click Apply.** If iTunes starts syncing your iPad, drag the Slide to Cancel slider on the iPad to stop it.

5. **Either click Music in the Library list or click a playlist that contains the tracks you want to sync.** If a track's check box is selected, iTunes syncs the track with your iPad. If a track's check box is deselected, iTunes doesn't sync the track with your iPad. If a track is already on your iPad, iTunes removes it.

6. **In the Devices list, click your iPad.**

7. **Click the Summary tab.**

8. **Click Sync.** iTunes syncs only the checked tracks.

You also can configure iTunes to let you drag tracks from the Music library (or any playlist) and drop them on your iPad. Here's how this works:

1. **Click your iPad in the Devices list.**

2. **Click the Summary tab.**

3. **Select the Manually manage music and videos check box.**

Note

When you select the Manually manage music and videos check box, iTunes auto-matically deselects the Sync Music check box in the Music tab. However, iTunes doesn't mess with the music on your iPad. Even when it syncs after a drag and drop, it only adds the new tracks; it doesn't delete any of your iPad's existing music.

4. **Click Apply.** If iTunes starts syncing your iPad, drag the Slide to Cancel slider on the iPad to stop it.

5. **Either click Music in the Library list or click a playlist that contains the tracks you want to sync.**

6. **Choose the tracks you want to sync like this:**

   - If all the tracks are together, Shift+click the first track, hold down Shift, and then click the last track.

   - If the tracks are scattered all over the place, hold down ⌘ (Mac) or Ctrl (Windows) and click each track.

7. **Click and drag the selected tracks to the Devices list, and drop them on the iPad icon.** iTunes syncs the selected tracks.

Caution

If you decide to return to playlist syncing by selecting the Sync Music check box in the Music tab, iTunes removes all tracks that you added to your iPad via the drag-and-drop method.

Syncing music via iCloud

As you've seen, if you purchase a song or album on your Mac or PC, getting that music onto your iPad requires you to connect your iPad to your computer and then run a sync. Even worse, if you purchase music on another device, such as your iPhone, getting that music over to your iPad means you have to first sync that device with your computer, and *then* sync your iPad. Too much work!

You can avoid all that hassle if you have an iCloud account because you can configure it to automatically download any new music purchases — whether they were bought on your Mac, your PC, your iPhone, your iPod touch, or even another iPad — directly to your iPad.

This is called automatic downloading. Follow these steps to set it up:

1. **On your iPad, tap Settings in the Home screen to open the Settings app.**
2. **Tap Store.**
3. **If you haven't signed in to the iTunes Store, tap Sign In and then type your iCloud username and password.**
4. **Tap the Music switch to On.**

Now, each time you purchase music via iTunes on another device, it is automatically sent to your iPad.

Syncing podcasts

In many ways, podcasts are the most problematic of the various media you can sync with your iPad. It's not that podcasts themselves pose any concern. Quite the contrary: They're so addictive that it's not unusual to collect them by the dozens. Why is that a problem? Because most professional podcasts are at least a few megabytes in size and many are tens of megabytes. A large-enough collection can put a serious dent in the storage space on your iPad, which is all the more reason to take control of the podcast-syncing process. Here's how you do it:

1. **Connect your iPad to your computer.**
2. **In iTunes, click your iPad in the Devices list.**
3. **Click the Podcasts tab.**
4. **Select the Sync Podcasts check box.**

5. **If you want iTunes to choose some of the podcasts automatically, select the Automatically include check box and proceed to Steps 6 and 7.** If you prefer to manually choose all the podcasts, deselect the Automatically include check box and skip to Step 8.

6. **Choose one of the following options from the first pop-up menu:**

   - **All.** Choose this item to sync every podcast.

   - ***X* most recent.** Choose this item to sync the *X* most recent podcasts.

   - **All unplayed.** Choose this item to sync all the podcasts you haven't yet played.

Note

A podcast episode is *unplayed* if you haven't yet played at least part of it either in iTunes or on your iPad. If you play an episode on your iPad, the player sends this information to iTunes when you next sync. Even better, your iPad also lets iTunes know if you paused in the middle of an episode; when you play that episode in iTunes, it starts at the point where you left off.

   - ***X* most recent unplayed.** Choose this item to sync the *X* most recent podcasts that you haven't yet played.

   - ***X* least recent unplayed.** Choose this item to sync the *X* oldest podcasts that you haven't yet played.

   - **All new.** Choose this item to sync all the podcasts published since the last sync.

   - ***X* most recent new.** Choose this item to sync the *X* most recent podcasts published since the last sync.

   - ***X* least recent new.** Choose this item to sync the *X* oldest podcasts published since the last sync.

Genius

To mark a podcast episode as unplayed, in iTunes choose the Podcasts library, right-click (or Control+click on a Mac) the episode and then choose Mark as New.

7. **Select one of the following options from the second pop-up menu:**

   - **All podcasts.** Choose this option to apply the option from Step 5 to all your podcasts.

● **Selected podcasts.** Choose this option to apply the option from Step 5 to only the podcasts you select, as shown in Figure 9.3.

9.3 To sync specific podcasts, choose the selected podcasts option and then select the check boxes for each podcast you want synced.

8. **Select the check box beside any podcast or podcast episode you want to sync.**

9. **Click Apply.** iTunes syncs the iPad using your new podcast settings.

Syncing audiobooks

The iTunes sync settings for your iPad have tabs for Music, Photos, Podcasts, and Video, but not one for Audiobooks. What's up with that? It's not, as you might think, some sort of antibook conspiracy or even forgetfulness on Apple's part. Instead, iTunes treats audiobook content as a special type of playlist which, confusingly, doesn't appear in the iTunes Playlists section. To get audiobooks on your iPad, follow these steps:

1. **Connect your iPad to your computer.**

2. **In iTunes, click your iPad in the Devices list.**

3. **Click the Books tab.**

4. **Select the Sync Audiobooks check box.**

5. **Select the Selected audiobooks option.**

6. **Select the check box beside each audiobook you want to sync.**

7. **Click Apply.** iTunes syncs your audiobooks to your iPad.

If you've opted to manually manage your music and video, you need to choose the Audiobooks category of the iTunes library. Next, drag and drop the audiobooks you want to sync on your iPad.

Getting More Out of the Music App

Your iPad is a full-fledged music player thanks to its Music app, which you can fire up any time you want by tapping the Music icon in the Home screen Dock.

You navigate the Music app using the *browse buttons* on the bottom of the screen — Playlists, Songs, Artists, and Albums, and tap More to see Genres, Composers, Podcasts, and Audiobooks — each of which represents a collection of media files organized in some way. For example, tapping the Songs browse button displays a list of all the songs on your iPad or in the currently selected playlist.

In the next couple of sections, I cover a few useful techniques that help you get more out of the Music app.

Creating a playlist on your iPad

The playlists on your iPad are those you've synced via iTunes. These playlists are either generated automatically by iTunes or they're playlists you've cobbled together yourself. However, when you're out in the world and listening to music, you might come up with an idea for a different collection of songs. It might be girl groups, boy bands, or songs with animals in the title.

Whatever your inspiration, don't do it the hard way by picking out and listening to each song one at a time. Instead, you can use your iPad to create a playlist on the fly. To create a playlist using the Music app, follow these steps:

1. **Open the Music app.**

2. **Tap the Playlists browse button.**

3. **Tap New.** The Music app displays the New Playlist dialog.

4. **Type the name of your playlist, and then tap Save.** The Music app displays the Add songs to the "*Name*" playlist screen (where *Name* is the name of your playlist), which contains a list of all your songs. You can also click one of the browse buttons to find your music.

5. **Scroll through the list and tap each song you want to add to your playlist.** Your iPad turns a song gray when you add it, as shown in Figure 9.4.

6. **When you've added all the songs you want, tap Done.** The Music app displays the playlist in Edit mode.

7. **Tap Done.**

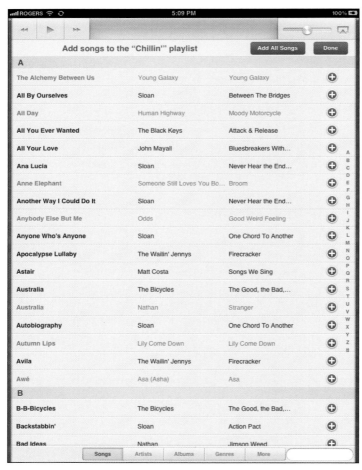

9.4 Tap each song that you want to add to your playlist.

Your playlist isn't set in stone by any means. You can get rid of songs, change the song order, or add more songs. Follow these steps to edit your Playlist:

1. **Open the Music app.**

2. **Tap the Playlists browse button.**

3. **Tap your playlist.**

4. **Tap Edit.** This changes the list to the editable version, as shown in Figure 9.5.

9.5 A playlist in Edit mode.

5. **To remove a song, tap the red Delete icon (-) to the left of the song, and then tap the Delete button that appears.** If you change your mind, tap the red Delete icon again to cancel.

6. **To move a song within the playlist, slide the drag icon (next to each song on the right) up or down to the position you prefer.**

7. **To add more tracks, tap Add Songs, and then tap each song you want to add.**

8. **When you finish editing, tap Done.** This sets the playlist.

Note If your playlist is a bit of a mess or if your mood suddenly changes, you can delete the entire playlist and start over. Tap the Playlists browse button, tap and hold the playlist, and then tap the Delete button (the X) that appears.

Creating a Genius playlist on your iPad

You saw earlier how to create a Genius playlist in iTunes. You also can use this seemingly magical feature right on your iPad.

Here's how to create a Genius playlist:

1. **Tap the song you want to use as the basis of the Genius playlist.**

2. **Tap the Genius icon that appears on the right side of the Music app status area.** iTunes creates the Genius playlist.

3. **Tap Playlists.**

4. **Tap Genius Playlist.** The Music app displays the 25 songs it chose for the playlist.

5. **Tap Save.** The Music app renames the playlist to the name of the original song. Figure 9.6 shows an example.

In the Genius playlist screen, you can perform the following actions to mess around with your shiny new playlist:

- **Tap Refresh to re-create the playlist.**
- **Tap a song to play it.**
- **Tap Edit to delete songs or change the song order.**

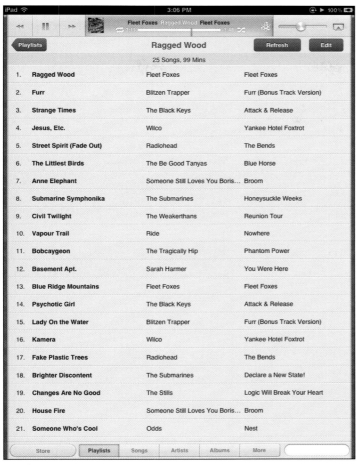

9.6 An example of a Genius playlist.

Listening to a Shared iTunes Library

You may be familiar with an iTunes feature called Home Sharing. It enables you to share your iTunes library with other people on your network as long as you're all logged in with the same Apple ID. Home Sharing is also available on the iPad, which means you can use your iPad to get wireless access to an iTunes library that's stored on a Mac or PC.

To set this up, you must first activate Home Sharing in iTunes. To do this, follow these steps:

1. **In iTunes on your Mac or PC, choose Advanced ➪ Turn On Home Sharing.** iTunes prompts you for an Apple ID.

2. **Type your Apple ID and password.**

3. **Click Create Home Share.** iTunes configures your library for sharing on the network.

4. **Click Done.**

Genius By default, iTunes shares the library with the name *User's* Library, where *User* is the first name of the current user account. To change that, choose iTunes ➪ Preferences, click the General tab, and then use the Library Name text box to type the new name.

With Your iTunes library set up for sharing, your next task is to configure your iPad with the same Home Sharing Apple ID and password. Here's what you do to configure it:

1. **On the iPad Home screen, tap Settings to open the Settings app.**

2. **Tap Music to open the Music screen.**

3. **In the Home Sharing section, use the Apple ID and Password boxes to type the same account information that you used to set up Home Sharing in iTunes.**

Now open the Music app on your iPad, tap More, and then tap Shared. As you can see in Figure 9.7, the Music app displays the Shared dialog, which lists the available shared libraries. Tap the library you want to access and the Music app displays the media in that library instead of the iPad media.

9.7 Tap More and then Shared to see a list of the available shared libraries.

Using AirPlay to stream iPad audio

If you have an Apple TV that supports AirPlay, you can use AirPlay to stream audio from your iPad to your TV or other audio device.

To set it up, follow these steps:

1. **Make sure your Apple TV is turned on.**

2. **On your iPad, start the audio you want to stream.**

3. **Use four or five fingers to swipe up.** Your iPad displays the multitasking bar. You can also double-click the Home button.

4. **Swipe the multitasking bar right to see the playback controls.**

5. **Tap the AirPlay button, which appears to the right of the Next/Fast**

9.8 Tap the AirPlay button on the multitasking bar to stream the audio to your Apple TV.

Forward button. Your iPad displays a menu of output choices, as shown in Figure 9.8.

6. **Tap the name of your Apple TV device.** Your iPad streams the video to that device and, hence, to your TV or receiver.

Rating a song on your iPad

If you use song ratings to organize your tunes, you may come across some situations like the following in which you want to rate a song that's playing on your iPad:

- You used your iPad to download some music from the iTunes Store and you want to rate it.

- You're listening to a song on your iPad and decide that you've given a rating that's either too high or low and you want to change it.

In the first case, you could sync the music to your computer and rate it there. In the second case, you could modify the rating on your computer and then sync with your iPad. However, these solutions are lame because you have to wait until you connect your iPad to your computer. If you're out and about, you want to rate the song *now* while it's fresh in your mind.

To do so, follow these steps:

1. **Locate the song you want to rate and tap it to start the playback.** The Music app displays the album art and the name of the artist, song, and album at the top of the screen.

2. **Tap the album art at the top of the screen.** The Music app displays the album art.

3. **Tap the screen to display the controls.**

4. **Tap the Details icon in the lower-right corner of the screen.** Your iPad turns the album art and displays a list of the songs on the album. Above that list are the five rating dots.

5. **Tap the dot that corresponds to the rating you want to give the song.** For example, to give the song a four-star rating, tap the fourth dot from the left.

6. **Tap the Details icon in the lower-right corner.** Your iPad saves the rating and returns you to the album art view.

The next time you sync your iPad with your computer, iTunes notes your new ratings and applies them to the same tracks in the iTunes library.

Getting More Out of Other iPad Audio Features

To close out this tour of your iPad audio features, the rest of this chapter takes you through a few useful techniques for redeeming iTunes gift cards, using audio accessories, and customizing the iPad audio settings.

Redeeming an iTunes gift card

If you've been lucky enough to receive an iTunes gift card or gift certificate for your birthday or some other special occasion (or just for the heck of it), you normally use the iTunes Store on your computer to redeem it. However, if you're not at your computer and the gift card is burning a hole in your pocket, don't fret: you can redeem it right on your iPad. To do so, follow these steps:

1. **Sign in to the iTunes Store on your iPad.** To do this tap Settings, tap Store, and then tap Sign In. Next, tap Use Existing Apple ID, and then type your iTunes Store username and password.

2. **On the Home screen, tap iTunes to open the iTunes app.**

3. **Tap Music in the menu bar.**

4. **Scroll to the bottom of the Music screen and then tap Redeem.** iTunes then displays the Redeem dialog, as shown in Figure 9.9.

5. **Use the Code box to type the code from the gift card or certificate.**

6. **Tap Redeem.** iTunes asks you to sign in to your account.

7. **Tap Continue.** iTunes prompts you for your account password.

8. **Type your iTunes password and then tap OK.** iTunes redeems the gift code and then displays your current account balance.

Redeem   Redeem

Enter your Gift Card or other iTunes Code:

Code

Redemption Terms and Conditions...

Redeem

9.9 Use the Redeem screen to redeem an iTunes gift card or certificate.

Using audio accessories with your iPad

When Apple announced the iPad, it also announced a few accessories, including an iPad-only dock, a keyboard dock, and a case. Of course, third-party vendors want a piece of the iPad pie, so we're now seeing a rather large cottage industry of iPad accessories, including headsets (wired and Bluetooth), external speakers, FM transmitters, and all manner of cases, car kits, cables, and cradles. Many places scattered all over the web sell iPad accessories, but the following sites are my faves:

- **Apple.** http://store.apple.com/us/browse/home/shop_ipad/family/ipad

- **Belkin.** www.belkin.com/iPad/

- **Griffin.** www.griffintechnology.com/iPad/

- **NewEgg.** www.newegg.com

- **EverythingiCafe.** http://store.everythingicafe.com/

Keep the following notes in mind when shopping for and using audio-related accessories for your iPad:

- **Look for the logo.** Despite the presence of the Music app, your iPad is not an iPod dressed up in fancy tablet clothes. It's a completely different device that doesn't fit or work with many iPod accessories. To be sure what you're buying is iPad-friendly, look for the *Works with iPad* logo.

- **Headsets, headphones, and earpieces.** The iPad uses a standard headset jack, so just about any headset that uses a garden-variety stereo mini-plug fits without requiring the purchase of an adapter.

- **External speakers.** You can also use the iPad headset jack to connect a set of external speakers. Note, too, that if you have either the iPad dock or the iPad keyboard dock from Apple, both come with an audio-out jack that you can use to connect to external speakers. There are also Bluetooth wireless external speakers that you can pair with your iPad.

- **FM transmitters.** These are must-have accessories for car trips because they send the iPad output to an FM station, which you then play through your car stereo. The FM transmitters that work with the iPod don't generally work with iPads, so look for one that's designed for the iPad.

- **Electronic interference.** Because your iPad is a transmitter (of Wi-Fi, Bluetooth and, in some cases, cellular signals), it generates a nice little field of electronic interference, which is why you need to switch it to Airplane mode when you're flying (see Chapter 1). That same interference can wreak havoc on nearby external speakers and FM transmitters, so if you hear static when playing audio, switch to Airplane mode to get rid of it.

Customizing the iPad audio settings

Audiophiles in the crowd don't get much to fiddle with in the iPad, but you can play with a few audio settings. Here's how to get at them:

1. **Press the Home button to get to the Home screen.**
2. **Tap the Settings icon.** The Settings screen opens.
3. **Tap Music.** Your iPad displays the Music settings screen.

The five settings you get to try out are the following:

- **iTunes Match.** If you have an iCloud account and you've shelled out the extra $24.99 per year for the iTunes Match service, tap this switch to On to activate it on your iPad. Any songs that you own that aren't available via the iTunes Store will be automatically synced to your iPad as soon as you upload them to iCloud.

- **Sound Check.** Every track is recorded at different audio levels, so invariably you get some tracks that are louder than others. With the Sound Check feature, you can set your iPad to play all your songs at the same level. This feature affects only the baseline level of the music and doesn't change any of the other levels, so you still get the highs and lows. If you use it, you don't need to worry about having to quickly turn down the volume when a really loud song comes on. To turn on Sound Check, in the Music settings screen, tap the Sound Check switch to the On position.

- **EQ.** This setting controls the built-in iPad equalizer, which is actually a long list of preset frequency levels that affect the audio output. Each preset is designed for a specific type of audio: Vocals, talk radio, classical music, rock, hip-hop, and lots more. To set the equalizer, tap EQ and then tap the preset you want to use (or tap None to turn it off).

- **Volume Limit.** You use this setting to prevent the iPad volume from being turned up too high and damaging your (or someone else's) hearing. You know, of course, that pumping up the volume while you have your earbuds in is an audio no-no, right? I thought so. However, I also know that when a great tune comes on, it's often a little too tempting to go for 11 on the volume scale. If you can't resist the temptation, use Volume Limit to limit the damage. Tap Volume Limit and drag the Volume slider to the maximum allowed volume.

- **Group By Album Artist.** Leave this setting On to group the Artists browse button based on the value in the Album Artist field, as opposed to the Artist field. For most albums, these two fields are the same, but some compilation albums use "Various" in the Artist field, and the names of the individual track artists in the Album Artist field. If you were to turn off this switch, you'd end up with all such albums listed under Various in the Artists browse button, which probably isn't what you want.

Genius

If you're setting up an iPad for a younger person, you should set the Volume Limit. However, what prevents the young whippersnapper from setting a higher limit? *You* can. In the Volume Limit screen, tap Lock Volume Limit. In the Set Code screen, tap out a four-digit code and then tap the code again to confirm. This disables the Volume slider in the Volume Limit screen.

How Can I Get More Out of Video on My iPad?

We seem to have solved the audio part of the hunt for the perfect portable media player rather nicely with the iPod (and the iPhone). However, the video mission is more problematic. Single-purpose video players are too, well, single purpose. The more versatile tools, such as the iPod touch and the iPhone, are too small for proper viewing. Now, the iPad is making a bid for portable media perfection, and its case is strong given the large, high-definition touchscreen interface, video recording capabilities, and FaceTime video calling. This chapter puts that case to the test.

Syncing Videos

Although you can use the iTunes app on your iPad to rent or purchase movies, TV shows, and music videos, it's more likely that the bulk of your video content resides on your computer. If watching any of that video on your computer while sitting in your office chair is unappealing, then you need to transfer it to your iPad for viewing in more comfy circumstances. The next few sections provide the not-even-close-to-gory details.

Making a video compatible with iPad

Your iPad is very video friendly, but only certain formats are compatible with it. Here's the list and the features of each compatible format::

- **H.264 video**. Up to 1080 pixels; 30 frames per second; H.264 High Profile Level 4.1 with AAC-LC audio up to 160 Kbps; 48 kHz; stereo audio in M4V, MP4, and MOV file formats.

- **MPEG-4 video**. Up to 2.5 Mbps; 640 × 480 pixels; 30 frames per second; Simple Profile with AAC-LC audio up to 160 Kbps; 48 kHz; stereo audio in M4V, MP4, and MOV file formats.

- **Motion JPEG video.** Up to 35 Mbps, 1280 ×720 pixels, 30 frames per second, audio in u-law PCM stereo audio in the AVI file format.

If you have a video file that doesn't match any of these formats, you may think you're out of luck. Not so. You can use iTunes to convert that video to an MPEG-4 file that's iPad friendly. To do so, follow these steps:

1. **If the video file isn't already in iTunes, choose File ⇨ Add to Library or press ⌘+O.** In Windows, choose File ⇨ Add File to Library or press Ctrl+O. The Add To Library dialog box appears. If the file is already in iTunes, skip to Step 3.

2. **Locate and choose your video file, and click Open.** iTunes copies the file into the library, which may take a while depending on the size of the video file. In most cases, iTunes adds the video to the Movies section of the library.

3. **In iTunes, click your movie.**

Note

Because the converted video has the same name as the original, you should probably rename one of them so you can tell them apart when it comes to syncing your iPad. If you're not sure which file is which, right-click one of the videos and then click Get Info. In the Summary tab, read the Kind value. The iPad-friendly file has a Kind setting of MPEG-4 Video File.

4. Choose Advanced ⇨ Create iPad or Apple TV Version. iTunes begins converting the video to the MPEG-4 format. This may take some time for even a relatively small video. When the conversion is complete, a copy of the original video appears in the iTunes library.

Syncing movies

The third-generation iPad screen is large (9.7 inches on the diagonal) and sharp (2048 × 1536 resolution at 264 pixels per inch), which makes it ideal for watching a flick while sitting on the front porch with a mint julep. The major problem with movies is that their file size tends to be quite large — even short films lasting just a few minutes weigh in at dozens of megabytes and full-length movies are several gigabytes. Clearly, there's a compelling need to manage your movies to avoid filling up your iPad, leaving no room for the latest album from your favorite band.

Syncing rented movies

If you've rented a movie from iTunes, you can move it to your iPad and watch it there. Note that you're *moving* the rented movie, not copying it. You can store rented movies in only one location at time, so if you sync it to your iPad, it is no longer available on your computer.

Follow these steps to sync a rented movie to your iPad:

1. Connect your iPad to your computer.

2. In iTunes, click your iPad in the Devices list.

3. Click the Movies tab.

4. In the Rented Movies section, shown in Figure 10.1, click Move beside the rented movie you want to shift to your iPad. iTunes adds the movie to the On *iPad* list (where *iPad* is the name of your iPad).

5. Click Apply. iTunes syncs the iPad using your new movie settings.

10.1 Click Move to move a rented movie to your iPad.

Syncing purchased or downloaded movies

If you've purchased a movie from iTunes or added a video to your iTunes library, follow these steps to sync some (or all) of those movies to your iPad:

1. **Connect your iPad to your computer.**

2. **In iTunes, click your iPad in the Devices list.**

3. **Click the Movies tab.**

4. **Select the Sync Movies check box.**

5. **If you want iTunes to choose some of the movies automatically, select the Automatically include check box and proceed to Step 6.** If you prefer to choose all the movies manually, deselect the Automatically include check box and skip to Step 7.

6. **Choose one of the following options from the pop-up menu:**

    - **All.** Choose this item to sync every movie.

    - **X Most Recent.** Choose this item to sync the X most recent movies you've added to iTunes.

    - **All Unwatched.** Choose this item to sync all the movies you haven't yet played.

Note
A movie is unwatched if you haven't yet viewed it either in iTunes or on your iPad. If you watch a movie on your iPad, the player sends this information to iTunes when you next sync.

    - **X Most Recent Unwatched.** Choose this item to sync the X most recent movies you haven't yet played.

    - **X Least Recent Unwatched.** Choose this item to sync the X oldest movies you haven't yet played.

7. **Select the check box beside any other movie you want to sync, as shown in Figure 10.2.**

8. **Click Apply.** iTunes syncs the iPad using your new movie settings.

Genius
To mark a movie as unwatched in iTunes, choose the Movies library, right-click the movie, and choose Mark as Unwatched.

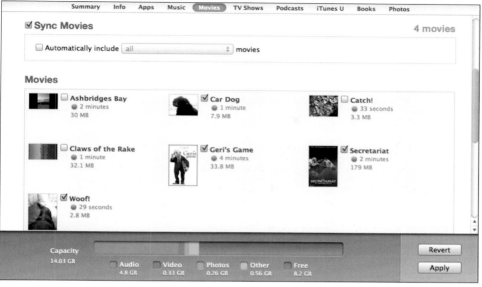

10.2 In the Movies tab, select Sync Movies and choose the films you want to sync.

Syncing TV shows

If the average iPad is at some risk of being filled up by a few large movie files, it's probably also at grave risk of being overwhelmed by a large number of TV show episodes. A single half-hour episode eats up approximately 250MB, so even a modest collection of shows consumes multiple gigabytes of precious iPad hard drive space.

This means it's crucial to monitor your collection of TV show episodes and keep your iPad synced with only the episodes you need. Fortunately, iTunes gives you a decent set of tools to handle this. Follow these steps to sync TV shows:

1. **Connect your iPad to your computer.**

2. **In iTunes, click your iPad in the Devices list.**

3. **Click the TV Shows tab.**

4. **Select the Sync TV Shows check box.**

5. **If you want iTunes to choose some of the episodes automatically, select the Automatically include check box and proceed to Steps 6 and 7.** If you prefer to choose all the episodes manually, deselect the Automatically include check box and skip to Step 8.

215

6. **Choose one of the following options from the drop-down menu:**

- **All.** Choose this item to sync every TV show episode.

- ***X* Most Recent.** Choose this item to sync the *X* most recent episodes.

- **All Unwatched.** Choose this item to sync all the episodes you haven't yet viewed.

Note A TV episode is unwatched if you haven't yet viewed it either in iTunes or on your iPad. If you watch an episode on your iPad, the player sends this information to iTunes when you next sync.

- ***X* Most Recent Unwatched.** Choose this item to sync the *X* most recent episodes you haven't yet viewed.

- ***X* Least Recent Unwatched.** Choose this item to sync the *X* oldest episodes you haven't yet viewed.

7. **Select one of the following options from the second pop-up menu:**

- **All Shows.** Choose this option to apply the choice from Step 5 to all of your TV shows.

- **Selected Shows.** Choose this option to apply the choice from Step 5 to only the TV shows you select, as shown in Figure 10.3.

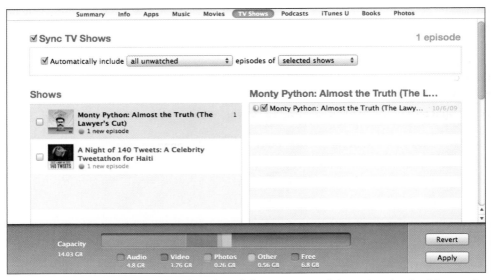

10.3 To sync specific TV shows, select the Selected Shows option and then select the check boxes of each show you want synced.

8. **Select the check box beside any TV show or episode you want to sync.**

9. **Click Apply.** iTunes syncs the iPad using your new TV show settings.

Genius

To mark a TV episode as unwatched, in iTunes, choose the TV Shows library, right-click the episode, and choose Mark as Unwatched.

Other Ways to Watch iPad Video

With a few movies and TV shows finally residing on your iPad, you get to kick back and watch some moving pictures in comfort. Your commute (meaning, of course, your commute as a *passenger*) doesn't have to be boring anymore. Just connect your headphones and fire up a show. The next few sections take you through a few techniques and tips to help you get a bit more out of the iPad video capabilities.

Playing videos on your TV

You can carry a bunch of videos with you on your iPad, so why shouldn't you be able to play them on a TV if you want? Well, you can. First, if you have an Apple TV that supports AirPlay, you can use AirPlay to stream a video from your iPad to your TV. On your iPad, start the video, tap the screen to display the controls, and then tap the Output button (which appears to the right of the Volume bar). As you can see in Figure 10.4, you can then tap your Apple TV to stream the video to that device and, hence, your TV.

If you don't have an Apple TV (or if you have an older Apple TV that doesn't support AirPlay), you have to buy another cable. However, that's the only investment you have to make to watch iPad videos right on your TV. To hook your iPad up to your TV, you have the following three choices:

- **Apple Digital AV Adapter.** This $39 cable has a 30-pin connector on one end that connects to the iPad or an iPad dock. The other end has another 30-pin connector so you can connect your iPad to a power outlet and an HDMI port that enables you to make a connection to the corresponding HDMI input on your HDTV.

- **Apple Composite AV cable.** This $39 cable plugs into the iPad dock connector on one end and the composite TV inputs at the other.

- **Apple Component AV cable.** This $39 cable has a dock connector on one end that plugs into the iPad dock connector, and component connectors on the other that connect to the component inputs of your TV.

10.4 While playing back a video, tap the screen and then tap the Output button to stream it to your Apple TV.

The cable you choose depends on the type of TV you have. Older sets have composite inputs, while more recent ones have component inputs and the latest have at least one HDMI port. After setting up your cables, set your TV to the input and play your videos as you normally would.

Mirroring the iPad screen on your TV

In previous versions of iOS, if you have a third-generation iPad or an iPad 2, the Apple Digital AV Adapter provides you with a *mirrored* display. This means what you see on your iPad is also displayed on your TV in HD. That worked well enough, but it was a drag having your iPad tethered to your TV via the HDMI cable. iOS 5, in one of its most outstanding features, solves that problem by offering wireless AirPlay mirroring through Apple TV. As long as you have a second-generation Apple TV (and it has been updated with the latest software), you can use AirPlay mirroring not only to send videos to your TV, but also photos, slide shows, websites, apps, games, and anything else you can display on your third-generation iPad or iPad 2.

Follow these steps to start mirroring the iPad screen on your TV:

1. **Turn on your Apple TV device.**

2. **On your iPad, use four or five fingers to swipe up and display the multi-tasking bar.** You can also double-click the Home button.

3. **In the multitasking bar, swipe right to reveal the playback controls.**

4. **Tap the AirPlay button, which appears to the right of the Next/Fast Forward button.** Your iPad displays a menu of output choices.

5. **Tap the name of your Apple TV device.**

6. **Tap the Mirroring switch to On, as shown in Figure 10.5.** Your iPad streams the screen to Apple TV and indicates that AirPlay is active by displaying

10.5 Use the multitasking bar to tap AirPlay, tap your Apple TV, and then tap the Mirroring switch to On.

the AirPlay icon in the status bar. Note, too, that the status bar appears blue to indicate that mirroring is on (see Figure 10.6).

Watching videos from a shared iTunes library

If you have iTunes Home Sharing activated on your computer, you can use your iPad to tap in to that library and play its video content. I showed you how to activate iTunes Home Sharing in Chapter 9. Assuming that's done, your next task is to configure your iPad Videos app with the same Home Sharing Apple ID and password. (If you already did this using the Music settings, as I described in Chapter 9, then you can skip the steps that follow.) Follow these steps:

AirPlay icon

10.6 When AirPlay mirroring is on, you see the AirPlay icon in the status bar and it turns blue.

1. **On your iPad Home screen, tap Settings to open the Settings app.**

2. **Tap Video to open the Video screen.**

3. **In the Home Sharing section, use the Apple ID and Password boxes to type the same account information that you used to set up Home Sharing in iTunes.**

Now open the Videos app on your iPad and then tap Shared. As you can see in Figure 10.7, the Videos app displays icons for the available shared libraries. Tap the library you want to access and the Videos app displays that library's video content instead of your iPad videos.

10.7 With Home Sharing configured, tap Shared to see a list of the available shared libraries.

Customizing the iPad video settings

Your iPad offers a few video-related settings that you can try on for size. Follow these steps to get at them:

1. **Press the Home button to get to the Home screen.**
2. **Tap Settings to open the Settings screen.**
3. **Tap the Video icon.** The Video screen opens.

In addition to the Home Sharing options mentioned earlier in this chapter, you can also meddle with the following two settings:

- **Start Playing.** This setting controls what your iPad does when you stop and restart a video. You have two choices: Where Left Off (the default), which picks up the video from the same point where you stopped it; and From Beginning, which always restarts the video from scratch. Tap Start Playing, and then tap the setting you prefer.

- **Closed Captioning.** This setting toggles support for closed captioning on and off, when it's available. To turn on this feature, tap the Closed Captioning switch to the On position.

Recording and Editing Video

The third-generation iPad is a bit lighter and quite a bit thinner than the original, so it's easier to hold and has a more comfortable feel overall. However, even this more manageable iPad is still a slightly odd choice as a camcorder, so you probably won't find yourself using it to record video all that often. On the other hand, the rear camera does support recording 1080p HD at 30 frames per second, so if a must-record event suddenly arises and you don't have your digital camera (or iPhone) with you, then iPad video will certainly do in a pinch.

Recording video with an iPad camera

Of course, this being an iPad and all, it's no surprise that recording a video is almost criminally easy. Follow these steps:

1. **On the Home screen, tap the Camera button.** The Camera screen appears.

2. **Flick the Mode switch in the lower-right corner from Camera to Video.**

3. **Tap the screen to focus the video if necessary.**

4. **Tap the Switch Camera icon if you want to use the front camera rather than the rear camera.**

5. **Tap the Record button.** Your iPad starts recording video and displays the total recording time in the upper-right corner of the screen.

6. **When you're done, tap the Record button again to stop recording.** Your iPad saves the video to the Camera Roll.

Genius

If you have an AirPlay-friendly device, such as an Apple TV, you can stream your recorded iPad videos to that device. Make sure your AirPlay device is on, open the recorded video on your iPad, and then tap the Output button in the upper-right corner. In the menu that appears, tap the AirPlay device name (such as Apple TV) and away you go.

Editing recorded video

Okay, being able to record video at the tap of a button is pretty cool, but your iPad tops that by also letting you perform basic editing chores right on the device. It's nothing fancy — basically, you can trim video from the beginning and end of the file — but it sure beats having to first sync the video to your computer, and then fire up iMovie or some other video-editing software.

Here's how to edit a video right on your iPad:

1. **Open the Camera Roll album in one of the following ways:**

   - **In the Camera app, tap the Camera Roll button in the lower-left corner of the screen.**

   - **In the Photos app, display the Albums screen and then tap Camera Roll.**

Note

Video thumbnails show a video camera icon in the lower-left corner and the duration of the video in the lower-right corner.

2. **Tap the video you want to edit.** The Photos app displays the video.

3. **Tap anywhere to display the on-screen controls.** If the video is playing, tap Pause to stop the playback. You see a timeline of the video along the top of the screen.

4. **Tap and drag the left edge of the timeline to set the starting point of the video.**

5. **Tap and drag the right edge of the timeline to set the ending point of the video.** The trimmed timeline appears surrounded by orange, as shown in Figure 10.8.

10.8 Use the video timeline to set the start and end points of the video footage you want to keep.

Genius

If you need more precision when trimming the timeline, tap and hold either the start trim control or the end trim control. Your iPad expands the timeline to show more frames which enables you to make more precise edits.

6. **Tap Play to ensure you've set the start and end points correctly.** If not, repeat Steps 5 and 6 to adjust the timeline as needed.

7. **Tap Trim.** Your iPad trims the video and then saves your work.

Uploading a video to YouTube

Of course, the real reason you want to be able to instantly record something is because you want to upload it to YouTube and share it with the world.

Your iPad is happy to help here, too, as shown by the following steps:

1. **Open the Camera Roll album in one of the following ways:**

   - **In the Camera app, tap the Camera Roll button in the lower-left corner of the screen.**

   - **In the Photos app, display the Albums screen and then tap Camera Roll.**

2. **Tap the video you want to share.** Your iPad opens the video.

3. **Tap the Action icon in the menu bar.** The Action icon appears to the left of the Trash icon. If you don't see the menu bar, tap the screen to display the controls. The Share options appear.

4. **Tap Send to YouTube.** Your iPad compresses the video and prompts you to log in to your YouTube account.

5. **Type your YouTube username and password, and then tap Sign In.** The Publish Video screen appears.

6. **Tap a title, description, and tags for your video, and then choose a category.**

7. **If you want to upload a high-definition (HD) version of the video, tap HD.** HD versions of iPad videos are more than three times larger than standard-definition versions, so uploading them takes longer.

8. **Tap Publish.** Your iPad publishes the video to your YouTube account. This may take several minutes, depending on the size of the video. When the video is published, you see a dialog with a few options.

9. **Tap one of the following options:**

   - **View on YouTube.** Tap this option to cue up the video on the YouTube site.

   - **Tell a Friend.** Tap this option to send an e-mail message that includes a link to the video on YouTube.

   - **Close.** Tap this option to return to the video.

Video Calling with FaceTime

One of the most welcome features of the iPad 2 (and the third-generation iPad, of course) is the front-mounted camera. This means you can take advantage of the amazing Apple FaceTime feature, which lets you make video calls on your iPad and actually see the other person face to face. It's an awesome feature, but to use it the other person must also be using a third-generation iPad or an iPad 2, an iPhone 4 or 4S, or a Mac with a video camera and the FaceTime application installed.

Note

You might expect to be able to use FaceTime over the speedy 4G connection on your third-generation iPad. Alas, that's not the case. Unfortunately, you still need a Wi-Fi connection to use FaceTime.

The good news about FaceTime (besides how cool it is), is that the app is already installed on your iPad and it doesn't require anything for use other than an Apple ID.

Configuring FaceTime

The first time you launch FaceTime, you need to run through a one-time configuration procedure. Here's how it works:

1. **In your Home screen, tap FaceTime.** The FaceTime app appears.
2. **Type your Apple ID and password.**
3. **Tap Sign In.** FaceTime asks which e-mail address you want other people to use to call you.
4. **Change the displayed address, if necessary.**
5. **Tap Next.** FaceTime verifies your Apple ID and then displays the FaceTime screen.

Initiating a FaceTime call

To initiate a FaceTime call, tap the FaceTime icon (if the app isn't open already), and then use either of the following techniques:

- **If the other person is in your Contacts list, tap Contacts, and then tap the person you want to call.** If the person has multiple contact items (phone numbers and e-mail addresses), tap the item you want to use to place the call.
- **If you've recently made a FaceTime call to someone, tap the Recents icon, and then tap the FaceTime call.**

If another FaceTime user calls you, you see the message "*Name* would like FaceTime," (where *Name* is the caller's name if she is in your Contacts list) as shown in Figure 10.9.

Genius

If you FaceTime call someone frequently, add that person to the FaceTime app Favorites list. Tap the Favorites icon, tap the plus sign (+), tap the contact, and then tap the phone number or e-mail address you want to use.

10.9 When a FaceTime user calls you, tap Accept to initiate a FaceTime video call.

Tap Accept and your video call connects, just like that. You see your caller's (hopefully) smiling face in the full iPad screen and your own mug in a picture-in-picture (PIP) window, as shown in Figure 10.10.

Genius

Your PIP window appears by default in the upper-right corner. If you prefer a different position, tap and drag it to any corner of the screen.

225

10.10 Face-to-face calling on the iPad.

The FaceTime calling screen includes the following three buttons in the menu bar:

- **Mute.** Tap this icon (it's the one on the left) to mute the sound from your end of the conversation. You can still hear sound from the other person's end.
- **End.** Tap this button (it's the one in the middle) to end the call.
- **Switch cameras.** Tap this button to switch your video output to the rear camera (for example, to show your caller something in front of you).

Disabling FaceTime

There are times when you simply don't want a face-to-face conversation, no matter who's calling. Perhaps you're in a secret location or you just don't look your best that day. Whatever the reason, you can follow these steps to turn off FaceTime:

1. **In the Home screen, tap Settings.** The Settings app appears.

2. **Tap FaceTime.** The FaceTime screen appears.

3. **Tap the FaceTime switch to the Off position.**

Now, when people try to call you using FaceTime, they see a message saying that you're "not available for FaceTime."

How Can I Use My iPad to Manage Contacts?

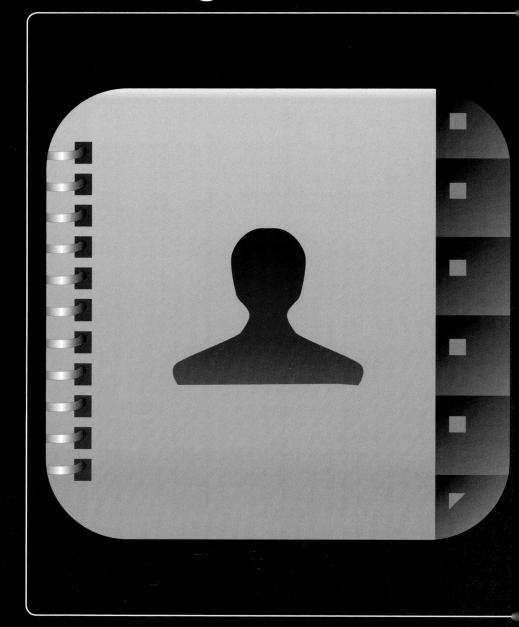

One of life's paradoxes is that as your contact information becomes more important, you store less of it in the easiest database system of all — your memory. Instead of memorizing phone numbers, you now store them electronically. This is because it's no longer just a landline number that you have to remember for each person — there's also a cell number, an e-mail or website address, and more. That's a lot, so it makes sense to go the electronic route. For the iPad, *electronic* means the Contacts app, which is loaded with useful features that can help you organize your contacts.

Syncing Your Contacts

Although you can certainly add contacts directly on your iPad — and I show you how to do just that a bit later in this chapter — adding, editing, grouping, and deleting contacts is a lot easier on a computer. So a good way to approach contacts is to manage them on your Mac or Windows PC, and then sync your contacts with your iPad.

Creating contact groups

However, do you really need to sync *all* of your contacts? For example, if you only use your iPad to reach out to friends and family, then why clog your iPad Contacts app with work colleagues and clients? I don't know!

You can control which contacts are sent to your iPad by creating groups of contacts and then syncing only the groups you want. Here are some quick instructions for creating groups:

- **Address Book (Mac).** Choose File ⇨ New Group, type the group name, and then press Return. Now populate the new group by dragging and dropping contacts onto it.

- **Windows Contacts (Windows 7 and Windows Vista).** Click New Contact Group, type the group name, and then click Add to Contact Group. Choose all the contacts you want in the group and then click Add. Click OK.

Note
If you're an Outlook user, note that iTunes doesn't support Outlook-based contact groups, so you're stuck syncing everyone in your Outlook Contacts folder. Also note that iTunes doesn't support Windows Live Mail at all, so you can't use that application to sync your contacts.

Running the sync

With your group (or groups) all figured out, follow these steps to sync your contacts with your iPad:

1. **Connect your iPad to your computer.**

2. **In iTunes, click your iPad in the Devices list.**

3. **Click the Info tab.**

4. **Turn on contacts syncing by using one of the following techniques:**

   - **Mac.** Select the Sync Address Book Contacts check box.

   - **Windows.** Select the Sync Contacts With check box and then use the list to choose the program you want to use (such as Outlook). For Yahoo! contacts, see Step 7; for Google contacts, see Step 8.

5. **Select an option:**

   - **All contacts.** Select this option to sync all of your Address Book contacts.

   - **Selected groups.** Select this option to sync only the groups you pick. In the Selected groups list, select the check box beside each group that you want to sync, as shown in Figure 11.1.

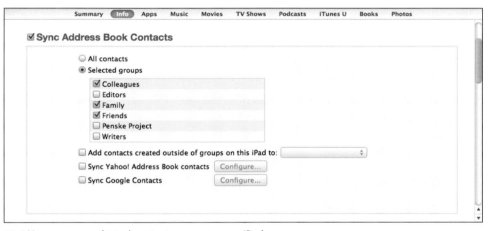

11.1 You can sync selected contact groups to your iPad.

6. **If you want to make the sync a two-way street, select the Add contacts created out-side of groups on this iPad to check box, and then choose a group from the menu.**

7. **In Mac OS X, if you have a Yahoo! account and you also want your Yahoo! Address Book contacts in on the sync, select the Sync Yahoo! Address Book contacts check box.** In Windows, use the Sync Contacts with list to select Yahoo! Address Book. In either case, you then type your Yahoo! ID and password, and click OK.

8. **In Mac OS X, if you have a Google account and you also want your Google Contacts in on the sync, select the Sync Google Contacts check box.** In Windows, use the Sync

Contacts with list to select Google Contacts. In either case, you then type your Google ID and password, and click OK.

9. **Click Apply.** iTunes syncs the iPad using your new contacts settings.

Getting Started with the Contacts App

You need the Contacts app up and running for this chapter, so head for the iPad Home screen and tap the Contacts icon. Figure 11.2 shows the Contacts app.

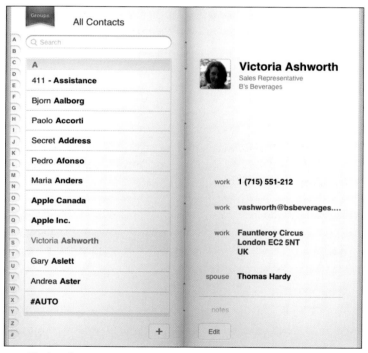

11.2 The handsome iPad Contacts app.

The Contacts app displays the All Contacts list on the left and the info for the currently selected contact on the right. If you have a healthy number of contacts, you need to know how to navigate the list. You have the following four choices:

- **By default, the Contacts app displays the All Contacts list.** To view a group of contacts, tap the Groups icon in the upper-left corner of the screen and then tap the group you want to view.

- **Flick up and down to scroll through the list.**

- **Tap a letter to leap directly to the contacts whose last names begin with that letter.**

- **Use the Search box at the top of the All Contacts list to type a few letters of the name of the contact with which you want to work, and then tap the contact in the search results.**

Creating and Editing Contacts

Syncing your computer's contacts program (such as Address Book or the Outlook Contacts folder) is, by far, the easiest way to populate your iPad Contacts app with a crowd of people. However, it might not include everyone in your posse. If someone's missing and you're not around your computer, you can add that person directly to the Contacts app.

Similarly, you might be messing around with the Contacts app and notice an error or old info for someone. No problem — you can edit a contact right on the iPad. Best of all, any changes you make within the Contacts app are automatically synced back to your computer the next time your iPad and iTunes get together for a sync session.

Creating a new contact

The next time you realize someone's missing from your contacts, you can fire up your trusty iPad and tap that person's vital statistics right into the Contacts app. Follow these steps:

1. **In the Home screen, tap the Contacts icon.** Your iPad opens the Contacts app.

2. **Tap the plus sign (+) at the bottom right of the screen.** The Info screen appears and your iPad displays the keyboard, as shown in Figure 11.3.

3. **The cursor starts off in the First box, so type the person's first name.** If you're jotting down the contact data for a company or some other inanimate object, skip to Step 5.

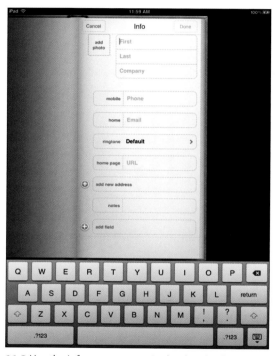

11.3 Use the Info screen to tap in the details of your contact.

4. **Tap the Last box and then type the person's last name.**

5. **If you want to note where the person works (or if you're adding a business to your Contacts list), tap the Company box and type the company name.**

Yup, I know there are still plenty of other fields to fill in, and we get to those in a second. For now, though, I want to interrupt your regularly scheduled programming to show you how to edit an existing contact. It will all make sense soon, trust me.

Editing an existing contact

Now that your new contact is off to a flying start, you can go ahead and fill in details such as phone numbers, addresses (e-mail, web, and real world), and anything else you can think of or have the patience to enter into your iPad (it can be a lot of tapping). The next few sections take you through the steps for each type of data.

Note

The one technique that I don't get into here is how to spruce up your contact with a photo. That's because I cover that in Chapter 7.

However, the steps I show also apply to any contact that's already residing in your iPad. Here, then, are the steps required to open an existing contact for editing:

1. **In the Home screen, tap the Contacts icon to open the All Contacts screen.**

2. **Tap the contact you want to edit.**

3. **Tap Edit.** Your iPad displays the contact's data in the Info screen.

4. **Make your changes, as described in the next few sections.**

5. **Tap Done.** Your iPad saves your work and returns you to the All Contacts screen.

Assigning phone numbers to a contact

Everyone has a phone number, so you, no doubt, want to augment a contact by entering his phone data. Sure, but *which* number: Work, home, cell, or fax? Fortunately, there's no need to choose just one because your iPad is happy to store all of these, plus a few more if need be.

Here are the steps to follow to add one or more phone numbers for a contact:

1. **In the Info screen, examine the label box in the Phone field to see if the default label is the one you want.** For a new contact, the default label is *mobile*, but you might see a different one if you're editing an existing contact. If you're okay with the existing label, skip to Step 4.

2. **Tap the Phone field label.** The Contacts app displays a list of phone labels, as shown in Figure 11.4.

11.4 Tap the label you want to use for a contact's phone number

3. **Tap the label that best applies to the phone number you're adding, such as mobile, iPhone, home, or work.** The Contacts app displays the new label.

4. **Tap inside the Phone field and then type the phone number with area code first.** Note that you only need to type the numbers — the Contacts app helpfully adds extra stuff, like parentheses around the area code and the dash. When you begin typing the phone number, the app automatically adds another Phone field below the current one.

5. **Repeat Steps 1 to 4 to add any other numbers you want to store for this contact.**

Assigning e-mail addresses to a contact

It makes sense that you might want to add multiple phone numbers for a contact, but would you ever need to enter multiple e-mail addresses? Well, sure you would! Most people have at least a couple of addresses — usually for home and work — and some Type A e-mailers have a dozen or more. Life is too short to type that many e-mail addresses, but you do need at least the important ones if you want to use the iPad Mail app to send a note to your contacts.

Follow these steps to add one or more e-mail addresses for a contact:

1. **In the Info screen, check out the default label in the Email field.** For a new contact, the default is *home*, but you might see a different one if you're editing an existing contact. If you want to use the existing label, skip to Step 4.

2. **Tap the Email field label to display a list of e-mail labels.**

3. **Tap the e-mail label you want to use, such as home or work.** The Contacts app applies the new label.

4. **Tap inside the Email field and type the person's e-mail address.** Note that the on-screen keyboard now displays the handy @ and period (.) keys. While you type the e-mail address, the Contacts app sneakily adds another Email field below the current one.

5. **Feel free to repeat Steps 1 to 4 as often as necessary to add other e-mail addresses for this contact.**

Assigning web addresses to a contact

Who on Earth doesn't have a website these days? It could be a humble home page, a blog, a Tumblr page, a home business site, or it could be someone's corporate website. Some busy web beavers may even have all five! Whatever web home a person has, it's a good idea to toss the address into her contact data because, later on, you can simply tap the address, and your iPad (assuming it can see the Internet from here) immediately fires up Safari and takes you to the site. Does your pal have multiple websites? No sweat — your iPad is happy to take you to all of them.

You can add one or more web addresses for a contact by making your way through these steps:

1. **In the Info screen, eyeball the current label for the URL field.** If you're okay with it, skip to Step 4.

2. **Tap the URL field label to get yourself a list of web address labels.**

3. **Tap the label that suits the web address you're entering (such as home page, home, or work).** The Contacts app adds the new label.

4. **Tap inside the URL field and then tap the person's web address.** In Figure 11.5, note that the on-screen keyboard now includes several useful URL-friendly keys, including slash (/), dot (.), underscore (_), dash (-), and .com. Note, too, that when you start typing the web address, the Contacts app surreptitiously inserts another URL field below the current one.

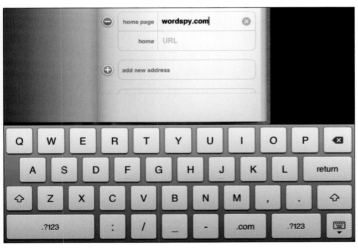

11.5 Don't forget to take advantage of the on-screen keyboard URL-related keys, such as slash (/) and .com.

5. **Repeat Steps 1 to 4 to add other web addresses for this contact as you see fit.**

Genius

To save some wear and tear on your tapping finger, don't bother adding the http:// stuff at the beginning of a URL. Your iPad adds those characters automatically any-time you tap an address to visit a site — same with the www. prefix. So if the full address is http://www.wordspy.com, you need only enter wordspy.com.

Assigning social network data to a contact

These days, many of us are far more likely to contact others via social networks (such as Twitter, Facebook, and LinkedIn) than we are via more traditional methods like e-mail. The Contacts app in iOS 5 reflects this new reality by enabling you to save social network data for each contact, including data for Twitter, Facebook, LinkedIn, Flickr, and Myspace. Here are the steps to follow to add one or more social network details to a contact:

1. **In the Info screen, tap Add Field to open the Add Field dialog.**

2. **Tap Twitter.** Yes, you need to tap Twitter even if you are entering data for some other social network. Your iPad is quirky that way.

3. **If you want to use a different social network, tap the Twitter label to see a list of social networks, as shown in Figure 11.6.**

11.6 Tap Twitter to see the social networks supported by the Contacts app.

4. **Tap the label that suits the social network data you're entering, such as Facebook or Flickr.** The Contacts app adds the new label.

5. **Tap inside the field and then tap the person's username for the chosen social network.** Note that as soon as you tap at least one character, Contacts adds a new social network field.

6. **If necessary, use the new social network field to add another social network, repeating as needed.**

Assigning physical addresses to a contact

With all this talk about cell numbers, e-mail addresses, and web addresses, it's easy to forget that people actually live and work somewhere. You may have plenty of contacts where the location of that somewhere doesn't much matter, but if you ever need to get from here to there, taking the time to insert a contact's physical address really pays off. Why? Because you need only tap the address and your iPad displays a Google map that shows you the precise location. From there you can get directions, see a satellite map of the area, and more. (I talk about all this great map stuff in Chapter 13.)

Tapping out a full address is a bit of work, but as the following steps show, it's not exactly painful:

1. **In the Info screen, tap Add New Address.** The Contacts app displays fields for the street address, city, state, postal code, and country.

2. **Examine the address label to see if the default *home* label is the one you want.** If you're okay with the existing label, skip to Step 5.

3. **Tap the address label.** The Contacts app displays a list of address labels.

4. **Tap the label that best applies to the address you're entering, such as home or work.** The Contacts app displays the new label.

5. **Tap the Street field and then type the person's street address.** When Contacts realizes you're typing a street address, it automatically adds a second Street field.

6. **If necessary, tap the second Street field and then type even more of the person's street address.**

7. **Tap the City field and then type the person's city.**

8. **Tap the State field and then type the person's state.** Depending on what you later select for the country, this field might have a different name, such as Province.

9. **Tap the ZIP field and then type the ZIP code.** Again, depending on what you later select for the country, this field might have a different name, such as Postal Code.

10. **Tap the Country field to open the Country list and then tap the contact's country.**

11. **Repeat Steps 1 to 10 if you feel like entering another address for your contact.**

Getting More Out of the Contacts App

Adding and editing data using the Contacts app is blissfully linear: Tap a field label to change i and then tap inside a field to add the data. If you remember to take advantage of the on-screen keyboard context-sensitive keys (such as the .com key that materializes when you type a web address), then contact data entry becomes a snap.

The Contacts app is straightforward on the surface, but if you dig a bit deeper, you find some use ful tools and features that can make your contact management duties even easier.

Creating a custom label

When you fill out your contact data, your iPad insists that you apply a label to each tidbit: home work, mobile, and so on. If none of the predefined labels fits, you can always just slap on the generic *other* label, but it seems so, well, dull. If you've got a phone number or address that you can't shoehorn into any of the iPad prefab labels, get creative and make one up. To do so, follow these steps:

1. **In the Info screen, tap the label for the field with which you want to work.** The Label list appears.

2. **Tap Add Custom Label.** If you're working with a social network field, tap Add Custom Service, instead. The Custom Label (or Custom Service) dialog appears.

3. **Type the custom label.**

4. **Tap Save.** The Contacts app saves your custom label and returns you to the Info screen.

You can apply your custom label to any type of contact data. For example, you can create a labe named college and apply it to a phone number, e-mail address, web address, or physical address

Deleting a custom label

If a custom label wears out its welcome, follow these steps to delete it:

1. **In the Info screen, tap the label for any field.** The Label list appears.

2. **Tap Edit.** The Contacts app puts the Label list into Edit mode.

3. **Tap the red Delete icon to the left of the custom label you want to remove.** The Contacts app displays a Delete button to the right of the field.

4. **Tap Delete.**

5. **Tap outside the Label list.** The Contacts app returns you to the editing screen.

Adding extra fields to a contact

The New Contact screen (which appears when you add a contact) and the Info screen (which appears when you edit an existing contact) display only the fields you need for basic contact info. However, these screens lack quite a few common fields. For example, you might need to specify a contact's prefix (such as Dr. or Professor), suffix (such as Jr., Sr., or III), or job title.

Thankfully, your iPad is merely hiding these and other useful fields where you can't see them. The following are the 14 hidden fields that you can add to any contact:

- **Prefix**
- **Phonetic First Name**
- **Phonetic Last Name**
- **Middle**
- **Suffix**
- **Nickname**
- **Job Title**
- **Department**
- **Twitter**
- **Profile**
- **Instant Message**
- **Birthday**
- **Date**
- **Related People**

11.7 The Add Field list shows the hidden fields that you can add to any contact.

The iPad is only too happy to let you add as many of these extra fields as you want. Here are the steps involved:

1. **In the Info screen, tap Add Field.** The Add Field list appears, as shown in Figure 11.7.

2. **Tap the field that you want to add.** The Contacts app adds the field to the contact.

3. **If the field has a label, tap the label box to choose a new one if needed.**

4. **Type the field data.** In the case of the Related People field, tap the label (the default value is *mother*), tap the relationship (such as spouse or manager), tap the blue More Info icon, and then tap the related contact.

5. **Repeat Steps 1 to 4 to add more fields as needed.**

Keeping track of birthdays and anniversaries

Do you have trouble remembering birthdays? If so, then I feel your pain because I, too, used to be pathetically bad at keeping birthdays straight. And no wonder: These days you not only have to keep track of birthdays for your family and friends but, increasingly more often, you also have to remember birthdays for staff, colleagues, and clients, as well. It's too much! My secret is that I simply gave up and outsourced the job to my iPad Contacts app, which has a hidden field that you can use to store birth dates.

To add the Birthday field to a contact, follow these steps:

1. **In the Contacts app, tap the contact with which you want to work.**

2. **Tap Edit.** The Info screen appears.

3. **Tap Add Field.** The Contacts app opens the Add Field list.

4. **Tap Birthday.** The Contacts app adds a birthday field to the contact and displays the nifty scroll wheels shown in Figure 11.8.

11.8 Use these fun scroll wheels to set the contact's birth date.

5. **Scroll the left wheel to set the month for the birth date.**

6. **Scroll the middle wheel to set the day of the month for the birth date.**

7. **Scroll the right wheel to set the year of the birth date.**

8. **Tap outside of the scroll wheels.** The Contacts app saves the birthday info.

Everyone has a birthday, naturally, but lots of people have anniversaries, too. It could be a wedding date, a quit-smoking date, or the date that someone started working at the company. Whatever the occasion, you can add it to the contact info so that it's staring you in the face as a friendly reminder each time you open that contact.

Follow these steps to include an anniversary with a contact:

1. **In the Contacts app, tap the contact you want to edit.**

2. **Tap Edit.** The Contacts app shows the Info screen.

3. **Tap Add Field.** The Add Field list appears.

4. **Tap Date.** The Contacts app adds a Date field to the contact and displays the same scroll wheels that you saw earlier in Figure 11.8.

5. **Scroll the left wheel to set the month for the anniversary.**

6. **Scroll the middle wheel to set the day of the month for the anniversary.**

7. **Scroll the right wheel to set the year of the anniversary.**

8. **The label box should already show the anniversary label.** If not, tap the label box and then tap anniversary.

9. **Tap outside of the scroll wheels.** The Contacts app saves the anniversary.

Note
Although you can only add one birthday to a contact (not surprisingly), you're free to add multiple anniversaries.

Creating a new contact from a vCard

Typing a person's contact data is a tedious bit of business at the best of times, so it helps if you can find a faster way to do it. If you can cajole a contact into sending his or her contact data electronically, then you can add that data with just a couple of taps. What do I mean when I talk about sending contact data electronically? The world's contact management gurus long ago came up with a standard file format for contact data: the vCard. It's a kind of digital business card that exists as a separate file. People can pass this data along by attaching their (or someone else's) card to an e-mail message.

If you get a message with contact data, you see an icon for the VCF file, as shown in Figure 11.9.

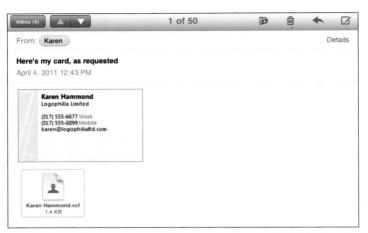

11.9 If your iPad receives an e-mail message with an attached vCard, an icon for the file appears in the message body.

To get this data into your Contacts list, follow these steps:

1. **In the Home screen, tap Mail to open the Mail application.**

2. **Tap the message that contains the vCard attachment.**

3. **Tap the icon for the vCard file.** Your iPad opens the vCard.

4. **Tap Create New Contact.** If the person is already in your Contacts list, but the vCard contains new data, tap Add to Existing Contact, and then tap the contact.

Sorting contacts

By default, the Contacts app displays your contacts sorted by last name (or company name, for businesses) and then by first name (to resolve cases where people have the same last name). That makes sense in most cases, but you might prefer a more friendly approach that sorts contacts by first name and then by last name. Here's how to make it so:

1. **Return to the iPad Home screen and tap Settings.** The Settings screen appears.

2. **Tap Mail, Contacts, Calendars.** The Mail, Contacts, Calendars screen appears.

3. **Scroll down to the Contacts section.**

4. **Tap Sort Order to display the Sort Order options.**

5. **Tap First, Last.** The Contacts app now sorts your contacts by first name.

Deleting a contact

It feels good to add new contacts but, unfortunately, you don't get a lifetime guarantee with these things. Friends fall out or fade away; colleagues decide to make a new start at another firm; clients take their business elsewhere; and some of your acquaintances simply wear out their welcome after a while. You move on and so should your Contacts list.

Follow these steps to delete a contact:

1. **In the Contacts list, tap the contact you want to delete.**

2. **Tap Edit.** The Info screen appears.

3. **Tap the Delete Contact button at the bottom of the screen.** The Contacts app asks you to confirm the deletion.

4. **Tap Delete Contact.** The Contacts app removes the contact and returns you to the All Contacts screen.

How Can I Use iPad to Track My Appointments?

Do you, like the White Rabbit in Lewis Carroll's *Alice's Adventures in Wonderland*, find yourself constantly saying, "My ears and whiskers, how late it's getting"? Well, you've come to the right place because iPad can help. Not only can you can use it to read *Alice's Adventures in Wonderland* (that will just make you later than you already are, though), but you can also take advantage of the efficient Calendar app. It turns your iPad into an electronic administrative assistant that stores your appointments and even reminds you when they're coming up. My ears and whiskers, how punctual you'll be!

Syncing Your Calendar

When you're tripping around town with your trusty iPad at your side, you certainly don't want to be late if you have a date. The best way to ensure that you don't miss an appointment, meeting, or rendezvous is to always have the event details at hand. This means adding those details to the iPad Calendar app. You could add the appointment to Calendar right on the iPad (a technique I take you through later in this chapter), but it's easier to create it on your computer and then sync it to your iPad. This gives you the added advantage of having the appointment listed in two places, so you're sure to arrive on time.

Most people sync all their appointments, but it's not unusual to keep track of separate schedules — for example, business and personal. You can control which schedule is synced to your iPad by creating separate calendars and then syncing only the calendars you want by doing one of the following:

- **Mac.** In the Mac iCal application, choose File ⇨ New Calendar, type the calendar name, and then press Return.

- **Windows.** In Outlook, click the Calendars tab, choose Folder ⇨ New Calendar, type the calendar name, and then click OK.

Now follow these steps to sync your calendar with your iPad:

1. **Connect your iPad to your computer.**
2. **In iTunes, click your iPad in the Devices list.**
3. **Click the Info tab.**
4. **Turn on calendar syncing by using one of the following techniques:**
   - **Mac.** Select the Sync iCal Calendars check box.
   - **Windows.** Select the Sync Calendars With check box and use the list to choose the program you want to use (such as Outlook).

Note iTunes doesn't support Windows Live Calendar (available with Windows 7) or Windows Calendar (available with Windows Vista), so you're out of luck if you use either one to manage your schedule.

5. **Select an option:**

   - **All calendars.** Select this option to sync all of your calendars.

   - **Selected calendars.** Select this option to sync only the calendars you choose. In the calendar list, select the check box beside each calendar that you want to sync, as shown in Figure 12.1.

12.1 You can sync selected calendars with your iPad.

6. **To control how far back the calendar sync goes, select the Do not sync events older than X days check box.** Next, type the number of days of calendar history you want to see on your iPad.

7. **Click Apply.** iTunes syncs the iPad using your new calendar settings.

Genius

If you have an iCloud account, iPad syncs completed iCloud events so you have a record of them. By default, iPad syncs events up to one month back. To change this, go to the Home screen, tap Settings, and then tap Mail, Contacts, Calendars. Scroll down to the Calendars section, tap Sync, and then tap how far back you want to go: Events 2 Weeks Back, Events 1 Month Back, Events 3 Months Back, Events 6 Months Back, or All Events.

Getting Started with the Calendar App

These days, when you ask someone how she is, the most common reply is a short one: "Busy!" We're all busy, and that places-to-go, people-to-see feeling is everywhere. All the more reason to keep your affairs in order, and that includes your appointments. Your iPad comes with a Calendar app that you can use to create items, called *events*, which represent your appointments, meetings, lunch dates, and so on. Calendar keeps track of all this stuff for you, leaving your brain free to concentrate on more important things.

You need the Calendar app up and running for this chapter, so head for the iPad Home screen and tap the Calendar icon. Figure 12.2 shows the Calendar app in landscape mode.

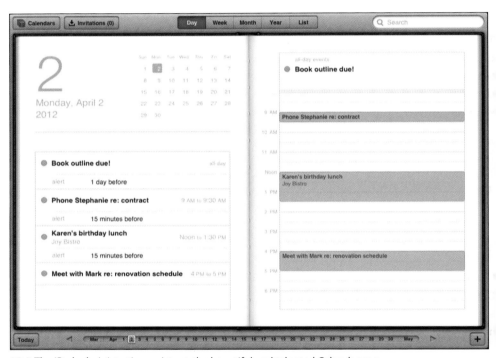

12.2 The iPad administrative assistant: the beautiful and talented Calendar app.

The key to getting around in the Calendar app efficiently is to take advantage of its various views, represented by the following five buttons found at the top of the screen:

- **Day.** This view shows the events of a single day. The schedule for that day appears on the right and the list of scheduled events is on the left.

- **Week.** This view shows all your events for the selected week.

- **Month.** This view shows the titles of all of your events for a given month.

- **Year.** This view shows a full calendar year. The dates on which you have scheduled events appear with a colored background.

- **List.** This view shows a list of all of your upcoming events on the left and the details of a selected event on the right.

The Calendar app also provides you with a Navigation bar at the bottom of the screen. This bar changes depending on the current view. For example, in Day view you can use the Navigation bar to tap a different day and in Month view you can tap a different month. You can also swipe left and right to navigate the current view. For example, if you're in Week view, swipe right to see the next week and swipe left to see the previous week.

Genius

Month view shows just the title of each event, along with a color-coded bullet that tells you in which calendar the event resides. To see more details for the events, drag your finger over them. Each time your finger passes over an event, Calendar displays details, such as the event time, location, notes, and attendees.

Tracking Your Events

I showed you how to sync your computer's calendar application (such as iCal on the Mac, or the Outlook Calendar folder) earlier in this chapter. That's the easiest way to fill your iPad with your events. However, something always comes up when you're running around, so you need to know how to add and edit events directly in your iPad Calendar. The next few sections provide the details.

Adding an event to your calendar

Follow these steps to add a basic event (the more advanced features, such as repeating events and alerts, are covered a bit later in this chapter):

1. **Select the date on which the event occurs.** In Day view, navigate to the date. In Week or Month view, tap the date.

2. **Tap the plus sign (+) in the bottom-right corner of the screen.** The Add Event screen appears, as shown in Figure 12.3.

3. **Tap the Title box and type a title for the event.**

4. **Tap the Location box and type a location for the event.**

5. **Tap the Starts/Ends/Time Zone box.** Calendar displays the Start & End screen.

6. **Tap Starts, and use the scroll wheels to set the date and time that your event begins.**

7. **Tap Ends, and use the scroll wheels to set the date and time that your event finishes.**

8. **Tap Done.** The Calendar app saves your info and returns you to the Add Event screen.

9. **If you have multiple calendars, tap Calendar, and then tap the calendar in which you want this event to appear.**

10. **Tap the Notes box, and type your notes for the event.**

11. **Tap Done.** The Calendar app saves the event info and displays the new event in the calendar.

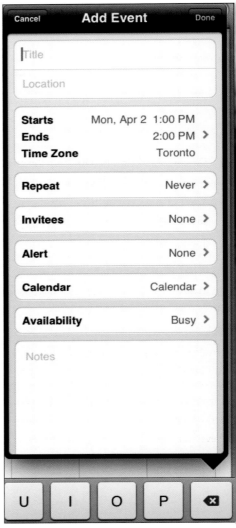

12.3 Use the Add Event screen to create your event.

Editing an existing event

Whether you've scheduled an event by hand or synced it from your computer, the event details might change: a new time, a new location, and so on. Whatever the change, you need to edit the event to keep your schedule accurate.

Genius If you just want to change the start or end time (or both), switch to either Day or Week view. Then, tap and hold the event until Calendar adds selection handles to it. Tap and drag the top selection handle to change the start time; tap and drag the bottom selection handle to change the end time; tap and drag any other part of the event to move it to a new time.

Follow these steps to edit an existing event:

1. **Display the date that contains the event you want to edit.** In Day view, navigate to the date. In Week or Month view, open the week or month that contains the date.

2. **Tap the event.** In Day view, tapping the event automatically opens it for editing, so skip to Step 4.

3. **Tap Edit.** Your iPad displays the event data in the Edit screen.

4. **Make your changes.**

5. **Tap Done.** Your iPad saves your work and returns you to the event details.

Setting up a repeating event

One of the truly great timesavers in Calendar is the repeat feature. This enables you to set up a single event and get Calendar to automatically repeat it at a regular interval.

For example, if you set up an event for a Friday, you can repeat it every week, which means that Calendar automatically sets up the same event to occur on subsequent Fridays. You can continue the events indefinitely, or end them after a certain number of repeats or on a specific date.

Follow these steps to configure an existing event to repeat:

1. **Display the date that contains the event you want to edit.** In Day view, navigate to the date. In Week or Month view, open the week or month that contains the date.

2. **Tap the event.** Calendar opens the event info.

3. **Tap Edit.** Calendar displays the event data in the Edit screen.

4. **Tap Repeat.** The Repeat Event list appears, as shown in Figure 12.4.

5. **Tap the repeat interval you want to use.**

6. **Tap Done.** Calendar returns you to the Edit Event screen.

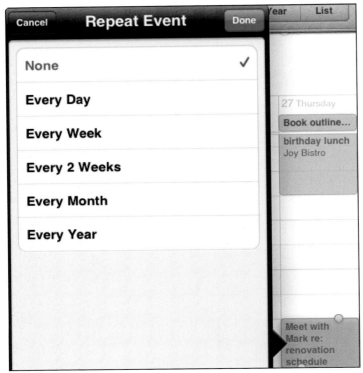

12.4 Use the Repeat Event list to decide how often you want your event to recur.

7. **Tap End Repeat.** The End Repeat list appears, as shown in Figure 12.5.

8. **You have the following two choices here:**

   • **Tap End Repeat to have the event repeats stop on a particular day.** Use the scroll wheels to set the day, month, and year that you want the final event to occur.

   • **Tap Repeat Forever to have the event repeat indefinitely.**

9. **Tap Done.** Calendar returns you to the Edit Event screen.

10. **Tap Done.** Calendar saves the repeat data and returns you to the event details.

Converting an event to an all-day event

Some events don't really have specific times that you can pin down. These include birthdays, anniversaries, sales meetings, trade shows, conferences, and vacations. What all these types of events have in common is that they last all day. In the case of birthdays and anniversaries, this is literally so, and in the case of trade shows and the like, *all day* refers to the entire workday.

Why is this important? Well, suppose you schedule a trade show as a regular event that lasts from 9 a.m. to 5 p.m. When you examine that day in the Calendar app Day or Week view, you see a big fat block that covers the entire day. If you also want to schedule meetings that occur at the trade show, Calendar lets you do that, but it shows these new events on top of this existing trade show event. This makes the schedule hard to read, so you might miss an event.

To solve this problem, configure the trade show (or whatever) as an all-day event. Calendar clears it from the regular schedule and displays it separately, near the top of the Day view or on the top part of the Week view.

12.5 Use the End Repeat list to decide how long you want the event to repeat.

Follow these steps to configure an event as an all-day event:

1. **Display the date that contains the event you want to edit.** In Day view, navigate to the date. In Week or Month view, open the week or month that contains the date.

2. **Tap the event.** Calendar opens the event info.

3. **Tap Edit.** Calendar switches to the Edit screen.

4. **Tap the Starts/Ends/Time Zone box.** Calendar displays the Start & End screen.

5. **Tap the All-day switch to the On position.**

6. **Tap Done.** The Calendar app saves the event, returns you to the calendar, and now shows the event as an all-day event.

Figure 12.6 shows Calendar in Day view with an all-day event added.

12.6 All-day events appear in the all-day section, near the top of the Day (as shown here) and Week views.

Adding an alert to an event

One of the truly useful secrets of stress-free productivity in the modern world is what I call the set-it-and-forget-it school of time management. That is, you set up an event electronically and then get the same technology to remind you when that event occurs. This way, your mind doesn't have to waste energy fretting about missing the event because you know your technology has your back.

The iPad technology of choice for this is the Calendar app and its alert feature. When you add an alert to an event, Calendar automatically displays a reminder of it in the form of a Notification Center alert that pops up on the screen. Your iPad also vibrates and sounds a few beeps to get your attention. You can also choose when the alert triggers (such as a specified number of minutes, hours, or days before the event).

Follow these steps to set an alert for an event:

1. **Display the date that contains the event you want to edit.** In Day view, navigate to the date. In Week or Month view, open the week or month that contains the date.

2. **Tap the event.** Calendar opens the event info.

3. **Tap Edit.** Calendar displays the event data in the Edit screen.

4. **Tap Alert.** The Event Alert list appears, as shown in Figure 12.7.

5. **Tap the number of minutes, hours, or days before the event you want to see the alert.** If you're editing an all-day event, you can set the alert at 9 a.m. the day before the event, at 9 a.m. two days before the event, or a week before the event.

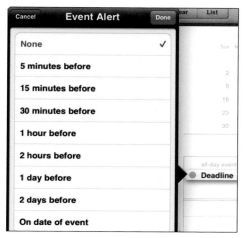

12.7 Use the Event Alert screen to tell Calendar when to remind you about your event.

6. **Tap Done.**

7. **To set up a backup alert, tap the Second Alert option.** Then, tap the number of minutes, hours, or days before the event you want to see the second alert.

Genius

You can save yourself some time by setting the default alert time for different types of events. Tap Settings in the Home screen, and then tap Mail, Contacts, Calendars. In the Calendars section, tap Default Alert Times, tap the type of alert you want to con-figure (Birthdays, Events, or All-Day Events), and then tap the default alert interval.

8. **Tap Done.** The Calendar app saves your alert choices and returns you to the calendar.

Figure 12.8 shows an example of an alert. Tap View Event to see the details or tap Close to dismiss the alert.

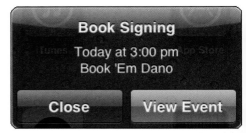

12.8 Your iPad displays an alert similar to this when it's time to remind you of an upcoming event.

Note

You can disable the alert chirps if you find them annoying. On the Home screen, tap Settings, tap General, tap Sounds, tap the Calendar Alerts, and then tap None.

Getting More Out of the Calendar App

The basic features of the Calendar app — multiple views, color-coded calendars, repeating events, all-day events, and event alerts — make it an indispensible time-management tool. But it has a few more tricks up its sleeve that you ought to know about and these are covered in the rest of this chapter.

Setting the default calendar

If you have multiple calendars on the go, each time you create a new event, the Calendar automatically chooses one of your calendars by default. It's no big whoop if every now and then you have to tap the Calendar setting and choose a different calendar. However, if you have to do this most of the time, it gets old in a hurry, particularly when I tell you there's something you can do about it. That is, you can configure the Calendar app to use a different default calendar. To do so, follow these steps:

1. **Return to the iPad Home screen, and tap Settings.** The Settings screen appears.

2. **Tap Mail, Contacts, Calendars.** The Mail, Contacts, Calendars screen appears.

3. **In the Calendars section, tap Default Calendar.** The Default Calendar screen appears.

4. **Tap the calendar you prefer to use as the default.** The Calendar app now uses that calendar as the default for each new event.

Creating a birthday or anniversary alert

If someone you know has a birthday coming up, you certainly don't want to forget! You can use the iPad Contacts app to add a Birthday field for that person, and that works great if you actually look at the contact. If you don't, you're toast. The best way to remember is to get your iPad to do the remembering for you.

Follow these steps to set up an alert for a birthday, anniversary, or any other important date:

1. **Display the date when the birthday occurs.** In Day view, navigate to the date. In Week or Month view, open the week or month that contains the date.

2. **Tap the plus sign (+) in the bottom right of the screen.** The Add Event screen appears.

3. **Tap the Title box and type a title for the event (*Karen's Birthday*, for example).**

4. **Tap the Starts/Ends/Time Zone box and use the scroll wheels to choose the birthday.**

5. **Tap the All-day switch to On.**

6. **Tap Done to return to the Add Event screen.**

7. **Tap Repeat and then tap Every Year.**

8. **Tap Alert and then tap 2 days before (9 AM).** This gives you a couple of days' notice, so you can go out and shop for a card and a present!

9. **Tap Done.** Calendar saves the event and you have another load off your mind.

Subscribing to a calendar

If you know someone who has published a calendar, you might want to keep track of that calendar within the iPad Calendar app. You can do that by subscribing to the published calendar. iPad sets up the published calendar as a separate item in the Calendar app, so you can easily switch between your own calendars and the published one.

To pull this off, you need to know the web address of the published calendar. This address usually takes the following form: *server.com/calendar.ics*.

Here, *server.com* is the address of the calendar server, and *calendar.ics* is the name of the iCalendar file (almost always preceded by a folder location). For calendars published to iCloud, the address always looks like this: ical.icloud.com/*member/calendar.ics*.

Here, *member* is the iCloud member name of the person who published the calendar. Here's an example address: ical.icloud.com/aardvarksorenstam/aardvark.ics.

Follow these steps to subscribe to a published calendar:

1. **On the Home screen, tap Settings.** Your iPad opens the Settings screen.

2. **Tap Mail, Contacts, Calendars.** The Mail, Contacts, Calendars screen appears.

3. **Tap Add Account.** The Add Account screen opens.

4. **Tap Other.** Your iPad displays the Other screen.

5. **Tap Add Subscribed Calendar.** You see the Subscription screen.

6. **Use the Server text box to type the calendar address.**

7. **Tap Next.** Your iPad connects to the calendar.

8. **Tap Save.** Your iPad adds an account for the subscribed calendar.

To view the subscribed calendar, tap Calendar on the Home screen to open the Calendar app, and then click Calendars to open the Calendars screen. Your new calendar appears in the Subscribed section, as shown in Figure 12.9. Tap the calendar to view its events.

Displaying a list of upcoming events

The Month view in the Calendar app indicates your upcoming events by displaying banners that show the event titles on the day each event occurs. This is a useful way to eyeball your schedule, but you might find you have lots of blank days where you have nothing set up, which can be distracting. If you really want to focus on your upcoming events, you can have Calendar do the work for you by displaying a list of what's scheduled over the next few days or weeks. Just tap the Calendar icon in the Home screen to open the Calendar app and then tap the List button. The Calendar app displays a list of your upcoming events. Tap an event to see its details.

12.9 Your calendar subscriptions appear in the Subscribed section of the Calendars screen.

Handling Microsoft Exchange meeting requests

If you've set up a Microsoft Exchange account in your iPad, there's a good chance you're using its push features. This means that the Exchange Server automatically sends incoming e-mail messages to your iPad, as well as new (or changed) contact and calendar data. If someone back at headquarters adds your name to a scheduled meeting, Exchange generates an automatic meeting request, which is an e-mail message that tells you about the meeting and asks if you want to attend.

How will you know? Tap Calendar in the Home screen and examine the top left of the screen. In the Calendar app toolbar, the Invitations icon tells you how many meeting requests you have waiting for you, as shown in Figure 12.10.

If you don't see the Invitations icon, you need to turn on syncing for your Exchange calendar. I show you how to do this in Chapter 6.

It's best to handle such requests as soon as you can, so here's what you do:

1. **Tap the inbox-like icon in the top-left corner of the screen.** Calendar displays your pending meeting requests.

2. **Tap the meeting request you want to respond to and then tap Details.** Calendar displays the meeting details, as shown in Figure 12.11.

3. **Tap one of the following responses:**

    - **Maybe.** Tap this button if you're not sure and will decide later.

    - **Decline.** Tap this button to confirm that you can't attend the meeting.

    - **Accept.** Tap this button to confirm that you can attend the meeting.

12.10 The Calendar Invitations icon shows you how many Exchange meeting requests you have.

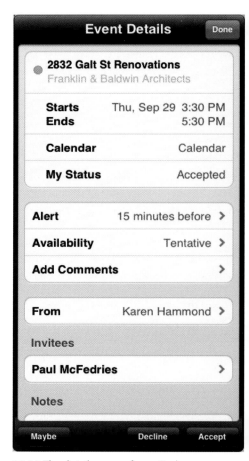

12.11 The details screen for an Exchange meeting request.

Note Meeting requests show up as events in your calendar and you can recognize them thanks to their gray text. Another way to open the meeting details is to tap the meeting request in your calendar.

Working with Reminders

The Calendar app is an excellent tool for tracking appointments, meetings, and other events. By adding an alert to an event you get a digital tap on the shoulder to remind you when and where your presence is required.

However, our days are littered with tasks that could be called *sub-events*. These are things that need to be done at a certain point during your day, bit don't rise to the level of full-fledged events: returning a call, taking the laundry out of the dryer, turning off the sprinkler. If you need to be reminded to perform such a sub-event, it seems like overkill to crank out an event using the Calendar app.

Fortunately, iOS 5 offers a better solution: the Reminders app. You use this app to create *reminders*, which are simple nudges that tell you to do something, to be somewhere, or whatever. These nudges come in the form of Notification Center banners that appear on your screen at a time you specify or when your iPad reaches a particular location. If you have an iCloud account, you can sync your reminders between your iPad, your Mac, your iPhone, and any other supported device.

Setting a reminder

Here are the steps to follow to set up a reminder that alerts you at a specific time:

1. **On the iPad Home screen, tap Reminders.** The Reminders app appears.

2. **On the left side of the screen, tap the list you want to use to store the reminder.**

3. **Tap the plus sign (+) in the upper-right corner of the screen.** The Reminders app creates a new reminder.

4. **Type the reminder text and then tap Return.**

5. **Tap the reminder.** The Details dialog appears.

6. **Tap Remind Me.** The Remind Me dialog appears.

7. **Tap the On a Day switch to On.**

8. **Tap the date that appears, and then use the scroll wheels to set the date and time of the reminder.**

9. **Tap Done.**

10. **Tap Show More to expand the Details dialog, as shown in Figure 12.12.**

11. **Use the Repeat setting to set up a repeat interval for the reminder.**

12. **Use the Priority setting to assign one of the following priorities to the reminder: None, Low, Medium, or High.**

13. **Use the List setting to choose which list you want to use to store the reminder.**

14. **Use the Notes text box to add some background text or other information about the reminder.**

15. **Tap Done.**

12.12 Tap Show More to see the full Details dialog options.Creating a new list

Creating a new list

The Reminders app comes with the following three preset lists that you can use: Reminders, Home, and Work. The default is Reminders, but you can select a different list if it's more suitable, or if you want to keep your personal and business reminders separate. If none of these three prefab lists are exactly right for your needs, feel free to create your own list by following these steps:

1. **In the Reminders app, tap Edit.** The Reminders app puts the left pane into Edit mode.

2. **Tap Create New List.** Reminders converts the Create New List button into a text box and displays the keyboard.

3. **Tap the name of your list.**

4. **Tap Done.** The Reminders app adds the list to the left pane.

5. **Tap Done.** Reminders exits Edit mode.

Deleting a reminder

If you no longer need a reminder, it's a good idea to delete it to keep your reminder lists neat and tidy. To delete a reminder, follow these steps:

1. **In the Reminders app, tap the list that contains the reminder you want to delete.** The Reminders app displays the list's reminders.

2. **Tap the reminder you want to delete.** The Reminders app opens the reminder for editing.

3. **Tap Delete.** The Reminders app asks you to confirm.

4. **Tap Delete.** Reminders deletes the reminder.

Navigate My World?

Dedicated GPS (Global Positioning System) devices have become gasp-inducingly popular over the past few years because it's not easy finding your way around in a strange city or an unfamiliar part of town. Deciphering hastily scribbled directions or a possibly out-of-date map is too hard and error prone. However, dedicated devices, whether they're music players, eBook readers, or GPS receivers, are going the way of the dodo. They're being replaced by multifunction devices that can do it all, including display maps. In this chapter, you take advantage of your iPad's multifunction prowess to learn about the amazingly useful Maps app.

Finding Your Way with Maps and GPS

When you're out in the real world trying to navigate your way between the proverbial points A and B, the questions often come thick and fast: *Where am I now? Which turn do I take? What's the traffic like on the highway? Can I even get there from here?* Fortunately, the answers to these and similar questions are now just a few finger taps away.

That's because your iPad comes loaded not only with a way-cool Maps app brought to you by the good folks at Google, but it also has a GPS receiver built in. Now your iPad knows exactly where it is (and so, by extension, you know where you are, too) and it can help you get where you want to go. However, just to be clear about this, note that your iPad only has GPS if you have the cellular model. If you have the Wi-Fi-only version, there's no GPS for you. However, Wi-Fi-only iPads can still use Maps and other location services because the iPad uses the locations of nearby Wi-Fi hotspots to get an approximate fix on your current whereabouts.

To get the Maps app on the job, tap the Maps icon in the iPad Home screen. Figure 13.1 shows the Maps screen.

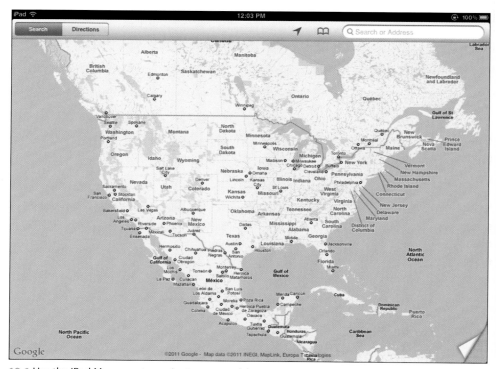

13.1 Use the iPad Maps app to navigate your world.

Viewing your destination

When you want to locate a destination using Maps, the most straightforward method is to search for it by following these steps:

1. **Tap inside the Search box in the upper-right corner of the screen.**

2. **Type the name, address, keyword, or a phrase that describes your destination.**

3. **In the on-screen keyboard, tap Search.** The Maps app locates the destination, moves the map to that area, and drops a pin on the destination, as shown in Figure 13.2.

Google Street View

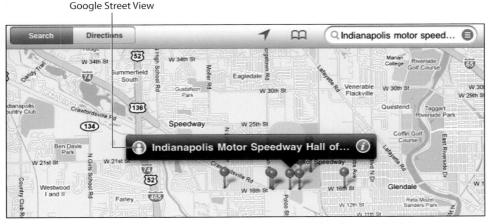

13.2 When you search for a destination, Maps displays a pin to mark its location on the map.

Now that you have pinpointed your destination (literally!), you can read the map to find your way by looking for street names, local landmarks, nearby major intersections, and so on. You also can use the Maps app to get specific directions and I show you how that works later in this chapter.

However, it's always hard to transfer the abstractions of a map to the real-world vista you see out-side your car window (or whatever) when you're close to the destination. Fortunately, Maps can bridge that gap. If Google Street View is available in that area, you see a red icon on the left side of the destination pushpin (pointed out in Figure 13.2).

Tap that icon, and Maps immediately shows you the destination in all its Street View glory, as shown in Figure 13.3. To get your bearings, flick the screen left or right to get a full 360-degree view of the area surrounding your destination.

13.3 Tap the Google Street View icon to see a real-world representation of your destination.

Displaying your current location

When you arrive at an unfamiliar shopping mall and you need to get your bearings, your first instinct might be to seek out the nearest mall map and look for the inevitable *You Are Here* marker. This gives you a sense of your current location with respect to the rest of the mall, so locating Pottery Barn shouldn't be all that hard.

When you arrive at an unfamiliar part of town or a new city, have you ever wished you had something that could provide you with that same *You Are Here* reference point? If so, you're in luck because you have exactly that waiting for you right in your iPad. Tap the Tracking icon in the Maps app menu bar, as pointed out in Figure 13.4. If this is the first time you've used the Tracking icon, Maps requests permission to use your current location, so be sure to tap OK.

Tracking icon

13.4 Tap the Tracking icon to see your precise location as a blue dot on a map.

That's it! Your iPad examines Wi-Fi hotspots and — if your iPad is cellular-equipped — uses GPS coordinates and nearby cellular towers to plot your current position. When it completes the necessary processing and triangulating, your iPad displays a map of your current city, zooms in on your current area, and then adds a blue dot to the map to pinpoint your current location, as shown in Figure 13.4. Amazingly, if you happen to be in a car, taxi, or other moving vehicle, the blue dot moves in real time.

Genius

Knowing where you are is a good thing, but it's even better to know what's nearby. Suppose you're in a new city and you're dying for a cup of coffee. Tap Search in the Search box, type *coffee,* and then tap Search. The Maps app drops a bunch of pins on nearby locations that match your search. Tap a pin to see the name, and tap the blue More Info icon to see the location's phone number, address, and website.

Displaying a map of a contact's location

In the old days (that is, a few years ago), if you had a contact located in an unfamiliar part of town or in another city altogether, visiting that person required a phone call or e-mail asking for directions. You'd then write down the instructions, get written directions via e-mail, or perhaps even get a crudely drawn map faxed to you. Those days, fortunately, are long gone thanks to myriad online resources that can show you where a particular address is located and even give you driving directions to get there from here (wherever *here* may be).

271

Even better, your iPad takes it one step further and integrates with Google Maps to generate a map of a contact's location based on the person's contact address. So, as long as you've typed (or synced) a contact's physical address, you can see where he or she is located on the map.

To display a map of a contact's location, follow these steps:

1. **In the Home screen, tap the Contacts icon to open the Contacts application.**

2. **Tap the contact with which you want to work.** Your iPad displays the contact's data.

3. **Tap the address you want to map.** Your iPad switches to the Maps app and drops a pushpin on the contact's location.

Note You also can display a map of a contact's location by using the Maps app itself. In the menu bar, tap the Bookmarks icon (it's to the left of the Search box). Tap Contacts and then tap the contact you want to map. The Maps app maps the contact's address.

Mapping an address from an e-mail

Addresses show up in all kinds of e-mail messages these days. Most commonly, folks include their work or home addresses in their e-mail signature at the bottom of each message. Similarly, if the e-mail is an invitation, your correspondent almost certainly includes the address for the event somewhere in the message.

If you need to know where an address is located, you might think that you need to copy the address from the message and then paste it into the Maps app. Sure, that works, but it's way too much effort! Instead, just do this:

1. **In the Mail app, locate the message that includes the address.** If your iPad is in portrait mode, tap Inbox to see the messages.

2. **Tap and hold on the address in the message.** Your iPad displays a list of actions.

3. **Tap Open in Maps.** The Maps app opens and drops a pushpin on the address.

Saving a location as a bookmark

If you know the address of the location you want to map, you can add a pushpin for that location by opening the Maps app and running a search on the address. That is, you tap the Search box in the menu bar, type the address, and then tap the Search button.

That's no big deal for one-time-only searches, but what about a location you refer to frequently? Typing that address over and over gets old in a hurry, I assure you. You can save time and tapping by telling the Maps app to save that location on its Bookmarks list, which means you can access it, usually, with just a few taps.

The Bookmarks screen also comes with a Recents button in the menu bar. Tap this button to see your last few searches, locations entered, and driving directions requested. To get the Maps app to run any item again, just tap it.

Follow these steps to add a location to the Maps app Bookmarks list:

1. **Search for the location you want to save.** The Maps app marks the location with a pushpin, and displays the name or address of the location in a banner above the pushpin.

2. **Tap the blue More Info icon in the banner.** The Maps app displays the Info screen with the following details about the location:

   ● **If the location is in your Contacts list, you see the contact's data.**

   ● **If the location is a business or institution, you see the address as well as other data, such as the organization's phone number and web address.**

   ● **For all other locations, you see just the address.**

3. **Tap Add to Bookmarks.** The Maps app displays the Add Bookmarks screen.

4. **Edit the name of the bookmark if you want to and then Tap Save.** The Maps app adds the location to the Bookmarks list.

To map a bookmarked location, follow these steps:

1. **Tap the Bookmark icon in the menu bar.** The Maps app opens the Bookmarks screen.

2. **Tap Bookmarks in the menu bar.**

3. **Tap the Bookmarks button.** The Maps app displays your list of bookmarked locations, as shown in Figure 13.5.

4. **Tap the location you want to map.** The Maps app displays the appropriate map and adds a pushpin for the location.

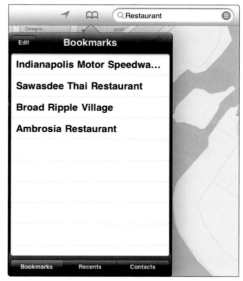

13.5 You can access frequently used locations with just a few taps by saving them as bookmarks.

Specifying a location when you don't know the address

Sometimes you have only a vague notion of where you want to go. In a new city, for example, you might decide to head downtown to look for a coffee shop or restaurant. That's fine, but how do you get downtown from your hotel in the suburbs? Your iPad can give you directions, but it needs to know the endpoint of your journey and that's precisely the information you don't have. Sounds like a conundrum, for sure, but there's a way to work around it. You can drop a pin on the map in the approximate area where you want to go. The Maps app can then give you directions to the dropped pin.

Follow these steps to drop a pin on a map:

1. **In the Maps app, display a map of the city with which you want to work in one of the following ways:**

   - **If you're in the city now, tap the Tracking icon in the lower-left corner of the screen.**

   - **If you're not in the city, tap the Search box, type the name of the city (and perhaps also the name of the state or province), and then tap the Search button.**

2. **Use finger flicks to pan the map to the approximate location you want to use as your destination.**

3. **Tap the Actions button in the lower-right corner of the screen.** The Maps app displays a list of actions.

4. **Tap Drop Pin.** The Maps app drops a purple pin in the middle of the current map.

5. **Drag the purple pin to the location you want.** The Maps app creates a temporary bookmark called Dropped Pin that you can use when you ask the iPad for directions (as described next).

Getting directions to a location

One possible navigation scenario with the Maps app is to specify a destination (using a contact, an address search, a dropped pin, or a bookmark), and then tap the Tracking icon. This gives you a map that shows both your destination and your current location. Depending on how far away the destination is, you may need to zoom out (by pinching the screen or tapping it with two fingers) to see both locations on the map. You can then eyeball the streets to see how to get from here to there.

Eyeball the streets? Hah, how primitive! The Maps app can bring you into the 21st century by not only showing you a route to the destination, but also by providing you with the distance and time it should take. It also gives you street-by-street, turn-by-turn instructions. It's one of the sweetest iPad features, and it works like so:

1. **Use the Maps app to add a pushpin for your destination.** Use whatever method works best for you: the Contacts list, an address search, a dropped pin, or a bookmark.

2. **Tap Directions in the menu bar.** The Maps app opens the Directions screen. As shown in Figure 13.6, you should see Current Location in the Start box at the top of the screen and your destination address in the End box.

Genius Instead of getting directions to the destination, you might need directions *from* the destination. No sweat! When you map the destination, tap the blue More Info icon, and then tap Directions From Here. If you're already in the Directions screen, tap the Swap icon in between the Start and End boxes. The Maps app swaps the locations.

3. **If you want to use a starting point other than your current location, tap Current Location in the Start box.** Then, type the address of the location you want to use.

4. **In the Overview area at the bottom of the screen, tap the mode of transportation: car, transit, or walking.** The Maps app shows the trip distance and approximate time.

5. **Tap Start.** The Maps app displays the directions for the first leg of the journey.

6. **Tap the Next (right arrow) key.** You see the directions for the next leg of the journey. Repeat to see the directions for each leg. You also can tap the Previous (left arrow) key to go back.

Note Instead of seeing the directions one step at a time, you may prefer to see them all at once. On the left side of the Overview area at the bottom of the screen, tap the List icon to display the Directions screen.

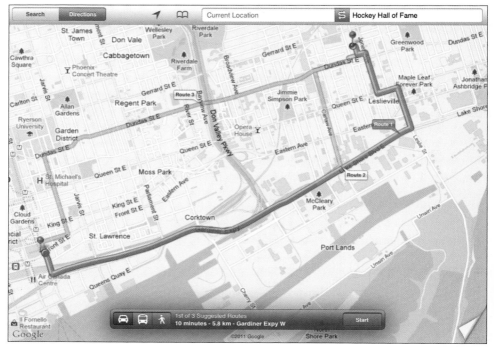

13.6 Use the Directions screen to specify the start and endpoints of your trip, and to see all routes to your destination.

Showing alternate routes

When you map a journey to a location, the main route is shown on the map using a thick blue line, as shown in Figure 13.6. However, if you look carefully you notice that (in this case) two other routes are shown using lighter blue lines. They are labeled Route 2 and Route 3, and they're alternate routes suggested by the Maps app. So, for example, if you happen to know that Route 1 goes through a construction zone or is particularly busy at this time of day, tap an alternate route that avoids the congestion.

Getting live traffic information

Okay, it's pretty darn amazing that your iPad can tell you precisely where you are and how to get somewhere else. However, in most cities, it's the getting somewhere else part that's the problem. Why? One word: traffic. The Maps app may tell you the trip should take 10 minutes, but that could easily turn into a half hour or more if you run into a traffic jam.

That's life in the big city, right? Maybe not. If you're on a highway in a major North American city, the Maps app can most likely supply you with — wait for it — real-time traffic conditions. This is really an amazing tool that can help you avoid traffic messes and find alternative routes to your destination.

To see the traffic data, tap the Action icon in the lower-right corner of the screen and then tap the Traffic switch to the On position. As you can see in Figure 13.7, the Maps app uses four colors to illustrate the traffic flow.

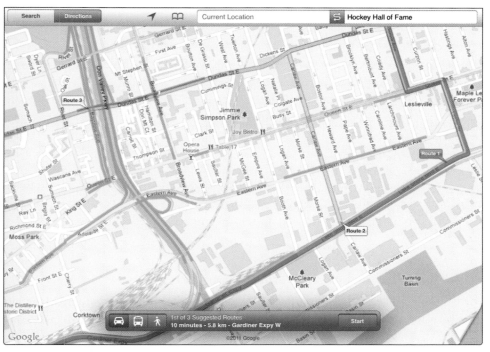

13.7 The color of the route tells you the current speed of the traffic.

Here is what each color means:

- **Green.** Routes where the traffic is moving at 50 mph or faster.
- **Yellow.** Routes where the traffic is moving between 25 and 50 mph.
- **Red.** Routes where the traffic is moving at 25 mph or slower.
- **Gray.** Routes that currently have no traffic data.

Now you don't have to worry about finding a news radio station and waiting for the traffic report. You can get real-time traffic information whenever you need it.

Configuring Location Services

On your iPad, *Location Services* refers to the features and technologies that provide apps and system tools with access to location data. This is a handy and useful thing, but it's also something that you need to keep under your control because your location data, particularly your current location, is fundamentally private and shouldn't be given out willy-nilly. Fortunately, your iPad comes with a few tools for controlling and configuring Location Services.

Turning off Location Services

The next couple of sections show you how to turn off Location Services for individual apps as well as individual system services. That fine-grained control is the best way to handle Location Services, but there may be times when you prefer a broader approach that turns off Location Services altogether. For example, if you're heading to a secret rendezvous (how exciting!) and you've brought your iPad along, you might feel more comfortable knowing that no app or service on your iPad is tracking your whereabouts. On a more mundane level, Location Services uses up battery power. So, if your iPad battery is getting low — or if you just want to maximize the battery (on a long bus ride, for example) — turning off Location Services can help.

Follow these steps to turn off all Location Services on your iPad:

1. **On the Home screen, tap Settings.** The Settings app appears.
2. **Tap Location Services.** The Location Services settings appear.
3. **Tap the Location Services switch to the Off position.** If you have the Find My iPhone feature activated (see Chapter 3), your iPad asks you to confirm.
4. **Tap Turn Off.** Your iPad shuts off all location services.

Controlling app access to GPS

When you open an app that comes with a GPS component, the app displays a dialog like the one shown in Figure 13.8 to ask your permission to use the iPad location hardware and determine your current location. Tap OK if that's just fine with you; tap Don't Allow if you think that your current location is none of the app's business.

However, after you make your decision, you might change your mind. For example, if you deny your location to an app, that app might lack some crucial functionality. Similarly, if you allow an app to use your location, you might have second thoughts about compromising your privacy.

13.8 When you first launch a GPS-aware app, it asks your permission to use your current location.

Whatever the reason, you can control an app's access to GPS by following these steps:

1. **In the iPad Home screen, tap Settings.** The Settings app appears.

2. **Tap Location Services.** The Location Services screen appears, as shown in Figure 13.9.

13.9 Use the Location Services screen to control which apps have access to your location.

3. **Configure app access to GPS as follows:**

- **If you want to deny your current location to all apps, tap the Location Services switch to Off.**

- **If you want to deny your current location to specific apps, for each app tap the On/Off switch to Off.**

Enabling or disabling system Location Services

Your iPad also provides location services to various internal system services that perform tasks, such as calibrating the iPad compass, setting the time zone, and serving up iAds that change depending on location data. If you don't want your iPad providing any of these services, you can turn them off this way:

1. **On the Home screen, tap Settings to open the Settings app.**

2. **Tap Location Services.** The Location Services screen appears.

3. **Tap System Services.** The Settings app displays the System Services screen, as shown in Figure 13.10.

13.10 Use the System Services screen to control which system tools have access to your location.

4. **For any system service that you don't want to provide access to location data, tap its switch to Off.**

Sharing Map Data

If you want to show someone where you live, where you work, or where you want to meet, you could just send the address, but that's so last century. The more modern way is to send your friend a digital map that shows the location. With your iPad this a snap — you can send a map via e-mail or text message, or post a map on Twitter.

To share a map, follow these steps:

1. **Use the Maps app to add a pushpin for the location you want to send.** Use whatever method works best for you: the Contacts list, an address search, a dropped pin, or a bookmark. If you want to send your current location, display it and then tap the blue dot.

2. **Tap the blue More Info icon.**

3. **Tap Share Location.** Your iPad displays a list of ways to share the map.

4. **Tap the method you want to use to share the map: Email, Message, or Tweet.** The Maps app creates a new e-mail, text message, or tweet that includes a Google Maps link to the location.

5. **Fill in the rest of your message or tweet and send it.**

How Do I Fix My iPad?

Your iPad may *look* like an iPod touch on steroids, but its sophisticated innards tell a different story. This is one fancy device, and it's more complex than an iPod touch. The good news is the iPad is a full-blown computer and you can use it to perform some pretty amazing tricks. The bad news is the iPad is a full-blown computer and most computers eventually have problems. There's a good chance that some day your iPad will behave strangely or not at all. This chapter gives you some general troubleshooting techniques and also tackles a few specific problems.

General iPad Troubleshooting Techniques

If your iPad is behaving oddly or erratically, it's possible that a specific component inside the device is the cause. In that case, you don't have much choice but to ship your iPad back to Apple for repairs. Fortunately, most glitches are temporary and can often be fixed by using one or more of the following techniques:

- **Restart your iPad.** By far the most common solution to an iPad problem is to shut down and restart the device. By rebooting the iPad, you reload the entire system, which is often enough to solve many problems. You restart your iPad by pressing and holding the Sleep/Wake button for a few seconds until you see the Slide to Power Off screen (at which point you can release the button). Drag the Slide to Power Off slider to the right to start the shutdown. When the screen goes completely black, your iPad is off. To restart, press and hold the Sleep/Wake button until you see the Apple logo, and then release the button.

- **Reboot the iPad hardware.** When you restart your iPad by pressing and holding Sleep/Wake for a while, what you're really doing is rebooting the system software. If that still doesn't solve the problem, you may need to reboot the iPad hardware as well. To do that, press and hold the Sleep/Wake button and the Home button. Keep them pressed until you see the Apple logo (it takes about 8 seconds or so), which indicates a successful restart.

Genius

The hardware reboot is also the way to go if your iPad is really stuck and holding down just the Sleep/Wake button doesn't do anything.

- **Recharge your iPad.** It's possible that your iPad battery is completely discharged. Connect your iPad to your computer or the dock. If it powers up and you see the battery logo (note that this may take 10 to 20 seconds), then it's charging just fine and will be back on its feet in a while.

- **Shut down a stuck app.** If your iPad is frozen because an application has gone haywire, you can usually get the iPad back in the saddle by forcing the application to quit. Press and hold the Sleep/Wake button until you see the Slide to power off screen. Next, press and hold Home button for about 6 seconds. Your iPad shuts down the application and returns you to the Home screen. If an app is frozen but your iPad works fine otherwise, double-click the Home button to display the multitasking bar. Press and hold any icon until you see the app icons jiggling, tap the red Delete icon that appears in the upper left corner of the stuck app's icon, and then click Home.

- **Check for iPad software updates.** If Apple knows about the problem you're having, it will fix it (eventually) and make the patch available in a software update. I tell you how to update your iPad a bit later in this chapter.

- **Check for app updates.** It's possible that a bug in an app is causing your woes. On the Home screen, tap App Store and check the Updates icon to see if any updates are available. If so, tap each app and tap the Update button to make it so. If you have quite a few updates ready, an easier route is to tap the Updates icon, and then tap Update All to automatically process all of them.

- **Erase and restore your content and settings.** This may seem like drastic advice, but it's possible to use iTunes to perform a complete backup of everything on your iPad. You can then reset the iPad to its original, pristine state, and then restore the backup. I explain this rather lengthy process later in the chapter.

- **Reset your settings.** Sometimes your iPad goes down for the count because its settings have become corrupted. In that case, you can restore the iPad by restoring its original settings. If iTunes doesn't recognize your iPad, then the backup-and-restore option is out. However, you can still reset the settings on the iPad itself. Tap Settings in the Home screen, tap General, tap Reset, and then tap Reset All Settings. When your iPad asks you to confirm, tap Reset.

Genius

If resetting your iPad doesn't get the job done, it could be some recalcitrant bit of content that's causing the problem. In that case, tap Settings in the Home screen, tap General, tap Reset, and then tap Erase All Content and Settings. When your iPad asks you to confirm, tap Erase.

Troubleshooting connected devices

You can connect devices to your iPad in only a few ways: Using the headset jack, the Dock connector, or Bluetooth. So, although the number of devices you can connect is relatively limited, that doesn't mean you might never have problems with those devices.

If you're having trouble with a device attached to your iPad, the good news is that a fair chunk of those problems have a relatively limited set of causes. You may be able to get the device back on its feet by attempting a few tried-and-true remedies that work quite often for many devices. If it's not immediately obvious what the problem is, then your hardware troubleshooting routine should always start with these very basic techniques:

- **Check connections, power switches, and so on.** Some of the most common (and embarrassing) causes of hardware problems are the simple physical things, so make sure the device is turned on and that the cable connections are secure. If you can't access the Internet through the iPad Wi-Fi connection, make sure your network router is turned on, and that the cable between your router and the ISP's modem is properly connected.

- **Replace the batteries.** Wireless devices, such as headsets, really chew through batteries. If such a device is working intermittently or not at all, always try replacing the batteries to see if that solves the problem.

- **Turn the device off and then on again.** You *power cycle* a device by turning it off, waiting a few seconds for its innards to stop spinning, and then turning it back on again. You'd be amazed how often this simple procedure can get a device back up and running. For a device that doesn't have an On/Off switch, try either unplugging the device from the power outlet, or removing and replacing the batteries.

- **Reset the default settings for the device.** If you can configure a device, then perhaps some new setting is causing the problem. If you recently made a change, try returning the setting to its original value. If that doesn't do the trick, most configurable devices have some kind of Restore Default Settings option that enables you to quickly return it to its factory settings.

- **Upgrade the device's firmware.** Many devices come with *firmware*, a small program that runs inside the device and controls its internal functions. For example, all routers have firmware. Check with the manufacturer to see if a new version exists. If it does, download it and see the manual for the device to learn how to upgrade the firmware.

Updating the iPad operating system

The iPad operating system should update itself from time to time when you connect it to your computer (provided the computer has an Internet connection). This is another good reason to sync your iPad regularly. The problem is, you might hear about an important update that adds a feature you're really looking forward to or perhaps fixes a gaping security hole. What do you do if iTunes isn't scheduled to check for an update for a few days? In that case, you take matters into your own hands and check for updates yourself.

In iOS 5, you can check for updates right on your iPad by doing the following:

1. **On the Home screen, tap Settings to open the Settings app.**

2. **Tap General.** Your iPad displays the General screen.

3. **Tap Software Update.** Your iPad begins checking for available updates. If you see the message "Your software is up to date," then you can move on to bigger and better things.

4. **If an update is available, tap Download and Install.** Your iPad downloads the update and then proceeds with the installation, which takes a few minutes.

Here's the iTunes route:

1. **Connect your iPad to your computer.** iTunes opens and connects to your iPad.

2. **Click your iPad in the Devices list.**

3. **Click the Summary tab.**

4. **Click Check for Update.** iTunes connects to the Apple servers to see if any iPad updates are available. If an update exists, you see the iPad Software Update dialog, which offers a description of the update.

5. **Click Next.** iTunes displays the Software License Agreement.

6. **Click Agree.** iTunes downloads the software update and installs it.

Backing up or restoring iPad data and settings

Sometimes your iPad goes down for the count because its settings have become corrupted. In that case, you can restore the iPad by restoring its original settings. The best way to go about this is to use the Restore feature in iTunes, because that enables you to make a backup of your settings. However, it does mean that your iPad must be able to connect to your computer and be visible in iTunes.

If that's not the case, see the instructions for resetting in the next section. Otherwise, follow these steps to do a backup and restore on your iPad:

1. **Connect your iPad to your computer.**

2. **In iTunes, click your iPad in the Devices list.**

3. **Click Sync.** This ensures that iTunes backs up your iPad and has copies of all of its data.

4. **Check that your iPad is backed up by choosing iTunes ⇨ Preferences, and clicking the Devices tab.** You should see your iPad in the Device backups list, as shown in Figure 14.1. When you finish, click OK to close the dialog.

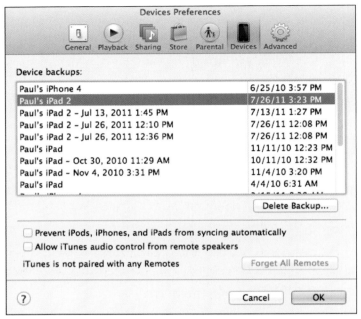

14.1 In the iTunes preferences, use the Devices tab to double-check that your iPad is backed up.

5. **Click the Summary tab.**

6. **Click Restore.** iTunes asks you to confirm you want to restore.

7. **Click Restore.**

8. **If the iPad Software Update dialog appears, click Next and then click Agree.** iTunes downloads the software, backs up your iPad, and then restores the original software and settings. When your iPad restarts, iTunes connects to it and displays the Set Up Your iPad screen.

9. **Select the Restore from the backup of option.**

10. **If you happen to have more than one iPad backed up, use the list to choose yours.**

11. **Click Continue.** iTunes restores your backed-up data, restarts your iPad, and then syncs the iPad.

12. **Go through the tabs, and check the sync settings to make sure they're set up the way you want.**

13. **If you made any changes to the settings, click Sync.** This ensures that your iPad has all its data restored.

Caution If you have confidential or sensitive data on your iPad, that data becomes part of the backup files and could be viewed by some snoop. To prevent this, select the Encrypt iPad backup check box in the Summary tab and then use the Set password dialog to specify your decryption password.

Taking Care of the iPad Battery

Your iPad comes with a large lithium-ion battery. Apple claims that the iPad gives you up to 10 hours of continuous usage and holds a charge in standby mode for 30 days. Those are impressive times, although count on getting less in the real world (particularly if you have a cellular model and you're surfing the web over a cellular connection).

The biggest downside to the iPad battery is that it's not, in Apple parlance, a *user-installable* feature. If your battery dies, you have no choice but to return it to Apple to get it replaced — all the more reason to take care of it and try to maximize its life.

Tracking battery usage

Your iPad doesn't give much battery data, but you can monitor both the total usage time (this includes all activities; surfing, reading eBooks, gaming, playing media, and so on) and standby time (when your iPad was in Sleep mode). To do so, follow these steps:

1. **On the Home screen, tap Settings.** The Settings screen appears.

2. **Tap General.** Your iPad displays the General screen.

3. **Tap Usage.** Your iPad displays the Usage screen.

4. **Tap the Battery Percentage On/Off switch to the On position.** Your iPad shows you the percentage of battery life left in the status bar beside the battery icon, as shown in Figure 14.2.

14.2 Turn on the Battery Percentage option to monitor battery life in the iPad status bar.

Extending battery life

Reducing battery consumption as much as possible on the iPad not only extends the time between charges but also extends the overall life of your battery. Here are a few suggestions:

- **Dim the screen.** The touchscreen drains lots of battery power, so dimming it reduces that power. On the Home screen, tap Settings, tap Brightness & Wallpaper, and then drag the slider to the left to dim the screen.

- **Cycle the battery.** All lithium-based batteries slowly lose their charging capacity over time. If you can run your iPad on batteries for eight hours today, later you'll only be able to run it for six hours on a full charge. You can't stop this process, but you can delay it significantly by periodically cycling the iPad battery. *Cycling* — also called reconditioning or recalibrating — a battery means letting it completely discharge and then fully recharging it again. To maintain optimal performance, you should cycle the iPad battery every one or two months.

Genius Paradoxically, the less you use your iPad, the more often you should cycle its battery. If you often go several days or even a week or two without using your iPad (I can't imagine!), you should cycle its battery at least once a month.

- **Slow the auto-check on your e-mail.** Having your e-mail poll the server for new messages eats up your battery. Don't set it to check every 15 minutes if possible. Ideally, set it to Manual check if you can. Tap Settings, tap Mail, Contacts, Calendars, tap Fetch New Data, and then tap Manually.

- **Turn off Push.** If you have a MobileMe account, consider turning off the Push feature to save battery power. Tap Settings, tap Mail, Contacts, Calendars, and then tap Fetch New Data. In the Fetch New Data screen, tap the Push setting to Off and tap Manually in the Fetch section, as shown in Figure 14.3.

- **Minimize your tasks.** If you aren't able to charge your iPad for a while, avoid background chores such as playing music or secondary chores such as organizing your contacts. If your only goal is to read all your e-mail, stick to that until it's done because you don't know how much time you have.

- **Manually put your iPad into Sleep mode, if necessary.** If you're interrupted — for example, the pizza delivery guy shows up on time — don't wait for your iPad to put itself to sleep because those few minutes use up precious battery time. Instead, put your iPad to sleep manually by pressing the Sleep/Wake button.

14.3 You can save battery power by turning off the iPad push features.

- **Avoid temperature extremes.** Exposing your iPad to extremely hot or cold tempera-tures reduces the long-term effectiveness of the battery. Try to keep your iPad within a reasonable range of temperatures.

- **Turn off Wi-Fi if you don't need it.** When Wi-Fi is on, it regularly checks for available wireless networks, which drains the battery. If you don't need to connect to a wireless network, turn off Wi-Fi to conserve energy. Tap Settings, tap Wi-Fi, and then tap the Wi-Fi setting to Off.

- **Turn off cellular if you don't need it.** If you have a cellular iPad, it constantly looks for nearby cellular towers to maintain the signal, which can use up battery power in a hurry. If you're surfing on a Wi-Fi network, you don't need cellular, so turn it off. Tap Settings, tap Cellular Data, and then tap the Cellular Data setting to Off.

- **Turn off Location Services if you don't need them.** When Location Services are on, iPad regularly exchanges data with the Wi-Fi and GPS systems which uses up battery power.

- **Turn off Bluetooth if you don't need it.** When Bluetooth is running, it constantly checks for nearby Bluetooth devices, which drains the battery. If you aren't using any Bluetooth devices, turn off Bluetooth to save energy. Tap Settings, tap General, tap Bluetooth, and then tap the Bluetooth setting to Off.

291

Genius

If you don't need all three (or four, if you have cellular) of the iPad antennae for a while, a faster way to turn them off is to switch your iPad to Airplane mode. Tap Settings, and then tap the Airplane Mode switch to the On position.

Solving Specific Problems

The generic troubleshooting and repair techniques that you've seen so far can solve all kinds of problems. However, specific problems always require specific solutions. The rest of this chapter takes you through a few of the most common of these.

The battery won't charge

If you find that your battery won't charge, here are some solutions:

- **If the iPad is plugged into a computer to charge via the USB port, it may be that the computer has gone into standby.** Waking the computer should solve the problem.

- **The USB port may not be transferring enough power.** For example, the USB ports on most keyboards don't offer much in the way of power. If your iPad is plugged into a keyboard USB port, plug it into a USB port on the computer itself.

- **Attach the USB cable to the USB power adapter, and then plug the adapter into an AC outlet.**

- **Double-check all connections to make sure everything is plugged in properly.**

- **Try an iPod cord if you have one.**

If you can't seem to locate the problem after these steps, you may need to send your iPad in for service. A replacement battery (if you live in the United States) costs $99 plus $6.95 shipping.

Note

To get your iPad repaired, you could take your device to an Apple store or send it in. Visit www.apple.com/support and follow the prompts to find out how to send your iPad in for repairs. Remember that the memory comes back wiped, so be sure to sync with iTunes, if you can. Also, if you have a cellular iPad, don't forget to remove your SIM before you send it in.

You can't access a Wi-Fi network

Wireless networking adds a whole new set of potential snags to your troubleshooting chores because of problems such as interference and device ranges.

Here's a list of a few things to check when you're trying to solve wireless connectivity problems:

- **Make sure the Wi-Fi antenna is on.** Tap Settings, tap Wi-Fi, and then tap the Wi-Fi switch to the On position.

- **Make sure the iPad isn't in Airplane mode.** Tap Settings, and then tap the Airplane Mode switch to the Off position.

- **Check the connection.** The iPad has a tendency to disconnect from a nearby Wi-Fi network for no apparent reason. Tap Settings. If the Wi-Fi setting shows as Not Connected, tap Wi-Fi and then tap your network in the list.

- **Renew the lease.** When you connect to a Wi-Fi network, the access point gives your iPad a Dynamic Host Control Protocol (DHCP) lease that allows it to access the network. You can often solve connectivity problems by renewing that lease. Tap Settings, tap Wi-Fi, and then tap the blue More Info icon to the right of the connected Wi-Fi network. Tap the DHCP tab, and then tap Renew Lease, as shown in Figure 14.4.

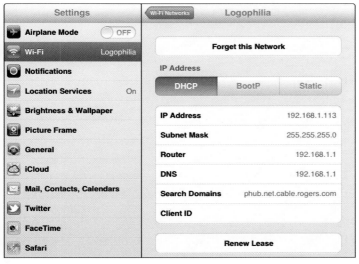

14.4 Open the connected Wi-Fi network settings and tap Renew Lease to get a fresh lease on your Wi-Fi life.

- **Reconnect to the network.** You can often solve Wi-Fi network woes by disconnecting and then reconnecting to the network. Tap Settings, tap Wi-Fi, and then tap the blue More Info icon to the right of the connected Wi-Fi network. Tap the Forget This Network button to disconnect and then reconnect to the same network.

- **Reset the iPad network settings.** This removes all stored network data and resets everything to the factory state, which might solve the problem. Tap Settings, tap General, tap Reset, and then tap Reset Network Settings. When your iPad asks you to confirm, tap Reset.

- **Reboot and power cycle devices.** Reset your hardware by performing the following tasks in order: Restart your iPad, reboot the iPad hardware, power cycle the wireless access point, and power cycle the broadband modem.

- **Look for interference.** Devices such as baby monitors and cordless phones that use the 2.4 GHz radio frequency (RF) band can play havoc with wireless signals. Try either moving or turning off such devices if they're near your iPad or wireless access point.

- **Check your range.** If you're getting no signal or a weak signal, your iPad could be too far away from the access point. If you have an 802.11n access point, the theoretical range is about 230 feet. If you have an older access point (such as 802.11g), you usually can't get much farther than about 115 feet away from it before the signal begins to degrade. Either move closer to the access point or turn on the access point range booster feature, if it has one. You also could install a wireless range extender.

- **Update the wireless access point firmware.** The wireless access point firmware is the internal program that the access point uses to perform its various chores. Wireless access point manufacturers frequently update their firmware to fix bugs, so you should see if an updated version of the firmware is available. See your device documentation to learn how this works.

- **Reset the router.** As a last resort, reset the router to its default factory settings (see the device documentation to learn how to do this). Note that if you do this, you need to set up your network from scratch.

Caution

You should keep your iPad and wireless access point well away from microwave ovens, which can jam wireless signals.

iTunes doesn't see your iPad

When you connect your iPad to your computer, iTunes should start and you should see the iPad in the Devices list. If iTunes doesn't start when you connect your iPad, or if iTunes is already running but the iPad doesn't appear in the Devices list, it means that iTunes doesn't recognize your iPad. Here are some possible fixes:

- **Check the connections.** Make sure the USB connector and the Dock connector are fully seated.

- **Try a different USB port.** The port you're using may not work, so try another one. If you're using a port on a USB hub, trying using one of the built -in USB ports on the computer.

- **Restart your iPad.** Press and hold the Sleep/Wake button for a few seconds until the iPad shuts down, and then press and hold Sleep/Wake until you see the Apple logo.

- **Restart your computer.** This should reset the computer's USB ports which might solve the problem.

- **Check your iTunes version.** You should be using at least iTunes version 10.2 to work with the iPad.

- **Check your operating system version.** On a Mac, your iPad requires OS X 10.5.8 or later. On a Windows PC, your iPad requires Windows 7, Windows Vista, or Windows XP Service Pack 3 or later.

iTunes won't sync your iPad

If iTunes sees your iPad, but you can't get it to sync, you probably have to adjust some settings. See Chapter 2 for some troubleshooting ideas related to syncing. Another possibility is that your iPad is currently locked. That's not usually a problem for iTunes, but it is sometimes confused by a locked iPad. The easy remedy is to unplug the iPad, unlock it, and then plug it in again.

You have trouble syncing music or videos

You may run into a problem syncing your music or videos to your iPad. The most likely culprit here is that your files are in a format that the iPad can't read. WMA, MPEG-1, MPEG-2, and other formats aren't readable to the iPad. First, convert them to a format that the iPad does understand using converter software. Then put them back on iTunes and try to sync again. This should solve the problem.

iPad-supported audio formats include: AAC, HE-AAC (V1 and V2), and Protected AAC; AIFF; Audible formats 2, 3, 4, and Audible Enhanced Audio; Apple Lossless; MP3, MP3 VBR, and WAV. iPad-supported video formats include: H.264, MPEG-4, and Motion JPEG.

Your iPad doesn't recognize the SIM

If you have a cellular iPad and it doesn't detect your SIM, try this:

1. **Eject the SIM tray from the side of your iPad using a SIM tool (if you have one), a paper clip, or a pin.** Gently press the tool into the little hole on the tray and pull out the tray.

2. **Make sure the SIM is free of dirt and debris.**

3. **Reseat the SIM in the tray and slide the tray back in.**

If this doesn't solve the problem, then your problem is a larger one, and you need to contact Apple or your cellular provider.

An app is taking up too much space

The iPad is so useful and so much fun it's easy to forget that it has limitations, especially when it comes to storage. This is particularly true if you have a 16GB model. However, even a big 64GB iPad can fill up in a hurry if you've stuffed it with movies, TV shows, and tons of magazine subscriptions.

You can tell how much free space your iPad has left either by connecting it to iTunes, or by tapping Settings, then General, then Usage. In iOS 5, the Usage screen not only shows you how much storage space you have available, it also shows you how much space each app is using, as shown in Figure 14.5.

If you see that your iPad is running low on space, check the apps to see if any of them are taking up more than their fair share of hard drive real estate. If you see a hard drive hog, you can choose one of the following two ways to delete its data and give your iPad some room to breathe:

- **Third-party apps.** For an app you picked up via the App Store, tap the app, tap Delete App, and then tap Delete App when your iPad asks you to confirm.

- **Built-in apps.** For an app that came with your iPad (such as Music or Video), tap the app to display a list of the data it's storing on your iPad, and then tap Edit. This puts the list in edit mode, as shown in Figure 14.6. To remove an item, tap the red Delete button to the left of it, and then tap the Delete button that appears.

14.5 In iOS 5, the Usage screen tell

s you how much storage space remains
on your iPad.

14.6 In iOS 5, you can free up storage space by deleting individual items
from some of the built-in apps.

Glossary

3G A third-generation cellular network that supports download speeds up to 7.2 Mbps. It is supported in iPad 2 Wi-Fi + 3G models, as well as third-generation iPads for data delivery over the cellular network.

4G See *LTE*.

802.11 See *Wi-Fi*.

accelerometer The component inside the iPad that senses the device's orientation in space and adjusts the display accordingly (such as switching Safari from portrait view to landscape view).

access point A networking device that enables two or more devices to connect over a Wi-Fi network and to access a shared Internet connection.

ad hoc wireless network A wireless network that doesn't use an access point.

Airplane mode An operational mode that turns off the transceivers for the cellular iPad, Wi-Fi, and Bluetooth features, and puts the device in compliance with federal aviation regulations.

AirPlay A wireless technology that enables you to stream iPad video or audio to an Apple TV device, and see or hear it on your TV or audio receiver.

AirPrint A wireless technology that enables you to send a web page, e-mail message, or other text from your iPad to a printer.

alert A notification message that pops up on the iPad screen and must be dealt with before you can resume what you were doing.

app An application that is designed for and runs on a specific device (such as an iPad), or a set of related devices (such as an iPad, iPhone, and iPod touch).

authentication See *SMTP authentication*.

Auto-capitalization A keyboard feature that automatically activates the Shift key after you tap a sentence-ending character, such as a period or question mark.

Auto-correction A keyboard feature that automatically corrects errors as you type.

badge A small red icon that appears in the upper-right corner of an app icon to let you know that some new activity or data awaits you.

banner A notification message that appears at the top of the iPad screen, but lets you keep working.

Bluetooth A wireless networking technology that enables you to exchange data between two devices using radio frequencies when the devices are within range of each other (usually within about 33 feet/10 meters).

bookmark An Internet site saved in Safari so you can access it quickly in future browsing sessions.

cache An area of memory where Safari stores web page text and images for faster loading when you revisit that page.

cloud The collection of icloud.com networked servers that store your iCloud data and push any new data to your iPad, Mac, or Windows PC.

cropping Removing unneeded or distracting elements from a photo.

cycling Letting the iPad battery completely discharge and then fully recharging it again.

data roaming A cellular provider feature that enables you to perform activities, such as checking for e-mail when you're outside of your provider's normal coverage area.

digital rights management (DRM) Technology that restricts the usage of content to prevent piracy.

discoverable Describes a device that has its Bluetooth feature turned on so other Bluetooth devices can connect to it.

double tap To use a fingertip to quickly press and release the iPad screen twice.

EDGE (Enhanced Data rates for GSM [Global System for Mobile communication] Evolution) A cellular network that's older and slower than 3G, although still supported by iPad.

event An appointment or meeting that you've scheduled in the iPad Calendar.

flick To quickly and briefly drag a finger across the iPad screen.

FM transmitter A device that sends iPad output to an FM radio frequency, which you then play through your car stereo.

GPS (Global Positioning System) A satellite-based navigation system that uses wireless signals from a GPS receiver — such as the one in the iPad — to accurately determine the receiver's current position.

group A collection of Address Book contacts. See also *Smart Group*.

headset A combination of headphones for listening and a microphone for talking.

Home screen The main screen on your iPad, which you access by pressing the Home button.

Home Sharing An iTunes feature that enables you to share the iTunes library on your Mac or PC with your iPad.

IMAP (Internet Message Access Protocol) A type of e-mail account where incoming messages, as well as copies of messages you send, remain on the server. See also *POP*.

keychain A list of saved passwords on a Mac.

location services The features and technologies that provide apps and system tools with access to location data.

LTE (Long-Term Evolution) The cellular transmission standard which supports theoretical maximum download speeds of 73 Mbps, and is supported by the third-generation iPad.

magnetometer A device that measures the direction and intensity of a magnetic field.

Mbps Megabits per second or millions of bits per second; a unit of data transmission speed.

memory effect The process in which a battery loses capacity over time if you repeatedly recharge it without first fully discharging it.

mirroring Displaying your iPad screen on your TV.

Multitouch A touchscreen technology that can detect and interpret two or more simultaneous touches, such as two-finger taps, spreads, and pinches.

notification Data that an app sends to let you know that it has recent activity for you to check out.

pair To connect one Bluetooth device with another by typing a passkey.

pan To slide a photo or other image up, down, left, or right.

passcode A four-digit code used to secure or lock an iPad.

piconet An ad hoc wireless network created by two Bluetooth devices.

pinch To move two fingers closer together on the iPad screen. See also *spread*.

playlist A collection of songs that you create using iTunes.

POP (Post Office Protocol) A type of e-mail account in which incoming messages are only stored temporarily on the provider's mail server. When you connect to the server, the messages are downloaded to the iPad and removed from the server. See also *IMAP*.

power cycle A method of rebooting your iPad in which you turn the device off, wait a few seconds for its inner components to stop spinning, and then turn it on again.

preferences The options, settings, and other data that you configure for your Mac via System Preferences.

private browsing A web browsing mode in which Safari doesn't add sites to the History list, doesn't store site data in the cache, and doesn't save searches or passwords.

push To send data immediately without being prompted.

Reader A Safari feature that removes ads and other distractions from a web page.

ringtone A sound that plays when an incoming call is received.

RSS feed A special file that contains the most recent information added to a website.

side switch The sliding switch that appears on the side of your iPad beside the volume rockers.

silent mode An operational state in which the iPad plays no sounds except alerts set with the Clock application.

slide To drag a finger across the iPad screen.

Smart Group A collection of Address Book contacts in which each member has one or more things in common. Address Book adds or deletes members automatically as you add, edit, and delete contacts. See also *group*.

SMS (Short Message Service) A wireless messaging service that enables the exchange of short text messages between mobile devices.

SMTP (Simple Mail Transfer Protocol) The set of protocols that determines how e-mail messages are addressed and sent.

SMTP authentication The requirement that you must log on to a provider's SMTP server to confirm that you're the person sending the mail.

SMTP server The server that an Internet service provider uses to process outgoing e-mail messages.

spread To move two fingers apart on the iPad screen. See also *pinch*.

SSID (Service Set Identifier) The name that identifies a network to Wi-Fi devices.

synchronization (syncing) A process that ensures that data (such as contacts, e-mail accounts, and events) on your computer is the same as the data on your iPad.

tap To use a fingertip to quickly press and release the iPad screen.

text shortcut A short sequence of characters that represent a longer phrase.

touchscreen A screen that responds to touches such as finger taps and finger slides.

transceiver A device that transmits and receives wireless signals.

trim To edit the start and/or endpoints of a video recording or voice memo.

two-fingered tap To use two fingertips to quickly press and release the iPad screen.

undock To move the keyboard to a more convenient part of the screen.

user-installable A component that an end user can remove and replace.

vCard A file that contains a person's contact information.

VCF (.vcf) The file extension used by a vCard.

wallpaper The background image you see when you unlock your iPad.

Web Clip A Home screen icon that serves as a link to a web page, and preserves the page's scroll position and zoom level.

Wi-Fi (Wireless Fidelity) A wireless networking standard that enables wireless devices to transmit data and communicate with other devices using radio frequency signals that are beamed from one device to another.

Index

Numerics

3G
  defined, 298
  overview, 11
  turning off antenna, 12
  turning off to preserve battery, 291
5X digital zoom feature, 162
802.11. *See* Wi-Fi

A

accelerometer, 298
Accept button, 262
Accept Cookies option, 100
access point, 298
accessories for audio, 207–208
Account Summary screen, 33
accounts
  e-mail
    adding manually, 109–112
    default, specifying, 113
    deleting, 115
    switching, 113–114
    syncing, 108–109
    temporarily disabling, 114–115
  iCloud service, 29–31
  Twitter
    signing in to, 75–76
    Tweeting web pages, 98–99

activating
  Bluetooth feature, 63–64
  Find My iPhone app, 46
  multitasking gestures, 74–75
ad hoc wireless network, 298
Add Account screen, 112
Add Bookmark screen, 89
Add Custom Label option, 240
Add Location option, 159
Add New Address option, 239
Add New Shortcut option, 74
Add Subscribed Calendar option, 260
Add to Bookshelf option, 174
Add to Home Screen button, 58
Add to Reading List option, 91
addresses, assigning to contacts, 239
Advanced section, 26
Airplane mode
  defined, 298
  On/Off switch for, 13
  overview, 13
AirPlay technology
  defined, 298
  streaming audio using, 204–205
AirPrint technology
  defined, 298
  printing photos with, 154–155
  printing web pages with, 103–104
albums, photo, 151

The Genius is in.

iPad 2
PORTABLE GENIUS
Second Edition

978-1-118-17303-9

iPhone 4S
PORTABLE GENIUS
Also covers iPhone 4!

978-1-118-09384-9

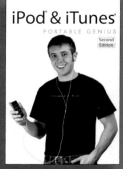

iPod & iTunes
PORTABLE GENIUS
Second Edition

978-0-470-64351-8

MacBook Air
PORTABLE GENIUS
Third Edition

978-1-118-18618-3

MacBook Pro
PORTABLE GENIUS
Third Edition

978-0-470-64204-7

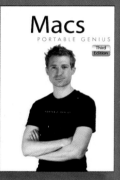

Macs
PORTABLE GENIUS
Third Edition

978-1-118-16433-4

iMac
PORTABLE GEN
Th Edit

978-1-118-14758-0

Mac OS X Lion
PORTABLE GENIUS

978-1-118-02239-9

iLife '11
PORTABLE GENIUS

978-0-470-64348-8

Aperture 3
PORTABLE GENIUS

978-0-470-38672-9

Microsoft
Office for Mac 2011
PORTABLE GENI

978-0-470-61019-0

The essentials for every forward-thinking Apple user are now available on the go. Designed for easy access to tools and shortcuts, the *Portable Genius* series has all the information you need to maximize your digital lifestyle. With a full-color interior and easy-to-navigate content, the *Portable Genius* series offers innovative tips and tricks as well as savvy advice that will save you time and increase your productivity.

WILEY
Now you know

e **Available in print and e-book formats.**